Lecture Notes in Computer Science 8215

Commenced Publication in 1973
Founding and Former Series Editors:
Gerhard Goos, Juris Hartmanis, and Jan van Leeuwen

T0242181

Junia C. Anacleto   Esteban W.G. Clua
Flavio S. Correa da Silva   Sidney Fels
Hyun S. Yang (Eds.)

Entertainment Computing – ICEC 2013

12th International Conference, ICEC 2013
São Paulo, Brazil, October 16-18, 2013
Proceedings

 Springer

Volume Editors

Junia C. Anacleto
Universidade Federal de São Carlos, SP, Brazil
E-mail: junia@dc.ufscar.br

Esteban W.G. Clua
Universidade Federal Fluminense, Rio de Janeiro, RJ, Brazil
E-mail: esteban@ic.uff.br

Flavio S. Correa da Silva
Universidade de São Paulo, SP, Brazil
E-mail: fcs@ime.usp.br

Sidney Fels
The University of British Columbia, Vancouver, BC, Canada
E-mail: ssfels@ece.ubc.ca

Hyun S. Yang
KAIST CS, Daejeon, Korea
E-mail: hsyang@cs.kaist.ac.kr

ISSN 0302-9743   e-ISSN 1611-3349
ISBN 978-3-642-41105-2   e-ISBN 978-3-642-41106-9
DOI 10.1007/978-3-642-41106-9
Springer Heidelberg New York Dordrecht London

Library of Congress Control Number: 2013948236

CR Subject Classification (1998): K.8, K.3, K.4, H.5, I.3, I.2, J.5, D.2

LNCS Sublibrary: SL 3 – Information Systems and Application,
incl. Internet/Web and HCI

Typesetting: Camera-ready by author, data conversion by Scientific Publishing Services, Chennai, India

Printed on acid-free paper

Springer is part of Springer Science+Business Media (www.springer.com)

Preface

We are pleased to present the proceedings of ICEC 2013, the 12th IFIP International Conference on Entertainment Computing, held for the first time in Brazil, Latin America. Brazil is considered to be one of the next leading countries in the world economy, along with Russia, India, China, and South Africa, forming what are being called the BRICS countries. ICEC 2013 was held in São Paulo, a cosmopolitan city well known for being the Brazilian hub for economics, one of the largest cities in the world, as well as a place for entertainment and leisure.

ICEC 2013 provided a leading international forum to bring together professionals from computer science, social and cultural sciences, psychology, art, design, education, and other disciplines to promote experience and knowledge exchange amongst researchers and developers in the interdisciplinary field of entertainment computing.

The ICEC 2013 proceedings contain exciting and inspiring research articles. We had 75 submissions, from which 13 were selected as full papers, 6 were selected as short papers, and 11 were selected as posters. We also had two demonstration papers, three workshops, three tutorials, and three art installations. The ICEC 2013 Program Committee was composed of 72 experts from 19 different countries, comprising a unique representation of the global entertainment computing community. We thank all the members of this committee and all the additional external reviewers for their work and commitment. The importance and credibility of these proceedings are sustained by the competence and dedication of these professionals.

We thank our sponsors CAPES (Brazilian Center of Support for Research and Education), FAPESP (São Paulo Supporting Agency for Research), and GRAND (Graphics, Animation, and New Media Center of Canada), as well as our supporters UFSCAR (Federal University of São Carlos), UFF (Fluminense Federal University), LIA (Advanced Interaction Laboratory), and Mackenzie University. We also thank IFIP TC14 Committee for supporting ICEC 2013.

ICEC 2013 was co-located with the 12th Brazilian Symposium on Computer Games and Digital Entertainment (SBGames 2013), due to a partnership between IFIP and SBC (Brazilian Computing Society).

October 2013

Junia Anacleto
Esteban Clua
Flavio Soares Correa da Silva
Sidney Fels
Hyun Yang

ICEC 2013 Workshops

The New Ecology of Entertainment Devices: First, Second, and Multiple Screens in the Home Setting (Lyn Pemberton, Sanaz Fallahkhair, and Roseli de Deus Lopes)

Mechanics, Mechanisms, and Devices: To Inform, Reflect, and Change Behavior (Tim Marsh, Rainer Malaka, Jannicke Baalsrud Hauge, Sidney Fels, Christian Jones, Eunice Ma, Bonnie Nardi, Albert "Skip" Rizzo, and Erik van de Spek)

ICEC 2013 Tutorials

Digital Games – Their Production, Management, Consumer Market, and Business Models (Artur Lugmayr)

Game Accessibility (Jerome Dupire)

Hot Topics in Business Information Management and Systems in Entertainment Computation Industries – From Consumer Mining, Sentiment Analysis, Big Data, towards Social Media Networks (Artur Lugmayr)

Introduction to Creating New Interfaces for Musical Expression (Sidney Fels and Michael Lyons)

The Role of Interactive Audio in Multimedia Productions: The Video Game Experiences (Paulo Hecht and Junia Anacleto)

Organization

Organizing Committee

Conference Chairs

Junia Coutinho Anacleto   Federal University of São Carlos, Brazil
Esteban Walter Gonzalez Clua   Fluminense Federal University, Brazil

Program Chairs

Flavio Soares Correa da Silva   University of São Paulo, Brazil
Sidney Fels   University of British Columbia, Canada
Hyun Seung Yang   Korea Advanced Institute of Science and
     Technology, South Korea

Conference Advisory

Matthias Rauterberg   Technical University of Eindhoven,
     The Netherlands
Ryohei Nakatsu   National University of Signapore, Singapore

Workshop and Tutorial Chairs

David Geerts   Katholieke Universiteit Leuven, Belgium
Tim Marsh   James Cook University, Australia

Industry Chair

Stephane Natkin   Conservatoire National des Arts et Métiers,
     France

Doctoral Consortium Chair

Nuno Correia   New University of Lisbon, Portugal

Poster, Art, and Demo Chair

Letizia Jaccheri   Norwegian University of Science and
     Technology, Norway

Local Organizing Chairs

Janaína Cintra Abib   Federal University of São Carlos, Brazil
Andre Bueno   Federal University of São Carlos, Brazil
Vinícius Afonso Raimundo
   Ferreira   Federal University of São Carlos, Brazil
Rener Baffa da Silva   Federal University of São Carlos, Brazil
Marcelo Zamith   Fluminense Federal University, Brazil

Program Committee

Lynn Rosalina Gama Alves	State University of Bahia, Brazil
Valter Alves	Polytechnic Institute of Viseu, Portugal
Junia Coutinho Anacleto	Federal University of São Carlos, Brazil
Manuela Aparicio	Lisbon University Institute, Portugal
Regina Bernhaupt	University Paul Sabatier, France
Rafael Bidarra	Delft University of Technology, The Netherlands
Anne-Gwenn Bosser	Teesside University, UK
Ary Fagundes Bressane Neto	University of São Paulo, Brazil
F. Amílcar Cardoso	University of Coimbra, Portugal
Marc Cavazza	Teesside University, UK
Paolo Ciancarini	Università di Bologna, Italy
Esteban Walter Gonzalez Clua	Fluminense Federal University, Brazil
Simon Colton	Imperial College London, UK
Flavio Soares Correa da Silva	University of São Paulo, Brazil
Nuno Correia	New University of Lisbon, Portugal
Bruno Feijo	Pontifical Catholic University of Rio de Janeiro, Brazil
Sidney Fels	University of British Columbia, Canada
Mathias Funk	Eindhoven University of Technology, The Netherlands
Oscar Garcia Panyella	Universitat Ramon Llul, Spain
David Geerts	Katholieke Universiteit Leuven, Belgium
Chris Geiger	University of Applied Sciences Düsseldorf, Germany
Stefan Göbel	Technische Universität Darmstadt, Germany
Timo Gottel	University of Hamburg, Germany
Marco A. Gomez Martin	Universidad Complutense de Madrid, Spain
Pedro Gonzalez Calero	Universidad Complutense de Madrid, Spain
Nicholas Graham	Queen's University, Canada
Letizia Jaccheri	Norwegian University of Science and Technology, Norway
Javier Jaen Martinez	Polytechnic University of Valencia, Spain
Bill Kapralos	University of Ontario Institute of Technology, Canada
Börje Karlsson	Microsoft Research Asia, China
Haruhiro Katayose	Kwansei Gakuin University, Japan
Rilla Khaled	University of Malta, Malta
Christoph Klimmt	Hanover University of Music, Drama and Media, Germany
Rainer Malaka	University of Bremen, Germany
Ricardo Marroquim	Federal University of Rio de Janeiro, Brazil

Sponsors

Coordination for Enhancement of Higher Education Personnel (CAPES)
Foundation for Research Support of the State of São Paulo (FAPESP)
Graphics, Animation and New Media (GRAND)

Support

International Federation for Information Processing (IFIP)
Advanced Interaction Laboratory (LIA)
Brazilian Computer Society (SBC)
Federal University of São Carlos (UFSCar)
Fluminense Federal University (UFF)

Table of Contents

Full Papers

Short Papers

Posters

Demonstrations

Interactive Arts

Full Papers

An Empirical Examination of Behavioral Factors in Creative Development of Game Prototypes

Michail N. Giannakos[1], Letizia Jaccheri[1], and Sandro Morasca[2]

[1] Norwegian University of Science and Technology, Trondheim, Norway
{michailg,letizia}@idi.ntnu.no
[2] Università degli Studi dell'Insubria, Como, Italy
sandro.morasca@uninsubria.it

Abstract. In the last few years, several learning programs, workshops, technologies, and activities have been introduced and applied to game prototyping activities. The research goal of this work is to investigate how participants experience game prototyping activities. This paper presents a one-day intensive course consisting of both learning and hands-on sessions with open source software (OSS) tools, tangible materials, and sensor boards for creative development of games prototypes. The intensive course program was developed using the empirical experience of the instructors from numerous prior programs. We present the results of an empirical examination regarding participants' attitude towards the program. A group of 12 MSc/PhD students, teachers, and designers participated in the program in our empirical evaluation. We used a survey grounded in motivational factors for technology and open-ended questions to obtain both quantitative and qualitative data from the participants. Quantitative statistical analysis indicates that, in our study, participants' satisfaction and activity's usefulness are the most influential factors for participants' intention to attend similar activities in the future. Qualitative analysis suggests improvements on how to prepare the participants, introduce the software used in the courses, and enrich the variety of the materials in our program.

Keywords: Game Prototyping, Empirical Examination, Creative Development, Software Engineering Activities, Behavioral Factors, OSS for Entertainment.

1 Introduction

Computer games are highly engaging not only for game players but also for game developers. Here we mention The Gathering (http://www.gathering.org) as an example of a highly engaging environment for game players and developers. Thousands of youths have been meeting every year since 1992 at The Gathering, the second largest computer party in the world (second only to DreamHack). Events like The Gathering are a place for young creative people to engage in creative game development, in addiction to demo coding, music, graphics, animation, and game playing. These events receive a lot of attention by researchers and educators who aim at understanding this growing phenomenon of creative development of computer games.

J.C. Anacleto et al. (Eds.): ICEC 2013, LNCS 8215, pp. 3–8, 2013.

Modding, the practice and process of developing game mods, is typically a "Do It Yourself" (DIY) approach to game development [6] by reusing game software. For this purpose, well known and validated Software Engineering (SE) theories and techniques for development and innovation can be applied to game development. But little is known about how participants experience game prototyping activities. How easy it is for them to participate? Do they enjoy their participation to these activities? Do they intend to participate to future versions of such game prototyping activities?

In our approach, we developed and taught an intensive course for game prototyping and development and empirically evaluated it via the participants' feedback. Specifically, we employed a mixed (both quantitative and qualitative) approach to gain insights into participants' attitudes towards the intensive course, to examine any potential relations to the participants' intention to re-attend similar events in the future. In our work, we give insights regarding:

- *Behavioral factors about game prototyping activities.*
- *Potential improvements for the development of games prototyping courses.*

The clarification of participants' attitudes during these activities is expected to also shed a light on improvements on the course structure and development. We found that by increasing participants' satisfaction and connecting the activities with something more important (increase the activities' usefulness) allows instructors to increase participants' willingness to attend such intensive programs. In addition, participants complete the intensive course more successfully if they are provided with more information prior to the intensive course. In our case, such information included the OSS, sensor platform, and materials used.

2   Related Work

The previous decades have seen various attempts to introduce creative learning practices in CS and SE. Numerous projects focus on creativity and design using diverse software tools (e.g., VVVV, PD, Scratch, Processing, Panda3D, Alice, Wiring). Most of these projects build on the context of robotics, interactive installations, and creativity. The role of the active learner and project based learning with multidisciplinary teams in CS and SE have been explored in the literature [3] [6] [7] with great success. For example, one or more stakeholders to a project may have different backgrounds than the rest of a team, or when the given task is to "think outside the box" by developing creative solutions.

Games prototyping and development courses engage students through incorporating up-to-date technologies, providing the opportunity to work on projects that are relevant to them, and instructing students on the ethics and methods of research. Our activity can be characterized as a project-based learning activity and emphasizes in the challenging balance between production and process [1]. Related studies [6] [7] have proved the value of game prototyping in SE. While these studies address the issue of creative development of computer games, they do not explicitly explore how these activities are experienced by participants and can be potentially improved.

3   Methodology

3.1   The Intensive Course

A full-day intensive course was organized as a combination of a learning session and hands-on applied sessions with OSS tools for creativity [4]. The learning sessions derived from both related literature and the research experience [2] [5] of the two instructors (who are also the first two authors of this paper). The hands-on sessions had the goal of letting the participants experiment with software tools for creative game development while working in small groups to get to know each other in a creative and motivating atmosphere. The first half of the course included presentations on the background of the topics. The second half of the course included hands-on creative sessions. The participants worked in teams on small creative tasks using the methods presented earlier. The exact schedule of the intensive course can be found here: http://wp.me/PXD0L-tm. After the course we proceeded with the evaluation. Due to the schedule of the intensive course and the need to have a low ratio among instructors and participants, our evaluation was not a large scale one. To fill this gap, we used both qualitative and quantitative data to interpret and summarize our results.

3.2   Participants and Procedures

Twelve participants attended the one full-day intensive course. The participants were MSc/PhD students in Software Engineering, software designers, and software teachers. The participants formed four different teams. Each team made a character (e.g., Mr. Coffee in Figure 1) using physical materials (e.g., Lego objects, plastic, glass). They then imported the character in Scratch, developed a storyboard for the game, and programmed the game on Scratch. At the end of the course, four different projects had been developed based on the given theme, which concerned issues with the Earth's water systems. In Figure 1, we present an example storyboard and the corresponding game developed by one of the teams.

Storyboard
Sam is really tired! He needs a cup of coffee to wake up and go to work! Unfortunately, there is not enough water in the tap. Water flows from ponds which are filled by rain and dried by the sun.
Mr. Coffee is Sam's best friend! He tries to help Sam get water for his coffee machine in the following way:
1. Water flows from several ponds through pipes to Sam's coffee machine
2. If the sun shines on a pond it becomes dry
3. If the cloud rains into a pond it gets filled
4. Mr. Coffee carries an umbrella
5. Mr. Coffee can cover a pond with his umbrella to prevent it from drying up
6. Once there is enough water in Sam's machine a button starts making coffee

Controlling Mr. Coffee
a)   The slider moves Mr. Coffee sideways.
b)   By pressing the button he either takes or drops the umbrella.

Fig. 1. One team developed a Scratch game with the name Mr. Coffee, the interface of the game (left) and the Storyboard (right)

3.3   Measures

The research methodology included a survey composed of three parts: the first included questions on the demographics of the participants (occupation and age); the second part included measures of the various factors identified in the literature from previous research; and the third consisted of open-entry questions regarding the recommendations and feedback of the participants. The questionnaire factors were: a) Satisfaction-the degree to which the participant positively feels about the course, b) Intention to Re-attend-the degree of participant's willingness to re-attend the course, c) Easiness-how easy it is for participants to shop online, d) Enjoyment-the degree to which the course is perceived to be personally enjoyable, e) Usefulness-the degree to which the participant believes that attending the course is useful, f) Control-the degree to which a participant perceives how easy or difficult it would be to perform an operation in the course, g) Happiness-the degree to which a person felt happy during the activity, h) Anxiety-the degree to which the participant felt anxious during the course. In all cases, 7-point Likert scales were used to measure the variables. The participants completed the questionnaire at the end of the course.

4   Data Analysis and Results

We carried out quantitative and qualitative analyses on the data obtained from the survey. We first carried out a quantitative analysis, which was based on the factors measured in the questionnaire (Table 1). We proceed to test the reliability of each measure using Cronbach α coefficient. As Table 1 shows, the result of the test revealed acceptable indices of reliability in all the factors (> 0.7). We also computed descriptive statistics for the factors under investigation. The factors is found to be in satisfactory level; however, participants' intention to re-attend in similar course is not as high as we would like (see Table 1 for the exact values).

Table 1. Summary of measurement scales

Factors	Mean	SD	CR	STF	IRa	EAS	ENJ	USF	CON	HAP	ANX
Satisfaction (STF)	5.81	0.78	0.87	1.0							
Intention to Re-attend (IRa)	4.69	1.46	0.95	.78**	1.0						
Easiness (EAS)	5.48	0.94	0.74	-.17	-.16	1.0					
Enjoyment (ENJ)	5.77	0.82	0.85	.54	.46	-.19	1.0				
Usefulness (USF)	5.04	1.26	0.87	.52	.60*	.31	.20	1.0			
Control (CON)	6.04	0.58	0.85	.49	.13	.27	.58*	.16	1.0		
Happiness (HAP)	5.58	0.81	0.79	.45	.43	.23	.63*	.02	.67*	1.0	
Anxiety (ANX)	2.69	0.98	0.83	-.25	-.28	-.24	-.58*	.11	-.51	-.82**	1.0

SD, Standard Deviation; CR, Cronbach α; Correlation is significant at the ** 0.01 & * 0.05 level.

To investigate any possible relationships among the factors and explore factors that may be strongly related to participants' intention to re-attend the course, we used the Spearman's rank-correlation coefficient, statistically testing the null hypothesis which is equal to 0. Spearman's test suggests that some of the factors are related, in some cases relatively strongly. More precisely, the most important positive relationships involve intention to re-attend on the one side and satisfaction and usefulness on the other side. In addition, enjoyment is positively related to control and to happiness, and control is positively related to happiness. These relations revealed the important role of control over the course and its high influence on the participants' positive feelings during the course. Moreover, there is also one expected negative relation, that of happiness with anxiety. We present the results of Spearman's test in Table 1.

In addition to the above questions, we used free-entry questions to capture any additional information and suggestions from the participants. The responses from free-entry questions and the observations of the instructors during the course form the qualitative part of our study. After collecting the responses, we proceeded with a content analysis. Based on the free text responses, we summarize the following additions that will potentially improve the course:

1. It was difficult for the participants to start working with a software that was new to them: sending information regarding the software prior to the course will familiarize participants with the software, thereby making the intensive course more effective;
2. Longer, in-depth introduction of the software at the beginning of the course will also help the participants be more effective in the second (hands-on) part of the course;
3. The physical part was very important, and supplying participants with a wider range of physical materials may allow them to more quickly develop a more representative physical character.

5   Conclusions

In the course, the twelve participants were introduced to OSS practices and tools that are suitable for creators of interactive and playful systems. The course offered the participants an opportunity to create their physical character through OSS tools, such as Scratch and Pico-Boards, which motivate a broader participation of technical and non-technical users in the creative production of interactive systems.

The first step was to design and deploy a series of these activities. In particular, participants engaged in OSS Scratch and the hardware platform Pico-board, which enable them to engage in the world of creativity with digital games and stories. In the final step, we used the empirical data obtained from participants' experiences with the course to evaluate it and investigate any improvements.

This study, based on the quantitative analyses, particularly improves our understandings regarding creative development of games prototypes. The findings indicate that satisfaction and usefulness have positive relationships with participants' intention to participate in similar activities in the future. As such, by increasing their satisfaction and connecting the activity to something more important (increase activity's usefulness), we will be able to increase participants' willingness to attend such as intensive programs.

The qualitative analyses suggest guidelines regarding how to prepare the participants, how to introduce the OSS, and how to enrich the variety of the materials in our program. Specifically, educating participants about the software prior to the intensive course and conducting an in-depth introduction at the beginning will help them "buy time" from the intensive course, allowing for further progress. Moreover, as the cornerstone of our program is creativity, the supply of a wider range of physical materials will allow students to produce a physical object that is more advanced and closer to what they want, in a shorter amount of time.

As with most of the empirical studies, there are a few limitations. As for the internal validity of our study, the data are based on a self-reported method and instructors' observations. Other in-depth methods such as semi-structured interviews could provide a complementary picture of the findings through data triangulation. As for external validity, the subjects were MSc/PhD students, teachers and designers, which may somewhat limit the generalizability of our results. Nevertheless, the insights drawn are not connected with the subjects' background and can be applied on any population. Another direction of research is to apply the empirical framework proposed in this paper to the investigation of existing highly engaging environment for game players and developers, such as The Gathering.

Acknowledgements. We are grateful to the participants of the course and to K. Chorianopoulos and A.S. Nossum for their help on the prior versions of this program.

References

1. Chaffin, A., Barnes, T.: Lessons from a course on serious games research and prototyping. In: Proceedings of the Fifth International Conference on the Foundations of Digital Games (FDG 2010), pp. 32–39. ACM, NY (2010)
2. Chorianopoulos, K., Jaccheri, L., Nossum, A.S.: Creative and open software engineering practices and tools in maker community projects. In: Proceedings of the 4th ACM SIGCHI Symposium on Engineering Interactive Computing Systems, pp. 333–334. ACM (2012)
3. Holbert, K.E., Karady, G.G.: Strategies, challenges and prospects for active learning in the computer-based classroom. IEEE Trans. Educ. 52(1), 31–38 (2009)
4. Jaccheri, L., Giannakos, M.N.: Open Source Software for Entertainment. In: Herrlich, M., Malaka, R., Masuch, M. (eds.) ICEC 2012. LNCS, vol. 7522, pp. 604–607. Springer, Heidelberg (2012)
5. Jaccheri, L.: Open software and art: a tutorial. In: Anacleto, J.C., Fels, S., Graham, N., Kapralos, B., Saif El-Nasr, M., Stanley, K. (eds.) ICEC 2011. LNCS, vol. 6972, pp. 468–471. Springer, Heidelberg (2011)
6. Scacchi, W.: Modding as a basis for developing game systems. In: Proceedings of GAS 2011, pp. 5–8. ACM, NY (2011)
7. Wang, A.I.: Extensive Evaluation of Using a Game Project in a Software Architecture Course. Trans. Comput. Educ. 11(1), Article 5, 28 pages (2011), doi:1921607.1921612

A New Chess Variant for Gaming AI

Azlan Iqbal

College of Information Technology, Universiti Tenaga Nasional, Kampus Putrajaya,
Jalan IKRAM-UNITEN, 43000 Kajang, Selangor, Malaysia
azlan@uniten.edu.my

Abstract. In this article, we describe a newly-invented chess variant called Switch-Side Chain-Chess that is demonstrably more challenging for humans and computers than the standard, international version of the game. A new rule states that players have the choice to switch sides with each other if a continuous link of pieces is created on the board. This simple rule increases significantly the complexity of chess, as perceived by the players, but not the actual size of its game tree. The new variant therefore more easily allows board game researchers to focus on the 'higher level' aspects of intelligence such as perception and intuition without being constrained by a larger search space as they would be if using a game like Go or Arimaa. They can also immediately build upon the tried and tested approaches already being used in strong chess engines instead of having to start from scratch or a lower level of progress as is the case with other games of this type.

Keywords: Chess, variant, complexity, intelligence, intuition, perception.

1 Introduction

Chess variants may vary from the standard game in terms of factors like the types of pieces used, the shape and size of the board, and particularly the rules [1, 2]. The following provides a succinct description.

"Chess variants comprise a family of strategy board games that are related to, inspired by, or similar enough to the game we today call Chess. The game we commonly know today was based on earlier games, most immediately the Arabian game of Shatranj, itself descended from the Indian game of Chaturanga. Besides its direct ancestors, Chess has many cousins, the most popular being Shogi (in Japan), Xiangqi (in China), and Janggi (in Korea). The modern game of Chess has also inspired countless variants. Some have been created by Chess champions seeking new challenges. Some have been created by entrepreneurs who have provided commercial sets. Some have been created for fairy Chess problems without any intent of actually playing them. And most have been designed by creative people who like to try out new pieces, new rules, or new ideas." [2]

J.C. Anacleto et al. (Eds.): ICEC 2013, LNCS 8215, pp. 9–16, 2013.
© IFIP International Federation for Information Processing 2013

Our purpose was to challenge the field of artificial intelligence (AI) with a new Drosophila [3]. One of the problems with standard chess AI today is that computers are already able to play it well enough using efficient search techniques and well-designed heuristics. This has lead to the intensified study of board games with greater search spaces (i.e. the size of the game tree) such as Go and Arimaa in the hope that designing computer programs to play them as well as the best human players will lead to more advances in AI [4, 5]. Even so, many of the techniques that have worked for chess seem to also work well for these games [4]. Research into chess and computer chess has, in fact, yielded many benefits related to various fields such as molecular computing [6, 7], automated theorem proving [8], computer music composition [9], machine reading [10], cognitive development [11], the education of children [12, 13] and medicine, specifically with regard to Alzheimer's disease [14-16].

It is therefore not inconceivable that the right chess variant could be just as beneficial, if not more; and not only to AI. The advantage of our proposed variant, Switch-Side Chain-Chess (SSCC)[1] over more complex games and other chess variants is that it increases the human-perceived complexity without increasing the size of the original game's tree. This encourages the development of more sophisticated AI without the computational burden of a greater search space. In the following section, we explain the new rule of SSCC in some detail. In section 3, we discuss and illustrate with examples the impact and significance of the new variant in contrast to the standard game. We conclude in section 4 with some suggestions for further work.

2   The New Rule

In SSCC, the additional rule is simply that when a 'chain' or a link of pieces is formed on the board by the piece that moved last – enclosing at least two empty adjacent squares – the player has the right to switch armies with his opponent. Fig. 1 shows example configurations of chains. In (a), taken from a real game, the white knight has just moved from the *g6* square to *e7*, delivering check on the enemy king. The knight creates the chain *g5-h6-h7-g8-f7-e7-f6-g5* and now the player in control of the white army has the right to switch sides with the opponent, if so desired. The turn is then Black's, regardless of whom is now in control of that army. In this particular case, there is a *double* check created and therefore the enemy king *must* move.

Since the king is unable to create a new chain in the process in order to switch back, it may not make much sense for White to switch in the first place. In (b), a constructed position, it is shown how two empty squares diagonally adjacent may constitute a valid chain as well. Logically, with fewer than 6 pieces on the board, SSCC reverts back into the standard version's endgame. We could not find this particular concept of a chain in any existing variant. The simple addition of a new rule in SSCC introduces levels of complexity beyond the standard game without

---

[1] Iqbal, M. A. M. Apparatus for Playing a Chess Variant and Its Method. Malaysia Patent Application No. PI 2011006257. Filing Date: 23 December 2011.

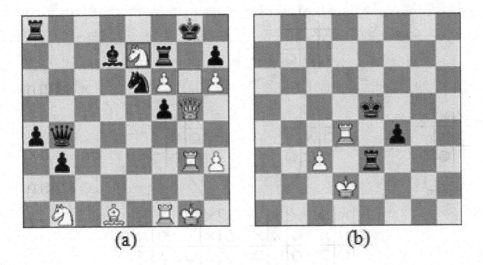

Fig. 1. Chains in the new variant

affecting the size of the original game's tree. It can be played on any standard chess set but a board that allows for easy rotation – or used in conjunction with a turntable device – would be preferable.

3   Increased Human-Perceived Complexity

If a computer program could play SSCC *well*, it would first need to include all the heuristics that work for standard chess (every chess game is an SSCC game) but also additional heuristics that deal with the complexities of 1) chain detection on the board, and 2) deciding whether or not to switch sides. First let us consider the standard game's tree and see why switching sides does not affect it. Consider the game tree of tic-tac-toe shown in Fig. 2[2] as a small-scale example.

If we consider 'X' to be the *player* in control of the white pieces and '0' to be the *player* in control of the black pieces, at any point, if a chain formed on the board and the players switched sides, the *tree itself* would be unaffected; i.e. no additional positions or nodes would be created. The switch is analogous to the players simply exchanging seats with each other. While this does not affect the 'physical' game tree, the players themselves are faced with additional challenges. It is interesting to note that, computationally, an implementation using a *larger* game tree is possible – e.g. by mapping player identity to piece color or treating the decision to switch as an extra 'move' – but this is not a necessity as the standard 'minimax' decision rule usually employed can be simply inverted at the appropriate time. This is the reason why a single computer chess engine can easily play a fair and unbiased game against itself.

---

[2] Adapted from: http://ozark.hendrix.edu/~burch/cs/150/test/fr/print.html

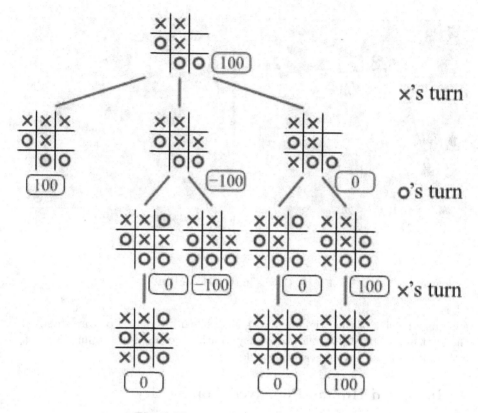

Fig. 2. The typical game tree structure

Experienced SSCC players, for instance (there are none at present), might find the variant easier than standard chess because they are particularly good at pattern recognition and exploiting opportunities on the board related to switching sides. Experienced standard chess players might find it much more difficult because they are simply not used to the new rule. Therefore, at this time, we can rely only on the logical argument that SSCC demands more from players. Computationally, the difficulties become more evident. A computer program requires heuristics that make chain detection both thorough and efficient. Even with knowledge of graph theory, there is no easy way for a computer to 'see' a SSCC chain (they can take many forms on the board) without repeatedly examining virtually every piece in a position and its surrounding squares since every piece is potentially the starting and ending vertex.

If one extends this concept to the millions of positions analyzed at every move, chain detection alone becomes too resource intensive. Here lies the first main challenge to gaming AI that will not lend itself easily to a brute-force solution. It may be acceptable for a human to miss certain chains but a computer must always be 'aware' of all possible chains to prevent the human player from cheating, or simply being able to proceed legally with a switch. Let us say that this first main challenge is met. The computer is then faced with the second main challenge in having to decide whether or not to switch sides. Earlier, it was mentioned that the minimax decision rule used in standard chess can be inverted should a chain be formed.

This means that, should a candidate move by the computer create a chain (and switching becomes possible), the computer should now consider the perspective of the opponent since it could assume immediate control of his army. But is this sufficient to play SSCC well? We developed a rudimentary prototype SSCC program using this inverted minimax or 'iminimax' decision rule and tested it informally against a few average chess players. Due to an inability to detect chains correctly and efficiently enough, the program played at a very poor level. However, even if it could detect chains well, what sort of switching heuristics would bring it to the 'world class' level? Consider the position shown in Fig. 3 which was taken from a real SSCC game between the author and his research assistant.

Why is Bf7 a critical mistake when, in standard chess, it looks perfectly sound compared to the Kd8 alternative? The following analysis – which was performed after the game – perhaps illustrates how complicated SSCC can get. The reader, with the aid of a chessboard and the information in section 2, might like to determine the best sequence of moves before looking at the analysis. '(S)' indicates the presence of a chain and the decision to switch. Where the chain is not easily apparent, it is included.

> **1. Qh5+ Bf7? 2. Qh6** (S) **Bh5** (S, this also removes the bishop as a defensive piece along the line and sets it up for capture by the queen) **3. Nxg5** (S, probably the only move that creates a valid chain in this position) **Qd8** (S, removing the d8 escape square of the king) **4. h4** (S, again probably the only chain move) **Nd7** (S, removes the last escape square) **5. Qxh5#**
> Alternatively, if **3. ... Qd8** was missed and **3. ... Qg4** played instead, **4. f4** (S, f4-g4-h5-h6-h7-g8-f8-e7-f6-g5-f4) **Nd7** (S) **5. Bh3** (S, h3-g4-h5-h6-h7-g8-f8-e7-f6-g5-f4-g3-h3; **5. Bf3** also works) **Rd8** (S) **6. Bxg4** (S) **c6** (S) **7. Qxh5#** (*5. Bxh5# also works and creates another chain but it is unnecessary at this point*)

The basic idea here is that once a player is able to switch and gains control of the opponent's army, he can 'set him up' to lose as long as a sequence of chains can be guaranteed to lead to checkmate. It should be clear from the above example that this is not always easy to do. What combination of new heuristics and associated 'weights' would work well in SSCC? The act of switching sides goes completely against the progressive build-up of material (usually measured in 'pawn units') that chess engines generally rely on. When should the computer 'gamble' all that has been gained, on a switch? Human players would typically use intuition and other subtle factors in conjunction with their pattern-recognition abilities to decide. In short, SSCC appears to combine the zero-sum

Fig. 3. *Qh5+* and black replies with the critical mistake of *Bf7*. Why?

perfect-information nature of standard chess with some amount of chance or unpredictability [17] (will there be an opportunity to switch back somewhere down the line?) without affecting the 'certainty' of the standard game's tree.

4   Conclusions

The new variant proposed poses new, interesting challenges to gaming AI without the computational burden of a larger search space. Concepts such as 'intuition' and 'perception' which are critical to high-level play (when it comes to humans) are definitely worthy of investigation in the *computational* domain. Further work in the area would benefit from a creative, mathematical demonstration of the increased strategic complexity of SSCC, as we have presently only 'logically' argued for it. This will not be trivial if it is to be sufficiently convincing. It may be analogous in difficulty to a 'proof' of the estimated maximum number of forced three-move mate sequences possible in standard chess.

Further work should also include some new, cleverly-designed heuristics related to chain detection and switching; their effectiveness demonstrated using prototype SSCC game engines. Eventually, these technologies would do well if they could be extended to other areas of research such as image processing and intelligent real-world systems where decisions need to be made relatively quickly with only limited information available.

Acknowledgements. We thank Boshra Talebi Haghighi and Sinan Qahtan Mohammad Salih for their contributions. This research was sponsored in part by the Ministry of Higher Education (MOHE) in Malaysia under their Fundamental Research Grant Scheme (FRGS/1/10/TK/UNITEN/02/2) and the Ministry of Science, Technology and Innovation (MOSTI) in Malaysia under their eScienceFund research grant (01-02-03-SF0240).

References

1. Gollon, J.: Chess Variations: Ancient, Regional, and Modern. Charles E. Tuttle Co. Inc., North Clarendon (1973)
2. Bodlaender, H.L., Howe, D.: The Chess Variant Pages (2002), http://www.chessvariants.com
3. McCarthy, J.: AI as Sport. Science 276, 1518–1519 (1997)
4. Hsu, F.-H.: Cracking Go. IEEE Spectrum 44(10), 50–55 (2007)
5. Wu, D.J.: Move Ranking and Evaluation in the Game of Arimaa. BA diss. Harvard College, Cambridge, MA (2011)
6. Cukras, A.R., Faulhammer, D., Lipton, R.J., Landweber, L.F.: Chess Games: A Model for RNA Based Computation. Biosystems 52(1-3), 35–45 (1999)
7. Faulhammer, D., Cukras, A.R., Lipton, R.J., Landweber, L.F.: Molecular Computation: RNA Solutions to Chess Problems. PNAS 97(4), 1385–1389 (2000)
8. Newborn, M.: Deep Blue's Contribution to AI. Annals of Mathematics and Artificial Intelligence 28, 27–30 (2000)

9. Friedel, F.: Ludwig - A Synthesis of Chess and Music. Chess Base News (December 4, 2006), http://www.chessbase.com/newsprint.asp?newsid=3522

10. Etzioni, O., Banko, M., Cafarella, M.J.: Machine Reading. AAAI Spring Symposium on Machine Reading. Technical Report SS-07-06, 1-5 (2007)

11. O'Neil, H.F., Perez, R.: Computer Games and Team and Individual Learning. Elsevier (2007) ISBN: 0080453430

12. Ferreira, D., Palhares, P.: Chess and Problem Solving Involving Patterns. TMME 5(2 & 3), 249–256 (2008)

13. AF4C: First Move Program Info. America's Foundation for Chess (2008), http://af4c.memfirstclubs.net/club/scripts/section/section.asp?NS=FMPI

14. Cavezian, C., Berquand-Merle, M., Franck, N., Demily, C.: Self-training for Cognitive Remediation in Schizophrenia. Schizophrenia Research 98(suppl. 1), 53 (2008)

15. Ciamarra, M.: Checkmating Alzheimer's Disease. FIDE (2013), http://www.fide.com/component/content/article/1-fide-news/7066-checkmating-alzheimers-disease.html

16. Dahl, M.: Being a Bookworm Boosts Your Brainpower into Old Age. Today Com. (July 3, 2013), http://www.today.com/health/being-bookworm-boosts-your-brainpower-old-age-6C10532642

17. Rubin, J., Watson, I.: Computer Poker: A Review. Artificial Intelligence 175(5-6), 958–987 (2011)

A Systematic Review of Game Design Methods and Tools

Marcos Silvano Orita Almeida[1] and Flávio Soares Corrêa da Silva[2]

[1] Federal Technologial University Paraná, Campo Mourão, PR, Brazil
marcossilvano@utfpr.edu.br
[2] Institute of Mathematics and Statistics, University of São Paulo,
São Paulo, SP, Brazil
fcs@ime.usp.br

Abstract. The game designers craft is very young if compared to film-making and software development. The knowledge base and formal techniques of these areas is far more comprehensive. Even after decades of evolution of the games production software, the range of design centered techniques and tools is still limited, as observed by many authors. Thereby, efforts have been made towards the establishment of game design formal methods. This paper presents a sys-tematization over the contributions of researchers and designers towards con-ceptual and concrete tools. These efforts converge to two approaches: the build of a shared design vocabulary and a game design modeling language. While valuable, the existing implementations of these approaches are not mature enough to gain industry adepts, serving only as reference to future works. Moreover, it is needed to discover the designers particular methods, which may contribute to-wards the constitution of a unified design toolbox.

Keywords: Game design, game design methods, game design tools.

1 Introduction

The game design is one of the key-areas to the digital entertainment industry. With the emergence of new technologies, production tools have evolved considerably, but little has been made to provide support to game design. Designers still use the same instruments from the beginning of the area and, although the industry has seen con-secutive successes in sales, researchers and professionals agree that the lack of tools, whether conceptual or software, imposes a barrier to any standardization attempt and hinders the knowledge transfer between generations of designers. They proposed conceptual and concrete tools that could complement or replace the design document, aiming improvements to the games creation process.

This paper presents a systematization of these efforts through a chronological overview of the main approaches and their implementations, in order to map them within the context of the state of art of design tools. Few studies have

J.C. Anacleto et al. (Eds.): ICEC 2013, LNCS 8215, pp. 17–29, 2013.

been published with a similar purpose. Kreimeier (2003) summarized the main methods proposed until 2003, analyzing them from the designer's perspective. Neil (2012) presented a discussion over the need to evaluate the proposed design tools.

2   The Game Design and Its Tools

The process of creating games has an intrinsic reliance on the designers creative skills. Books, movies, music and real world facts and culture serve as inspiration for games. Furthermore, existing games typically act as a foundation for new ideas. Ex-perimentation is an essential part of this process, which can be summarized in three steps: design, documentation and prototyping. The game design document is the main artifact produced by a game designer. It is used to communicate the designer's vision to the development team. It also acts as a guide to the whole development process and considered by many as a production method (Kreimeier, 2003).

As a key part of the game design activities, the design document has been subject of some efforts trying to establish more standardized content and format. However, no concrete results have been achieved. According to Dormans (2012), the lack of standards in design documentations inhibits the creation of a universal design methodology. Kreimeier (2003) points that while some designers highlight the need for the document others deny its practice. For Keith (2010), the document is rarely used by developers in later development stages, serving only as a contractual object. The size and format of the document can be factors that lead to such practice. Even with the use of visual aids, such as sketches and storyboards, Costykian (1994) points such tools are not enough to describe the design. Its static nature is also highlighted as a problem. Dormans (2012) points out that changes in the game concept are common and updating the document to reflect them becomes unproductive as the project progresses. Librande (2010) emphasizes that although the document has the purpose of communicating the designers vision throughout the development team, those involved in production feel little motivation to read it. The author emphasizes the need for visual languages, more expressive and compact.

Typically in a game development project, testing prototypes are produced in pre-liminary stages after the design document, with intense focus on gameplay and usually disregarding artistic presentation. They are commonly used as a concept proof tool and experimentation environment to evaluate and evolve the gameplay initially planned in the design document (Salen and Zimmerman, 2003). Game designers have unanimous agreement about the value of experimentation through prototyping, regarded a critical part of the game development process and considered the only reliable method of verifying the design quality (Neil, 2012).

With rare exceptions, designers are not able to build the game prototypes. Game creation toolkits are creatively too restrictive and analog prototypes, like board games, are ineffective for games with interaction mechanisms heavily based on real time actions (Sigman, 2005). Therefore, software prototypes are usually built by people involved in the production, like software developers and graphic artists, based on the documentation and guidance provided by the designers. This creates a gap between the conception of game ideas and the experimentation process that could attest them (Neil, 2012), turning prototyping into a costly and slow process, away from the direct control of the designer. Moreover, the prototype is commonly constructed after the completion of a significant part of the design document, making it impossible for designers to do instant gameplay experiments during the game conception phase.

Generally speaking, designers aim a tool that would allow them to build experi-mental prototypes directly from the definition of a set of game characteristics. This could provide a way to perform instant proofs of concepts while creating the design documentation, through an iterative process of design and testing of gameplay. In this environment, the ability to reuse existing elements of games as a design vocabulary would be an essential resource. A study of requirements gathering for design tools conduced by Nelson and Mateas (2009) confirms this direction. However, software tools are just facilitators for the use of practical and consolidated conceptual tools. The architecture and software engineering are examples of this scenario: the CAD software have been developed only to aid in the use of conceptual tools that already existed and were of common use. In this way, the first logical step would be the development of a conceptual tool box aimed at supporting the game design, which has been the main target of many studies in the area.

3   Early Discussions towards New Design Tools

Although widely adopted as the mainstream tool in the industry, there is a consid-erable lack of formalization and standardization in design document. Despite the visible success of the industry, researchers and professionals agree that the lack of tools, whether conceptual or software tools, hinders the knowledge transfer between generations of designers and the evolution of the design process itself (Neil, 2012). However, this is not a recent issue.

In 1994, Costikyan (1994) published a discussion about the need for greater for-malism on game design, suggesting the search of a common vocabulary that would allow designers to analyze and describe games. For him, designers should have a way to analyze games, understand them and identify the elements that make them good or bad. Therefore, Costikyan emphasizes the need for the creation of a shared language for game design. His discourse has been directly or indirectly echoed by many researchers and designers. For Church (1999), the main inhibitor of the design methods evolution lies in the lack of a common design vocabulary to describe games concepts, hindering the transfer of knowledge between generations of designers. Later, Fullerton (2008) also expressed the same opinion, pointing out the lack of a common vocabulary as one of the biggest problems faced by the games production industry of its time. Like Costikyan, Church advocates the creation of a vocabulary, an analysis and design tool that would allow an univocally identification of the elements that constitutes games, aiming to establish a collection of reusable design concepts. Through such vocabulary, Church hopes to be able to dissect a game, identify and separate its forming components, understand how they fit and balance together, and analyze which ones benefit or harm certain games or game genres.

Over the years, practitioners and researchers have identified the need for formal models and tools to support game design (Neil, 2012). In this context, "formal" does not refer to mathematical models, but to organized, standardized and structured models and tools to aid the game design methods. This paper presents a sys-tematization of the efforts made to date to build such models and tools, mapping them into the universe of approaches of game design tools and highlighting their specific contributions. This systematization is presented in the form of a state of art map of game design tools (Figure 1), which organizes the existing tools into two main groups: shared design vocabularies and visual design languages.

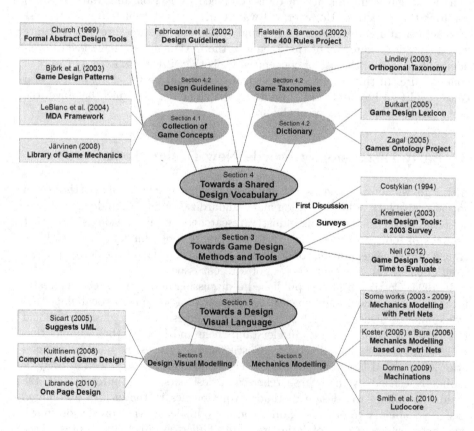

Fig. 1. State of art map of game design methods and tools

4 Towards Better Communication through a Unified Vocabulary

Many researchers and designers consider that a shared and unified vocabulary can bring significant benefits to the area (Neil, 2012). The fours approaches towards this accomplishment are discussed through this section (upper segment of Fig. 1. map).

4.1 Collections of Design Concepts

In 1999, Church (1999) proposed the creation of Formal Abstract Design Tools (FADT). They comprise a vocabulary of recurring game design concepts. Each term is presented by name and description. For the author, a FADT must be precise, unam-biguous and applicable to as many situations as possible. However, although Church has aimed to dissect the games in its forming parts the FADT do not define games components, but rather, abstract concepts and features. This can be noticed in one of only three terms defined by the author: "Perceivable Consequence: a clear reaction from the game world to the action of the player." In general, the model is too simple and relationships with games or genres are not covered. It also lacks information about the use implications of each FADT in a game. Its application relies too much on the abstraction ability of each designer. Kreimeier (2003) pointed out that in the end, only 25 FADT were documented and the work was discontinued. Dormans (2012) reported that between 1999 and 2002, the Gamasutra[1] site hosted a forum where people discussed and expanded Church's tool, although there are no reports of its use on real world projects. Although simple and short lived, Church's work repre-sented the first attempt towards a standardized collection of game design concepts.

In 2002, Kreimeier suggested the adoption of an approach similar to the Software Design Patterns of Gamma (1994) to document recurring concepts of game design. Following the same line, Björk et al (2003) proposed a model of Game Design Pat-terns (GDP) which, though inspired in Gamma, does not follow the approach of pairs "problem-solution" when structuring patterns. The GDP document recurring concepts of game design. The patterns represent games mechanics as well as transversal char-acteristics, like Church's FADT. Each design pattern is documented by a well-defined structure, which includes name, defini-tion, usage examples, application instructions, narrative aspects, consequences of use, and relationships with other patterns. Accord-ing to the authors, the GDP aim to provide a tool for analysis and design of games (Björk et al. 2003). The project has a wiki[2], in which there are 386 patterns collabora-tively documented, which shows the intention of making it a tool of practical use.

As a design technique, the Game Design Patterns represent an evolution over the FADT and the most significant contribution in trying to set up a database of design concepts. Its design patterns inspired structure allows highlighting the

---

[1] http://www.gamasutra.com/ (visited on 2013/03/13)
[2] http://gdp2.tii.se/index.php/Main_Page (visited on 2013/03/13)

relevant aspects of each pattern and their interrelationships. On the other hand, the project has short-comings that discourage its use. There is not enough correspondence between patterns and the games or genres that use them to allow a games-centered analysis. The wiki's documentation and navigation simplicity hinders both the understanding and the use of the patterns. It is common to find incomplete and contradictory docu-mentation on patterns, with disagreements between title, definition and usage exam-ples. Finally, there is a lack of graphical models to facilitate the patterns understanding and to allow the visualization of the hierarchy and relationships between patterns and games. These characteristics transform the GDP in a little intuitive scattered collection that requires a high learning curve.

LeBlanc et al. (2004) highlight the importance of considering both the perspective of the designer (producer) and the player (consumer) when designing games. Their work proposes a framework to analyze games in three different components: mechanics, that describe the static rules of the game system, described in the design document; dynamics, that represent the run-time behavior of the mechanics on a play session, present in games and prototypes, and; aesthetics, which comprehends the desired emotional responses of players, obtained from tests and experimentations with the prototype or game. This separation of components in rules, run-time and emotional responses highlights the focus on gameplay experiences when designing the game rules, and with it, the importance of building software prototypes for testing the outcome of the designed concepts. Moreover, it ratifies a very common practice of designers: the investigation of the emotional result of mechanics implemented in the existing games. Thus, as part of their work, designers must constantly experience a vast amount of games in an analytical way, which is quite costly. Thereby, the importance of building a database of design concepts drawn from existing games becomes evident, though neither of the existing implementations has been successful.

Similar approaches to the ones of Church (1999) and Bjork et al. (2003) were dis-cussed in the work of Järvinen's mechanics library (Järvinen, 2008) and the definition of game mechanics inspired by the object-orientated paradigm of Sicart (2008). There is also a collection of game concepts documented in the Giant-Bomb[3] site, which although presents an informal approach and a focus clearly aimed at end users, without the apparent intention of establishing a tool for designers, features a simple and functional solution based on collaborative construction. On the site's database, the understanding of the concepts is facilitated through the use of illustrations. Moreover, it has a considerable range over the library of available games, relating them to the concepts used. Although devoid of formalism, this collection of game concepts presents functional characteristics that may inspire future works in the area.

---

[3] http://www.giantbomb.com/concepts/ (visited on 2013/03/13)

4.2   Other Approaches and Their Implementations

Unlike the attempts focused on building a collection of design concepts, Falstein and Barwood initiated the "The 400 Rules Project" in 2002 (Falstein, 2002). Its aim was to identify, record and share practical experiences of designers indicating direc-tions to be taken or avoided on a game project. From the initial planning of 400 rules, only 112 were documented on the project's website[4] through the collaboration of various designers. As in the Game Design Patterns project, this work demonstrated a clear intention to provide an artifact of practical use. In a similar approach, Fabricatore, Nussbaum and Roses (2002) proposed design guidelines from an analysis of the influence of gameplay mechanisms in player's motivations. Regardless of the obtaining method, the documentation of design guidelines can assist in the knowledge transfer between generations of profession-als, especially during the training of new designers. Moreover, it has an intrinsic practical nature, considering that portrays the concrete learning of the designer's craft. On the other hand, guidelines cannot constitute a tool that actually supports the idiosyncratic crea-tive process of game design.

Burkart (2005) and Zagal et at. (2005) started distinct projects aiming to create shared design dictionaries in order to provide unambiguous definitions for terms commonly used in game design documents. These dictionaries would be available in a digital encyclopedia for online access and stored in a database to be embedded in documents through markup languages, such as XML. Of these, the Games Ontology Project of Zagal et al. (2005) was published in a wiki[5], where 179 definitions of spe-cific game design terms are documented. Although dictionaries alone cannot become design tools, Kreimeier (2003) states they are necessary complements to any method or conceptual tool. For him, even if recurring design concepts patterns, mechanics and games components do define part of a vocabulary, not every term defines a design concept but must be uniquely defined. Thus, dictionaries of terms can be seen as a lower abstraction layer, serving as a foundation for other approaches. Much like the design guidelines discussed above, a shared dictionary of terms has a concrete value of practical application in the designer's everyday, especially when writing doc-uments and communicating, but cannot surface as a design tool by itself.

A common language practiced by the industry and academia is resultant of the games taxonomy (Järvinen, 2008). Age, target audience, purpose and genre are examples of criteria that lead to different classifications. Of these, the gen-res classification is perhaps the most concrete example of value and practical application of a games vocabulary, structuring games with similar interaction characteristics under the same group. This classification helps to define the typ-ical elements of each game genre and to understand how the mixing between genres occurs. Some authors suggest that not all games can be framed in a hi-erarchical system of categories and subcategories (Björk, 2003). Among them, Lindley (2003) proposed an orthogonal taxonomy for games that defines a spa-tial system of characteristics, where games and genres are positioned according

---

[4] http://www.finitearts.com/Pages/400page.html (visited on 2013/03/13)
[5] http://www.gameontology.com/index.php/Main_Page (visited on 2013/03/13)

to their proximity to these characteristics. As an example, the author presents spaces of one, two or three dimensions applied to various characteristics such as simulation, ludology and narratology. Further studies could relate the taxonomies in games and the collections of design concepts in order to investigate which quantitative and qualitative relationships can be drawn between elements, market and user preferences. The outcome of these studies could suggest which elements are desirable for a particular game project that fit into a classification.

This section presented four different approaches and their implementations at-tempts to build a shared design vocabulary: collections of design concepts, design guidelines, dictionaries of terms and taxonomies in games (as seen in the upper seg-ment of the Fig. 1 map). Of these, the first has promising applications as a supporting tool for game analysis and design, allowing designers to create new games from an accumulated knowledge base. However, the existing implementations still do not allow this. The other approaches dictionaries, tax-onomies and guidelines have an intrinsically practical nature and although they cannot surface as tools, they are significant contributions to the conception and adoption of a common vocabulary. Overall, all approaches show an evident lack of maturity and computational support for adoption or even for experimentation in real world scenarios.

5   Towards Better Communication through Visual Game Design Modeling

Although of predominantly textual content, designers commonly use visual arti-facts as auxiliary tools in the design document (Neil, 2012). Game events and charac-ters behaviors are often expressed by diagrams and story boards. Conceptual illustra-tions are used to preview the game graphics. Furthermore, it is common for designers to create their own visual notations to express part of the game design in which they are working (Salen and Zimmerman 2003). The "One Page Design" schemes of Lib-rande (2012) are an example of this practice.

Designers have found in the visual modeling a strong ally to communicate their vi-sion of the game to other team members. Librande emphasizes that visual models are more synthetic, naturally communicative and scale better. For him, the diagramming practice forces the designers to extract the essence of the gameplay in few visual elements. Also, designers are driven to specify the relationships between the components of gameplay and to adopt a top-down approach, breaking larger problems into smaller pieces. In general, visual schemes create a game design map to the team, facilitating its understanding and update. However, the game design profession lacks a standard visual language and efforts have been made towards this approach. Along with the attempts to develop a common design vocabulary, the demand for visual design languages comprises the second main approach in which projects have followed towards design formal methods and tools (lower segment of Fig. 1). With this objective, two branches can be differentiated: the search for visual languages of design and languages for game mechanics modeling.

The use of visual languages for representing the design resembles the requirements and design modeling on the software engineering. This similarity has been noted by some authors, who discussed the use of UML diagrams to create design maps. Sicart (2008) presented a definition for game design based on the concept of object orienta-tion, suggesting the use of UML (Fowler, 2004) for modeling, although no examples were shown. Demachy (2003) discussed the use of Extreme Programming, an agile software development method, in the production of games. He also refers to UML as a design tool that can be used to describe game elements and the gameplay. Blumen-thal (2005) designed the Space Invaders game as a pedagogical demonstration, using UML to capture the requirements and design of the game. In general, though textual content documents are frequently used in software specification, visual languages are heavily used to enhance communication inside and outside of the development team. Likewise, the UML can be a convenient tool to communicate the design in a games project. However, further studies of UML application must be performed to make it suitably adapted to the needs of game design.

In order to generate design models based on Game Design Patterns of Björk (2003), Kuittinen (2008) implemented the software CAGE Computer-Aided Game Design one of the few initiatives already made to build concrete tools. His goal is to allow designers to select the patterns that will constitute the game concept and visual-ize their inter-relationships in a diagram. The descriptions of the used patterns are then integrated into the design document. Although simple and academic, this work represents an interesting attempt to apply a conceptual model and to integrate it to the method currently used in industry. In an opposite direction, the software Sketch-It-Up! (Karakaya, 2009) provides a visualization of the design narrative. Although not related to the design modeling, the software represents another attempt to bring computational support to game design. The central idea of the tool is to enable designers and developers to build a global view of the game through animatics (ani-mated story boards). In a brainstorming session, participants interact simultaneously by the software, controlling drafts of actors and objects in the game to create animated sequences of representations of the gameplay.

In contrast to the design modeling, academic approaches has focused on a lower level of abstraction, trying to put together a vocabulary of logical constructs that allow representation of game mechanics, a process that has been done textually in the design documents. Adaptations of Petri Nets for this purpose have been addressed by several authors, such as Brom & Abonyi (2006), Roque & Araujo (2009) and Natkin & Vega (2003). Koster (2005) and Bura (2006) also presented adaptations of Petri nets with several own customizations. Going a little farther, Joris Dorman (2009) built a software tool for mechanics modeling and simulation in real-time called Machinations. Using a visual language, designers specify the mechanics of the game. Once completed, the rules in the diagrams can be executed, allowing a "game simulation". Ludocore, a tool created by Smith, Nelson and Mateas (2010) follows a similar approach. However, instead of graphic constructions, designers use a textual programming language to create mechanics models, which can also be simulated in the environment. Although mechanics execution is apparently promising, the both tools use unknown and little intuitive languages. This is a fact that deserves attention, since the designers themselves use flowcharts to assist in the textual descriptions of mechanics. Additionally, the "game simulation" performed by these tools do not represents the player perspective, preventing the experimentation of the game aesthetic components.

The approaches presented in this section were distinguished into two groups: the constitution of languages for description and simulation of game mechanics, and the visual representation of the game concept through design modeling. In both, the goal is to act as a facilitator agent of communication in development teams and between generations of designers. In general, they represent the adoption of consolidated engi-neering approaches in game design. Although designers who heavily base their work on narrative techniques can provide resistance to the use of visual compositions, they represent a trend and a need already highlighted by researchers and practitioners.

6   Final Thoughts

The Game design lacks a shared tool box containing both broad application solu-tions and specific to certain genres of games. On one hand, professionals and compa-nies crave for tools that allow them to improve production and reduce the risks of investment in new projects. On the other, independent developers and beginners seek for tools that can bring them productivity and directions. Furthermore, the use of standardized tools can bring industry and academia closer, contributing to build a universal knowledge base of game design. The design document, the main tool cur-rently used, is considered by many authors as inappropriate to such aspirations.

In general, designers crave for productive and standardized tools and techniques that do not sacrifice the freedom and creativity inherent to their craft. Several attempts to set up these tools have been made and can be generalized under two approaches: the building of a design vocabulary and the development of visual languages for design modeling. Under the first group, researchers and designers have addressed topics such as dictionaries of design terms, taxonomies in games, design guidelines and collections of design concepts. The first three approaches can not be considered tools. Dictionaries are elementary, serving as a basis for communication between professionals and for project documents. Design guidelines help to transfer experiences to new generations of designers. Taxonomies help to organize the vast library of existing games and to compose a design vocabulary, besides essential to market studies. On the other hand, the collections of design concepts, addressed in the fourth topic, represent a promising possibility of a design toolbox and an important component in building a universal knowledge base of design.

Designers commonly build their work over the previous results of other professionals, through experiments and analysis of existing games. As a source of

inspira-tion, designers constantly use commercial and independent games in order to raise requirements to the project they are working on. This practice also
allows them to increase their knowledge about game mechanics and the gameplay
experiences they generate (their aesthetic components). Moreover, this process
of research and experi-mentation acts as a proof of concepts to the desired mechanics. In general, the goal of this practice is to extract the elements that can
lead games to success or failure, understand how they fit and balance, and assist
designers in the decision to include these elements into their projects. On the
other hand, the existing attempts of implementing this approach of collection of
design concepts FADT (Church, 1999), Game Design Patterns (Börjk, 2003),
Library of Mechanics (Järvinen, 2008) and Library of Concepts (GiantBomb[6])
do not meet the criteria raised. Together, these findings create a strong incentive for new attempts to build a collection of recurring design elements drawn
from existing games. Moreover, this approach is aligned with the needs raised
by Costikyan (1994) and Church (1999).

From the perspective of its development, games can be considered as the combination of filmmaking and software. So it would be natural that the tools coming
from these areas were borrowed for both development and design of games. From
the filmmaking, the loan occurs: designers use story boards, sketches and cameras and narration techniques to design and document game concepts. However,
the software development tools have very little influence over the designer work.
While software design and programming techniques are useless to the designer,
requirements analysis instruments can benefit them. From the perspective of requirements capture and analysis, game designers have a very similar role to the
system analysts, once they must understand and document the needs of users by
their perspectives. Thus, it would be expected that visual languages heavily used
by analysts, like UML, were adapted for game design, which does not occur in practice. Furthermore, although several authors agree with this perspective and others
highlight the benefits of using diagrams in the game design, little has been done.

Even criticizing the model of designing games as a whole, designers and
research-ers have been focusing solely on the creation of environments and languages for modeling and simulation of game mechanics, such as machinations
(Dormans, 2009) and Ludocore (Smith, Nelson and Mateas, 2010). In these implementations, the use of unfamiliar and counter intuitive languages, the high
learning curve required and the uncertainty of practical gains, keep the designers
away. Moreover, these tools have been validated in academic environments, applied to restricted work groups, usually composed by academics and beginners,
which does not reflect the area. Even its authors are uncertain about the gains
that such tools will bring to other designers and highlight the need to evaluate
them on the field. Neil (2012) proposed to carry out such evaluation.

Last but not least, in addition to recognizing the designers needs, it is needed
to know their particular methods, those not widely documented. The commercial
success of the industry cannot be overlooked, a fact that certainly contributes to
certify these methods. In particular, it is wanted to find out what are the tools

---

[6] http://www.giantbomb.com/concepts/ (visited on 2013/03/13)

the own designers create and use to work on particularities of their projects. It is possible that some significant importance tools have already been developed and abandoned at the end of a project. The design schemes on a single page of Librande (2012) are examples of an instrument carved from his needs. Becoming aware of such tools, created and used in specific design situations, can contribute with the approaches discussed in this paper to advance towards the constitution of a design toolbox. The fact that industry and academia agree about the needs of game designers indicates that both know what must be done, but the rejection of using the conceptual and physical implementations available, makes it clear they yet do not know how to do it.

References

1. Arajo, M., Roque, L.: Modeling Games with Petri Nets. Proceedings of 2009 Digital Games Research Association Conference (DiGRA). Brunel University (2009) **Brunel University**
2. Björk, S., Lundgren, S., Holopainen, J.: Game Design Patterns. In: Level Up - Proceedings of Digital Games Research Conference (DiGRA). Utrecht University (2003)
3. Blumenthal, R.: Space Invaders: A UML Case Study. Regis University, class notes (2005)
4. Bura, S.: A Game Grammar (2006), http://www.stephanebura.com/diagrams/
5. Brom, C., Abonyi, A.: Petri-Nets for Game Plot. In: Proceedings of AISB, vol. 3 (2006)
6. Burkart, P.: Discovering a lexicon for video games: New research on structured vocabu-laries. International Digital Media and Arts Association Journal 2(1), 18–24 (2005)
7. Church, D.: Formal Abstract Design Tools. Gamasutra (July 1999), http://www.gamasutra.com/view/feature/3357/ formal_abstract_design_tools.php
8. Costikyan, G.: I Have No Words & I Must Design. Interactive Fantasy, Eng. (2) (1994)
9. Demachy, T.: Extreme Game Development: Right on Time. Every Time, http://www.gamasutra.com/view/feature/2827/ extreme_game_development_right_on_.php
10. Dormans, J.: Engineering Emergence: Applied Theory for Game Design. Teste de Dou-torado. Amsterdam University of Applied Sciences (2012)
11. Gamma, E., et al.: Design Patterns: Elements of Reusable Object-Oriented Software. Addison-Wesley (1994)
12. Fabricatore, C., Nussbaum, M., Rosas, R.: Playability in Action Videogames: A Qualitative Design Model. Proceedings of Human-Computer Interaction 17(4), 311–368 (2002)
13. Falstein, N., Barwood, H.: More of the 400: Discovering Design Rules. Presentation at GDC (2002), http://www.gdconf.com/archives/2002/hal_barwood.ppt
14. Fowler, M.: UML Distilled: A Brief Guide to the Standard Object Modeling Language, 3rd edn. Addison-Wesley, Boston (2004)
15. Fullerton, T., Swain, C., Hoffman, S.: Game Design Workshop: Designing, Prototyping, and Playtesting Games. CMP Books, San Francisco (2004)

16. Järvinen, A.: Games Without Frontiers: Theories and Methods for Game Studies and Design. Tese de Doutorado. University of Tampere (2008)
17. Karakaya, B., Garcia, C., Rodriguez, D., Nityanandam, M., Labeikovsky, N., Al Tamimi, T.: Sketch-It-Up! Demo. In: Natkin, S., Dupire, J. (eds.) ICEC 2009. LNCS, vol. 5709, pp. 313–314. Springer, Heidelberg (2009)
18. Koster, R.: A Grammar of Gameplay. Presentation at GDC 2005, San Francisco CA (March 2005), http://www.raphkoster.com/gaming/atof/grammarofgameplay.pdf
19. Kreimeier, B.: Game Design Methods: A 2003 Survey. Gamasutra (March 2003), http://www.gamasutra.com/view/feature/2892/game_design_methods_a_2003_survey.php
20. Kuittinen, J.M.: Computer-Aided Game Design. Master's Thesis in Information Technology. University of Jyväskylä (January 19, 2008)
21. LeBlanc, M.: Formal Design Tools: Feedback Systems and the Dramatic Structure of Competition. In: Computer Game Developers' Conference (1999)
22. LeBlanc, M., Hunicke, R., Zubek, R.: MDA: A formal approach to game design and game research. In: Proceedings of the AAAI 2004 Workshop on Challenges (2004)
23. Librande, S.: One-Page Designs. Presentation at GDC 2010, San Francisco, CA (March 2010), http://stonetronix.com/gdc-2010/
24. Lindley, C.: Game Taxonomies: A High Level Framework for Game Analysis and Design (2003), http://www.gamasutra.com/view/feature/2796/game_taxonomies_a_high_level_.php
25. Natkin, S., Vega, L.: A petri net model for computer games analysis. International Journal of Intelligent Games Simulation 3(1), 37–44 (2004)
26. Neil, K.: Game Design Tools: Time to Evaluate. In: Proceedings of DiGRA Nordic 2012 Conference: Local and Global Games in Culture and Society (2012)
27. Nelson, J.M., Mateas, M.: A Requirements Analysis for Videogame Design Support Tools. In: Proceedings of the 4th IC-FDG 2009, Orlando, Florida, USA, April 26-30 (2009)
28. Salen, K., Zimmerman, E.: Rules of Play: Game Design Fundamentals. MIT Press (2003)
29. Sicart, M.: Defining Game Mechanics. Game Studies. The International Journal of Computer Game Research 8(2) (December 2008), http://gamestudies.org/0802/articles/sicart
30. Smith, A.M., Nelson, M.J., Mateas, M.: LUDOCORE: A logical game engine for modeling videogames. In: CIG 2010 IEEE Symposium, pp. 91–98 (2010)
31. Tremblay, J., Schneider, K., Cheston, G.: Game Case Study, ch. 17. Software Development in an Object-Oriented Domain, University of Saskatchewan (2010)
32. Zagal, J.P., Mateas, M., Fernadez-Vara, C., Hochhalter, B., Lichti, N.: Towards an Onto-logical Language for Game Analysis. In: Proceedings of the DiGRA, Canada (June 2005)

Augmented Home

Integrating a Virtual World Game in a Physical Environment

Serge Offermans and Jun Hu

Eindhoven University of Technology
Department of Industrial Design
The Netherlands
{s.a.m.offermans,j.hu}@tue.nl

Abstract. To combine these opportunities offered by both virtual words and the physical world, we have developed the Augmented Home, a game which combines the qualities of both worlds and integrates them into one. The Augmented Home draws the virtual world into the physical by binding it to the physical environment for children and parents to experience the virtual world together, being engaged in activities that benefit the child's educational, social and creative development.

Keywords: virtual worlds, physical play, educational games, development of children.

1 Introduction

A disadvantage of the recent development in computer games and virtual worlds is that children could be addicted to these virtual worlds and games [1]. This leads to problems such as social isolation [2] and obesity [3]. Most of these virtual worlds and games separate the children from their physical environments. This also means that other people from the physical world, such as parents, can hardly be involved in the virtual experiences. This paper presents 'the Augmented Home', a virtual world game that appears to be part of our everyday physicality, for parents and children to play together. This is a computationally generated and mediated world that is not bound to its generative medium - a personal computer, but rather is accessible in the physical world. It combines the qualities of both the physical and the virtual world.

The augmented home draws the virtual world into the physical by binding it to the physical environment and placing the virtual (objects and characters) in our physical world. Interaction with the world is made possible through a device that functions as a channel between the two worlds. It channels audio from one world to the other and allows you to 'feel' and manipulate the world through movement and touch, which stimulates the children's imagination. Through the interaction devices of the augmented home, the children can, together with the parents, participate in challenges and educational games, and experience narratives that stimulate the development of creativity, reasoning and social skills.

J.C. Anacleto et al. (Eds.): ICEC 2013, LNCS 8215, pp. 30–35, 2013.
© IFIP International Federation for Information Processing 2013

2   The Augmented Home

The Augmented Home is realized by creating an overlap of the virtual world over the physical environment [4], by integrating the values of both the virtual and the physical [5], and by making the virtual world available to all members of the family, allowing them to perceive it as part of their daily life.

2.1   Design Concept

A virtual world is designed to be an overlapped layer of the physical home, as a game platform for children (age between 4 and 12) to play together with parents at home. The story in this is about a group of characters live inside the house with some virtual objects. The users can communicate with the characters and do something with the objects. This is the basis for progression in the world, very similar to various digital virtual worlds. Different from the most of the virtual worlds available online, the Augmented Home is only apparent through sound and touch, allowing and encouraging the imagination of users and especially the children. The approach taken here is very similar to reading a book or telling a story; the visual aspect of the virtual world is constructed by the person listening to it or reading it [6]. This stimulation of imagination contributes to the child's development, especially in terms of creativity.

2.2   Scenario and Prototype

One scenario of the Augmented Home is worked out as a working prototype for user evaluation. The scenario and the prototype are briefly described next.

Scenario. The story is about a character called Dibbel who has lost his cat (Fig. 1, see also Fig. 3). Dibbel asks for cooperation from the user to help him find his cat and return the cat to him. There are however some difficulties. The cat is asleep and can't be found unless the user ring its bell in the same room. Furthermore, the cat is quite shy, and therefore tends to run away if the user approaches. If the user keeps the cat at ease with a cup of milk, the user can pick up the cat and return it to Dibbel. For the cup of milk the user needs to get it from Lilly, another character. She is somewhere in the house and the user has to find her first. If the user gets the milk from Lilly, the user has to walk carefully in order not to spill the milk from the cup.

Prototype. The prototype initiates the conversation with prerecorded sentences; the user can talk back to the virtual world through the channeling device (Fig. 2). Speech recognition is used to understand possible responses. The virtual objects that can be carried using the channeling device in the prototype are the bell, the milk and the cat. When carrying a virtual object, the user would feel the channeling device to be heavier. When carrying the bell, shaking it will create a ringing sound. When carrying a cup of milk, tilting the device will spill a bit of the virtual milk. When it is tilted too far, it will spill all the virtual milk and the user would feel the device to be lighter. The user has to return to Lilly to get new milk. When the cat is picked up, a purring sound would be heard from the channeling device.

The channeling device uses sound and tactile feedback to let the users experience the virtual world, and in turn, the users can influence the world via the same modalities. The users can talk to the characters in the virtual world. The sounds from the virtual world come out on one end of the channel, and are 'physically' output through the speaker on the other end. Speech from the user to the virtual world goes exactly the other way round.

The channeling device is also used for exploring the virtual world in the physical environment. The user can point the device at places around the room, until a character or an object is felt or heard. Distance to the virtual character or object can be felt through vibration with different levels of intensity. The closer, the stronger the vibration is. At the same time an identifier sound can be heard for the user to identify the character. The volume of the identifier also indicates the distance to the character.

When a virtual object is received, the channeling device can be felt heavier – the illusion is created using a weight distribution system inside. The virtual object can then be carried around and given to other characters by moving it closer. Depending on the object, having or using the object may also generate sounds. When the user would carry a bell, shaking the device will generate the sound as if the bell is ringing.

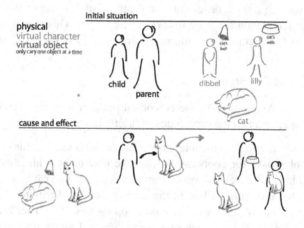

Fig. 1. Scenario

Fig. 2. Channeling device between the virtual and the physical in Augmented Home

3   Evaluation

The Augmented Home was evaluated with three groups of a child and one of the parents. The evaluation consisted of observations and semi-structured interviews.

3.1   Participants, Setup and Procedure

The children participating in the evaluation were all between the age of 5 and 9. These age limits were chosen together with a primary school teacher based on complexity of the challenge that was worked out in the prototype. Both the parent and child received a channeling device. Before the experiment started, the participants are given the opportunity to ask questions if there was anything not understood. They were also told that questions could be asked during the assignment if needed. The participants then performed the task (Fig. 3), after which a semi-structured interview took place with both the parent and the child together.

Fig. 3. User evaluation with the Augmented Home

3.2   Results

All children perceived the overlapping virtual world as very "real". After the evaluation, they indicated that they thought that Dibbel and the cat were still around. One of the children said: "I think they are playing together outside, because they are now reunited." This also indicates that the Augmented Home triggered the imagination of children as they came up with their own stories.

Two of three children tried to find the virtual cat, based on the behavior of real cats. They started by looking for the virtual cat in the couch and the bed, as these were the places where the real cats they knew would usually stay. One child also kept on reasoning after the evaluation, about how they could have done better by trying to understand the behavior of the virtual cat. Although one of them did not manage to find the cat at the beginning, "We might have found the cat if we were a bit more quiet, she might be scared". All children also immediately knew how to ring the bell with the channeling device when they were asked to do so by one of the characters.

All group showed roughly the same behavior concerning the division of their roles. The child did the primary conversations and took all the decisions that could be made, while the parent guided by asking rhetorical questions. The parents also carried the milk as that allowed their child to carry the cat; "I would not want to take the opportunity away from my son to carry the cat, so therefore I took the milk."

The cooperative nature of the game was considered to be a very positive aspect. Compared to the digital games that the participants played before, this was the first game where they could actually work together as equals in a team. "It allows you to do things together rather than play against each other or help from the sideline." Another parent stated that "It's a very social game..."

When asked about similarities and differences with other existing games, most comparisons were made with "hide and seek" for its explorative and surprising nature as well as for its physical part of the game. Comparisons were also made to other digital games. Similarities here were mainly the way you can progress through a narrative and the 'quest'-like setup. Having virtual characters was mentioned by two of the parents as one of the similarities. Differences were mainly the interaction, except when comparing it to Nintendo Wii, a system that two out of three couples had experienced. The parents saw similarities in the interaction as it is both relatively physically active. "It's like the Wii, but with this you can move around the house..."

Triggering the imagination of the children by removing the visual aspects of the virtual world and using only sound and tactile feedback was considered to be one of the strongest points of the design. One of the parents stated that "I didn't notice that it did not have a screen or something, now that you mention it I believe that really allows my son to imagine it for himself."

4   Discussion and Conclusion

The Augmented Home tries to integrate the qualities of both the physical and virtual worlds for the benefit of the development of children. The system was intended to be perceived as part of everyday reality, stimulating imagination and allowing children and parents to experience it together. In the evaluation of the Augmented Home, we have seen that the children perceived the virtual world as real and combined ideas presented in the virtual world with ideas from the physical world. This indicates that a clear distinction between the two was not made. The children were also able to imagine various aspects of the game that were not provided by the system such as character locations, activities and behavior. We have also seen a more cooperative relation emerge between parents and children. It allows the parents to support the development of the children while being engaged in a virtual world.

Furthermore the evaluation showed that children can be engage in a virtual world and benefit from its educative qualities without being separated from the 'real world'. The qualities of the virtual world, such as the tailored complexity and interactivity, were present and not compromised by the lack of physical qualities such as physical play and the ability to involve others in their activities.

One could argue that the system proposed still tends to pull the children out of their everyday reality and into the virtual world. We however believe that with the proposed integration, the distinction between virtual and real is no longer relevant. We already live our lives surrounded by –and immersed in– various virtual worlds in a broader sense. A reality is not determined by its material form, but by our common perception and agreement upon its existence.

The Augmented Home allows experiencing the designed virtual world with a large subset of its qualities in the everyday physical environment. Besides the combined qualities, there are some distinct qualities that are a result of this integration in the Augmented Home.

One of these distinct qualities is the cooperative opportunity that this approach offers. Parents and children can cooperate in an interactive narrative in their physical environment where they can together determine the path of the story whilst interacting with artificial actors and external influences. A second distinct quality is using sound and tactile feedback as interaction modalities, instead of the visual channel. Envisioning the virtual world requires and triggers imagination of children.

The proposition of the Augmented Home allows people to benefit from the qualities of virtual worlds in their physical daily live. In this paper this advantage is proposed as a part of the education development for children. This concept could however be implemented in a broader perspective, making the virtual available to in other everyday physical contexts. Similar benefits of the virtual world can be found for adults. The desire for such worlds can be observed in the popularity among adults of the online virtual worlds.

With the Augmented Home, we have done a first exploration of the design space, a preliminary evaluation of the system and the potential of its underlying principle. It would be interesting to see further explorations aiming at studying the effect of such systems in a more formal manner in the future.

References

1. Egger, O., Rauterberg, M.: Internet behaviour and addiction. Semester thesis (Swiss Federal Institute of Technology, Zurich, 1996) (1996)
2. Colwell, J., Kato, M.: Investigation of the relationship between social isolation, self-esteem, aggression and computer game play in Japanese adolescents. Asian Journal of Social Psychology 6(2), 149–158 (2003)
3. Trost, S.G., et al.: Physical activity and determinants of physical activity in obese and non-obese children. International Journal of Obesity and Related Metabolic Disorders: Journal of the International Association for the Study of Obesity 25(6), 822 (2001)
4. Rogers, Y., et al.: A conceptual framework for mixed reality environments: designing novel learning activities for young children. Presence: Teleoperators & Virtual Environments 11(6), 677–686 (2002)
5. Hu, J., Offermans, S.: Beyond L$: Values across the Virtual and the Real. In: International Conference on Advanced Infocomm Technology. Xi'an, China (2009)
6. Mendels, P., Frens, J.W.: The Audio Adventurer: Design of a Portable Audio Adventure Game. In: Markopoulos, P., de Ruyter, B., IJsselsteijn, W.A., Rowland, D. (eds.) Fun and Games 2008. LNCS, vol. 5294, pp. 46–58. Springer, Heidelberg (2008)

Debunking Differences between Younger and Older Adults Using a Collaborative Virtual Environment

Oswald D. Kothgassner[1,2,*], Anna Felnhofer[1,2,*], Helmut Hlavacs[2],
Leon Beutl[2], Jasmine Gomm[1], Nathalie Hauk[1], Elisabeth Kastenhofer[1],
and Ilse Kryspin-Exner[1]

[1] University of Vienna, Department of Applied Psychology: Health, Development,
Enhancement and Intervention
[2] University of Vienna, Research Group Entertainment Computing

Abstract. Collaborative virtual environments allow younger and older people to interact over long distances and stay in contact with their families and friends. Thus, these virtual environments are considered to be both, a crucial factor for active and healthy ageing and a great chance for future developments that may enhance and alter communication for specific age groups. Yet, to date there is a lack of studies examining differences between younger and older adults with special regards to technology usage factors, presence related factors as well as anxiety measures and psychophysiological arousal during social interactions in a collaborative virtual environment. Consequently, the objective of the current study was to evaluate the above mentioned factors in a group of 20 younger and 20 older adults using a slightly stressful collaborative virtual environment. The corresponding results indicate that virtual environments could indeed be beneficial tools for the communication of both, younger and older adults. Yet, older adults reported significantly lower levels of social presence during the interaction and were less able to handle the system than younger adults. Interestingly however, both groups did not differ in their technology related anxiety or regarding physiological measures of stress during the experience of the virtual environment.

1 Introduction

Over the course of time, many technology-aided communication forms have evolved from purely text typed messages to a more sophisticated, complex and thus, more demanding exchange which has undoubtedly altered social interactions via technology (e.g. virtual surroundings, virtual representations of the self, digital voices). The collaboration and interaction of many people around the world in virtual spaces using avatars as digital representations of the self are no longer limited to the field of commercial video games. So called collaborative

---

* Oswald D. Kothgassner and Anna Felnhofer contributed equally to this paper.

J.C. Anacleto et al. (Eds.): ICEC 2013, LNCS 8215, pp. 36–47, 2013.

virtual environments are also used for educational purposes, non-gaming virtual social communities like Second Life or the promising field of health related applications for therapy such as social skills trainings.

2 Related Work

Social participation as well as keeping in touch with family and friends are important factors for an active and healthy ageing. On the one hand the use of technological devices is discussed to be associated with a loss of quality in social contacts and with isolation. Yet, on the other hand social technologies like social network services or video games indicate the immense potential of technologies in increasing and enhancing social interaction with others [1]. Thus, collaborative virtual environments could act as an encouragement for people to stay in contact, play with their grandchildren or interact in a familiar environment with those who live far away. Nevertheless, collaborative virtual environments should not replace actual/physical visits of family members or significant others, but they could make these visits easer to communicate and get social support quicker and easier than through common paths of face-to-face interaction.

Several studies indicate that social interactions in collaborative virtual environments provoke behavioral and psychophysiological responses in users when interacting with avatars which are similar to responses when interacting with physically present "real-life" persons [2,12,25]. Recent studies illustrate the positive impact of social interaction and social support within virtual environments and provide evidence that virtually delivered social support can decrease the level of anxiety in stressful situations (e.g. [11]) as well as increase older adults' acceptance of virtual environments in particular [29].

Previous research [15] identified several factors which could act as barriers to the use of computer technology among older adults and could affect the quality of social interaction in collaborative virtual environments. Anxiety related to technological aspects has been identified as a key factor affecting the use of computer technology by older people [4]. Furthermore, prior computer experience has been shown to affect the performance of older people in virtual worlds [21]. Also, ease of use and perceived usefulness as well as the perception of accessibility of the product are seen as fundamental key factors for the user's intention to actually use the technology [8,24,28].

Other influencing factors factors (i.e. user characteristics) which have been repeatedly suggested to be responsible for the experience in and usage of collaborative virtual environments are related to the construct of (physical) presence. In contrast to immersion, which may be considered as a characteristic of technology [23], presence usually is broadly defined as the "perceptual illusion of nonmediation" [16]. While some researchers tend to define presence simply as the sense of "being there", other researchers differentiate between several separate aspects of presence including spatial presence, involvement and perceived realism (c.f. [16,10]). However, another element which is specifically necessary for the implementation of collaborative virtual environments is social presence.

Social presence refers to the degree in which the user believes to interact with another social entity and attributes mental states as well as personality to this social entity. It is a major contributing factor next to the so called behavioral realism in the Theory of social influence in virtual environments [3] which explains why people react to virtual others as if they were physically present. This theory underlines the importance of both, the evaluation of the virtual scenario (perceived realism) and the experience within the virtual environment (physical and social presence) in order for the collaborative virtual environment to be compelling and convincing.

To date, there is only little knowledge or evidence about differences between heterogeneous age groups using or interacting within collaborative virtual environments. Some findings revealed that older people seem to have greater difficulties in navigating and handling computer devices than younger adults [8]. Additionally, a study by Siriaraya and Ang [20] found that older adults showed significantly lower levels of social presence than younger adults, whereas physical presence produced inconclusive results [18,27,26]. Yet, a higher level of physical presence and social presence seem to be positive predictors of a general satisfaction with the collaborative virtual environments [9,20]. In sum, little is still known about age specific aspects of virtual reality experiences and about corresponding evaluations of the used technology.

3   Aim of the Study

Following the literature presented above, the scope of the present study was to evaluate a collaborative virtual environment and explore the potential differences between younger and older adults regarding their estimation of the virtual environment in terms of technology usage factors (intention to use, perceived usefulness, ease of use, perceived accessibility, and technology related anxiety).

Research question 1: Are there differences in the perception of technology usage factors between younger and older adults?

Consequently, presence related components like the sense of being there, perceived realism and social presence are said to be crucial in shaping the experience in collaborative virtual environments, yet results regarding possible age differences in the formation and degree of reported presence experiences are still inconclusive or non-existent. Therefore, the objective of the present study is to answer the following research question:

Research question 2: Are there differences in presence related factors between the two age groups in a collaborative virtual environment?

A third research question focuses on the subjectively perceived level of anxiety and corresponding psychophysiological responses during a social interaction in the virtual environment:

Research question 3: Are there differences between the age groups concerning the subjectively perceived level of anxiety and the psychophysiological stress level provoked during the social interaction in the virtual environment?

4   The VR-Cafe

Our virtual scenario consists of the following tasks: (i) learning how to control walking, (ii) entering a typical Viennese cafe and finding an empty table, (iii) interacting with the waiter, and (iv) interacting with strangers.

As a basis for the virtual cafe we modelled a typical Viennese cafe, including tables, seats, items on the tables, mirrors on the walls, textures, paintings, fotographs, news papers, vitrins etc. The result is a virtual representation of this cafe, being slightly larger inside. As modelling tools we used GIMP and Blender 3D, and for real time rendering we used the render engine OGRE3D. In order to create distinct looking avatars, we used our own head toolbox to model the heads of the research staff involved in this work.

The participant first has to learn how to control his avatar, seen from the first-person perspective. Since elderly people would most likely have troubles using off-the-shelf joypads for steering, we used an Android smart phone as input device. By tilting the phone, subjects could control their avatar. Learning to control their avatar's movements is done outside in an open area surrounded by buildings. The task is to follow a white rabbit (see Figure 1). We found that this natural gesture indeed also enables elderly people to control their avatar's movements smoothly.

After a certain time, the person should then enter the VR-cafe, and find an empty seat. In fact, all but one tables are taken, and the subject's task is to find this empty table and sit down. Again after some time, the waiter arrives and accepts an order, being either cafe or tea. Here, the psychologist can decide whether the waiter brings the correct order, or the wrong one.

After some time, a woman arrives and asks whether she can join the subject, the subject here may answer with yes or no (see Figure 2).

Fig. 1. Control training by following the white rabbit

Fig. 2. Social interaction inside the cafe

5   Experiments

5.1   Methods

The current study was conducted at the Department of Psychology at the University of Vienna in accordance with the current version of the Declaration of Helsinki. Prior to participation all participants signed an informed consent form indicating the experiment's procedure and the possibility to terminate participation at any time. All statistical analyses were conducted using SPSS Version 19 (SPSS, Inc. Chicago, USA) considering an alpha error of 5%.

5.2   Participants

The sample of younger adults (N=20) consisted of students who were recruited from several courses at the University of Vienna and received a course credit for their participation in the current study. In the group of the younger participants, 13 were female and 7 were male, with a mean age of 23.50 years (SD=2.782). The sample of older participants (N=20) consisted of healthy seniors. 10 older adults were female, 10 were male, with a mean age of 68.05 years (SD=8.275).

5.3   Procedure

All participants were invited to the laboratory on a weekday between 9 a.m. and 12 a.m. Upon their arrival, all participants signed the informed consent form and completed a short survey in a separate room. Following this, participants were guided to the laboratory where the physiological measures were applied. After a 5 minute resting period participants were instructed how to navigate through the virtual environment using the smart phone device (HTC Desire SV, Taoyuan) and the Head-mounted display (HMD, Sony HMZ-T1 3D Visor, Tokyo, Japan) with the externally applied head tracking system (TrackIR 5, NaturalPoint, Corvallis, USA). Subsequently, the participants started with a 5 minute preparation task, where they had to follow a virtual white rabbit through a virtual park. During the task they were given instructions via a pre-recorded male voice which guided them through the task. Following this preparation and training period the participants were invited to enter a virtual cafe which was located just across the street from the virtual park. There, the 5 minute experimental phase started, within which participants had to interact repeatedly with the two virtual characters (the waiter and a female guest). The last 5 minute phase was again a resting period, within which the participant was instructed to relax.

5.4   Measures

Several psychometric measures as well as psychophysiological measures were used to detect differences between younger and older adults and to evaluate the virtual environment. These measures are explained in more detail below.

Psychometric Measures: Five factors from the technology usage inventory (TUI, [13]) were used to evaluate participants estimations of the virtual environment: participants were asked to rate four statements for each factor on a 7-point-Likert scale (does apply - does not apply) after completing the tasks in the collaborative virtual environment for the first four factors (item examples in brackets): (1) perceived usefulness ("This technology would help me cope better with my daily duties", (2) ease of use ("The application of this technology is easy to understand"), (3) perceived accessibility ("I think that almost everyone can afford this technology") and (4) technology-related anxiety ("I think that the use of this technology is always associated with some risk"). The fifth factor (5) intention to use the virtual environment was assessed using three questions (e.g. "Would you use this technology?") which had to be rated on 1000 mm visual analog scales (VAS) (not at all - extremely). Additionally, a five item questionnaire [2] was used to assess social presence (e.g. "The person appears to be sentient, conscious and alive to me", strongly agree - strongly disagree), whereas two single 4-point-Likert-scaled items (strongly agree - strongly disagree) from the iGroup Presence Questionnaire (IPQ, [19]) were used to measure the sense of being there ("In the computer generated world I had a sense of 'being there'") and the perceived realism of the virtual environment ("How real did the virtual world seem to you?"). Participants completed these items immediately after the last resting period. Anxiety was assessed before the beginning of the simulation and short after the virtual experience using the 20-item 4-point-Likert-scaled (very - not at all) state version of the State-Trait Anxiety Inventory (STAI, [14]). One example for an item used in the STAI is: "I am calm".

Psychophysiological Measures: Heart rate variability (HRV) was selected as a measure of a participant's physiological arousal during the experiment. HRV was recorded via M-EXG (Schuhfried BFB 2000 x-pert, Moedling, Austria) using three one-way electrodes (3M Medica RedDot electrodes, Perchtoldsdorf, Austria). A time-domain measure for HRV was used to predominantly detect changes in the parasympathetic tone of the participants when being immersed in the collaborative virtual environment. In accordance with the recommendations of the Task Force of the European Society of Cardiology and the North American Society of Pacing and Electrophysiology [22] the root mean square of successive differences (rMSSD) was obtained as a time-domain measure reflecting a short-time measure of heart rate variability. The rMSSD values were calculated from beat-to-beat intervals for all 5 minute periods (for the detailed description of the experimental design see "procedure"). High rMSSD values represent low physiological arousal, whereas low values indicate higher physiological arousal and physiological stress.

6 Results

The main characteristics of younger and older adults participating in the current study are shown in Table 1. Neither the heart rate variability measure rMSSD during the first resting period ($T(28.636)=2.016$; $p=0.053$; $d=0.65$) nor the subjectively reported state anxiety measured by the state-version of the State-Trait

Table 1. User characteristics

	Younger adults (N=20)	Older adults (N=20)
computer experience (y/n)	100% / 0%	85% / 15%
educational level (in yrs)	12 (0.000)	13.55 (3.364)
weight (kg)	63.350 (10.321)	77.10 (14.881)
height (meters)	1.70 (0.061)	1.71 (0.081)

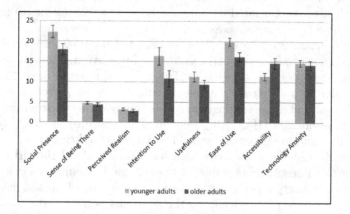

Fig. 3. Mean values (±SEM) of all psychological measures for younger (N=20) and older adults (N=20) (Values of the Intention to Use VAS were given in cm)

Anxiety Inventory (T(38)=1.660; p=0.105, d=0.54) did differ at a baseline level previous to the participants entering of the laboratory.[1]

6.1 Psychological Questionnaires

In order to estimate whether younger and older participants showed any difference on the technology usage scales and the assessments of presence related factors (sense of being there, perceived realism, social presence) group comparisons using Student t-tests were conducted. To correct the violation of the assumption of homogeneous variances for the two groups the Welch-Test was applied to the analysis. Results showed that the group of younger participants as compared to the older adults reported a significantly higher intention to use the collaborative virtual environment for social interaction (T(38)=1.865; p=0.070; d=0.59), and rated the handling of the virtual simulation as more usable than the

---

[1] Effect sizes d ranged between 0.20 and 0.49 indicate a small effect; effect sizes ranged between 0.50 and 0.79 indicate medium effects and effect sizes ranged over 0.80 indicate large effects. Effect sizes η^2 around 0.01 indicate small effects, while effect sizes around 0.06 indicate medium effects and all values over 0.14 indicate large effects.

older participants (T(37)=1.153; p=0.017; d=0.80). Additionally, the younger participants in the present study differed significantly from the group of older participants in terms of the perceived accessibility of the used system (T(35)=-2.087; p=0.044; d=0.69). However, no statistically significant differences were found regarding the participants' perceived usefulness of the virtual environment (T(37)=1.153; p=0.256; d=0.37) and their reported anxiety toward new technologies (T(37)=-0.409; p=0.685; d=0.13). Furthermore, the group of younger participants as compared to the older participants reported higher levels of social presence (T(38)=2.101; p=0.042; d=0.66), yet there was no difference between the two groups concerning other present related factors like the sense of being there (T(38)=0.663; p=0.511; d=0.21) or the perceived realism of the virtual environment (T(33.369)=0.670; p=0.508; d=0.22). The different distributions between the two groups (means±SEM) on the technology usage scales and the presence related factors are displayed in Figure 3. Furthermore, a repeated measures ANOVA was employed in order to compare the two groups of younger and older participants concerning their subjectively perceived levels of state anxiety (State-Trait Anxiety Inventory, STAI) before and after the experimental procedure. As shown in Figure 4, there is a symmetrical increase for both age groups regarding their perceived level of anxiety over the course of the experiment, including all four experimental phases (rest, preparation, social interaction, rest). The subsequent analysis of the reported anxiety levels indicates a significant main effect of time (F(1, 38)=5.811; p=0.021; η^2=0.13), but no differences between the two groups (F(1, 38)=2.166; p=0.149; η^2=0.05) and no significant interaction of time and group (F(1, 38)=0.096; p=0.758; η^2=0.03).

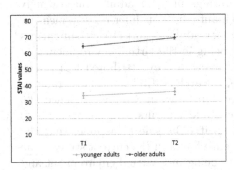

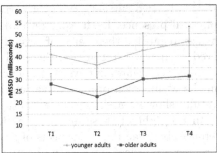

Fig. 4. Mean STAI-state anxiety values (±SEM) of younger (N=20) and older adults (N=20)

Fig. 5. Mean rMSSD levels (±SEM) of younger (N=20) and older adult (N=20) participants

6.2   Psychophysiological Measures

Similar ANOVAs were calculated for the autonomous responses (rMSSD, as a marker for changes in parasympathetic tone) over the course of the 4 experimental phases (rest, preparation, social interaction, rest). All results were corrected by the Greenhouse-Geisser procedure because of the violation of the sphericity assumption. Both groups responded symmetrically regarding their rMSSD scores during the whole experimental period. There was a decline in rMSSD values for the preparation period, when all participants became familiar with the system and its handling. Yet, there was neither a significant main effect of time $(F(1.914, 72.713)=2.632; p=0.081; \varepsilon=0.638; \eta^2=0.07)$ nor a significant effect of group $(F(1, 38)=3.127; p=0.085; \eta^2=0.08)$ or a significant interaction effect of time and group $(F(1.914, 72.713)=0.055; p=0.941; \varepsilon=0.638; \eta^2=0.01)$. Figure 5 depicts the rMSSD means $(\pm SEM)$ according to the four experimental phases (rest, preparation, social interaction, rest).

6.3 Discussion

Current literature indicates possible differences between younger and older adults regarding the nature of their experience when being immersed in a collaborative virtual environment [26,27]. These assumptions however, still prove to be inconclusive due to the lack of well balanced experimental designs and/or sufficiently well selected samples [18]. Thus, the present study aimed at debunking possible differences between healthy younger and older adults using a rather stressful virtual scenario within which the participants were asked to interact with two virtual characters represented by the computer.

In the present sample younger adults in contrast to their elderly counterparts were found to report significantly higher levels of social presence when being immersed in the collaborative virtual environment and when interacting with the virtual characters. This result is in line with some research [20] which also found significantly lower social presence ratings in older adults. Interestingly however, the two current groups of participants did not differ on any measure of physical presence. Both, younger and older adults reported very similar experiences regarding their sense of actually being in the virtual environment and showed comparable ratings on the level of realism they attributed to the virtual scenario. Regarding physical presence, research is still inconclusive, ranging from the assumption of a negative relationship between age and presence [26] to results showing a significant advantage of older adults over younger adults [18]. In the light of these diverging findings it is be safe to assume, that the differences between the two aspects of presence found in the current study – one embracing a physical experience of actually being in a virtual environment and the other comprising the attribution of sentience to a computer generated image of a person – might stem from different individual characteristics that may be subject to change over the course of life.

Another aspect that might shape or even determine to some extent the experience of presence is the evaluation of the virtual environment itself as well as of corresponding factors such as technology related anxiety [20]. The ratings obtained in the current study using the technology usage inventory [13] indicate significantly poorer evaluations of the technology by the group of elderly participants: In contrast to young adults older participants rated the virtual environment as being quite difficult to handle and not very accessible to them.

Also, older participants showed a much less pronounced intent to actually use the virtual environment than younger participants. Considering the presence experience as an illusion of nonmediation [16] it becomes obvious that a poor ease of use would draw the attention away from the virtual environment and its virtual characters and toward the handling of the hardware and thus, possibly hinder the formation of both, physical and social presence. It is interesting to note however, that although older adults rated the accessibility of the technology as quite low and showed an altogether lower intention to use it than their younger counterparts; they did not differ from the younger group regarding their perception of the technology's usefulness. Also, younger and older adults did not differ on their level of technology related anxiety. Similar to the level of technology related anxiety (see TUI, [13]), the two groups showed no significant differences in their subjectively reported state anxiety level as measured by the State-Trait Anxiety Inventory [14]. The significant increase over time (pre/post virtual experience) was symmetrical for both, younger and older adults. Self-reported Anxiety in this context may be seen as a perceived arousal stemming from the social interaction within the virtual environment and not from the virtual environment itself. Remarkably however, psychophysiological measures (rMSSD) had their peak during the preparation period, when participants learned how to handle the smart phone and how to navigate the virtual environment. In contrast, the physiological arousal levels were low during the virtual social interaction. Again, no group differences were found regarding heart rate variability measures indicating that younger and older participants were alike in their perception of the overall experience of the collaborative virtual environment.

6.4   Limitations

It is worth noting that the group of older participants in the present study predominantly consisted of highly educated older adults with a considerable amount of prior computer experience. Additionally, the experiment was conducted using a highly immersive interface technology, a head mounted display (HMD), which to date is still rather seldomly used in private households for entertainment purposes.

7   Conclusion

With respect to possible differences in emotional responsiveness and compassion between younger and older adults an additional measure of empathy might prove very insightful for the evaluation of social presence experiences when comparing older and younger adults in future studies. Also, the inclusion of personality factors [12] might shed more light on the relationship between the experience in virtual environments and its evaluation. Also, research has shown that there might be gender differences in the experience of presence [7]. Unfortunately, the current sample size did not allow for a thorough analysis of possibly existing differences, but future studies should account for probable differences between male and female users of virtual environments. In sum, the results of the current study indicate that older adults may benefit just as well from the experience of collaborative virtual environments as their younger counterparts. The relatively low levels of technology related anxiety in the current sample of older adults as well as their satisfying levels of presence all allow concluding that virtual worlds might also be a useful tool for social interaction in older adults.

Acknowledgements. This study was funded by the Austrian Research Promotion Agency (FFG), Projectnumber: 831199, ICARUS Project. We also thank Ellen Baumm, Antonia Scholz and Anna-K. Heinzle for their help.

References

1. Bailenson, J.N., Blascovich, J.: Virtual Reality and Social Networks Will Be a Powerful Combination: Avatars will make social networks seductive. IEEE Spectrum (2011)
2. Bailenson, J.N., Blascovich, J., Beall, A.C., Loomis, J.M.: Interpersonal distance in immersive virtual environments. Personality and Social Psychology Bulletin 29, 819–833 (2003)
3. Blascovich, J., Loomis, J., Beall, A.C., Swinth, K.R., Hoyt, C.L., Bailenson, J.N.: Immersive virtual environment technology as a methodological tool for social psychology. Psychological Inquiry 13(2), 103–124 (2002)
4. Czaja, S.J., Lee, C.C.: The Human Computer Interaction Handbook: Fundamentals, Evolving Technologies, and Emerging Applications. CRC Press (2007)
5. Cummings, J.J., Bailenson, J.N., Fidler, M.J.: How Immersive is Enough?: A Foundation for a Meta-analysis of the Effect of Immersive Technology on Measured Presence. In: Proceedings of the International Society for Presence Research, Philadelphia, USA (2012)
6. Felnhofer, A., Heinzle, A.-K., Kothgassner, O.D.: Game experience and behavior in young women: A comparison of interface technologies (in preparation 2013)
7. Felnhofer, A., Kothgassner, O.D., Beutl, L., Hlavacs, H., Kryspin-Exner, I.: Is virtual reality made for men only? Exploring gender differences in the sense of presence. In: Proceedings of the International Society on Presence Research, Philadelphia, USA (2012)
8. Goodman, J., Gray, P., Khammampad, K., Brewster, S.: Using landmarks to support older people in navigation. In: Brewster, S., Dunlop, M. (eds.) MobileHCI 2004, pp. 38–48 (2004)
9. Gunawardena, C.N., Zittle, F.J.: Social presence as a predictor of satisfaction within a computer-mediated conferencing environment. American Journal of Distance Education 11(3), 8–26 (1997)
10. IJsselsteijn, W.A., de Ridder, H., Freeman, J., Avons, S.E.: Presence: concept, determinants, and measurement. In: Electronic Imaging, pp. 520–529. International Society for Optics and Photonics (2000)
11. Kane, H.S., McCall, C., Collins, N.L., Blascovich, J.: Mere presence is not enough: Responsive support in a virtual world. Journal of Experimental Social Psychology 48(1), 37–44 (2012)
12. Kothgassner, O.D., Felnhofer, A., Beutl, L., Hlavacs, H., Lehenbauer, M., Stetina, B.: A virtual training tool for giving talks. In: Herrlich, M., Malaka, R., Masuch, M. (eds.) ICEC 2012. LNCS, vol. 7522, pp. 53–66. Springer, Heidelberg (2012)

13. Kothgassner, O.D., Felnhofer, A., Hauk, N., Kastenhofer, E., Gomm, J., Kryspin-Exner, I.: TUI. Technology Usage Inventory. FFG, Wien (2013), http://www.ffg.at/sites/default/files/allgemeine_downloads/thematische%20programme/programmdokumente/tui_manual.pdf
14. Laux, L., Glanzmann, P., Schaffner, C.D., Spielberger, C.D.: Das State-Trait-Angstinventar (STAI-G Form X 1 and STAI-G Form X 2). Belz, Weinheim (1981)
15. Lee, B., Chen, Y., Hewitt, L.: Age differences in constraints encountered by seniors in their use of computers and the internet. Computers in Human Behaviour 27(3), 1231–1237 (2011)
16. Lombard, M., Ditton, T.: At the heart of it all: The concept of presence. Journal of Computer Mediated Communication 3(2) (1997)
17. OBrien, E., Konrath, S.H., Grhn, D., Hagen, A.L.: Empathic concern and perspective taking: Linear and quadratic effects of age across the adult life span. The Journals of Gerontology Series B: Psychological Sciences and Social Sciences 68(2), 168–175 (2013)
18. Rand, D., Kizony, R., Feintuch, U., Katz, N., Josman, N., Rizzo, A.A., Weiss, P.L.: Comparison of two VR platforms for rehabilitation: Video capture versus HMD. Presence, Teleoperators and Virtual Environments 14(2), 147–160 (2005)
19. Schubert, T., Friedmann, F., Regenbrecht, H.: The experience of presence: Factor analytic insights. Presence: Teleoperators and Virtual Environments 10(3), 266–281 (2001)
20. Siriaraya, P., Ang, C.S.: Age differences in the perception of social presence in the use of 3D virtual world for social interaction. Interacting with Computers 24(4), 280–291 (2012)
21. Sjolinder, M., Hook, K., Nilsson, L.-G., Andersson, G.: Age differences and the acquisition of spatial knowledge in a three-dimensional environment: evaluating the use of an overview map as a navigation aid. International Journal of Human-Computer Studies 63(6), 537–564 (2005)
22. Force, T.: Heart rate variability: standards of measurement, physiological interpretation and clinical use. Task Force of the European Society of Cardiology and the North American Society of Pacing and Electrophysiology. Circulation 93(5), 1043–1065 (1996)
23. Usoh, M., Alberto, C., Slater, M.: Presence: experiments in the psychology of virtual environments, Department of Computer Science, University College London, UK (1996)
24. Venkatesh, V., Morris, M.G., Davis, G.B., Davis, F.D.: User Acceptance of Information Technology: Toward a Unified View. MIS Quarterly 27(3), 425–478 (2003)
25. Von der Pütten, A.M., Krämer, N.C., Gratch, J., Kang, S.H.: It doesn't matter what you are! explaining social effects of agents and avatars. Computers in Human Behavior 26(6), 1641–1650 (2010)
26. Weibel, D., Wissmath, B., Mast, F.W.: Immersion in Mediated Environments: The Role of Personality Traits. Cyberpsychology, Behavior, and Social Networking 13(3), 251–256 (2010)
27. Weiss, P.L., Rand, D., Katz, N., Kizony, R.: Video capture virtual reality as a flexible and effective rehabilitation tool. Journal of NeuroEngineering and Rehabilitation 1(12) (2004), doi:10.1186/1743-0003-1-12
28. Zajicek, M., Hall, S.: Solutions for elderly visually impaired people using the Internet. In: HCI, pp. 299–307 (2000)
29. Zancanaro, M., Gabrielli, S., Jameson, A., Leonardi, C., Not, E., Pianesi, F.: Virtual Helper or Virtual Card Player? Contrasting Responses of Older Users. In: Trappl, R. (ed.) Your Virtual Butler: The Making-of. LNCS, vol. 7407, pp. 70–78. Springer, Heidelberg (2013)

Exploring Opponent Formats
Game Mechanics for Computer-Supported Physical Games

Mads Møller Jensen, Majken Kirkegaard Rasmussen, and Kaj Grønbæk

Department of Computer Science, Aarhus University, Denmark
{mmjensen,denmike,kgronbak}@cs.au.dk

Abstract. The recent growth in development and research in computer-supported physical games has sprouted a wide variety of games merging qualities from both computer games and sports. Despite the increasing interest in this type of games, exploration of their specific game mechanics and the understanding of how the opponent format and relationships impact a game are almost absent in current research. Thus, this paper aims to elucidate how the perception of a competition differs, depending on the opponent format, by presenting a game mechanic framework. The paper furthermore presents an interactive football-training platform, as well as games designed to explore the different opponent formats. The games are qualitatively evaluated to illuminate the qualities of and distinctions between different types of opponent formats, proposed by the framework terminology.

Keywords: Sports, framework, game mechanics, exergames, competition.

1 Introduction

Every year, hundreds of new traditional computer games are being developed by game developer companies and embraced by consumers. Many of these games rely on several similar features known from computer game theory, and a vast amount of conceptual frameworks have emerged, providing game developers with guidelines and advice on how to create new games (e.g. [1, 3]). Sports, on the other hand, evolve slowly and new types of sports seldom appear. However, recently there has been an evolution, where computer games and traditional sports seem to fuse, creating new opportunities for game development, producing commercial computer gaming products, such as Nintendo Wii and Microsoft Kinect. A parallel increase in interest, has emerged in research communities, resulting in development of new games, e.g. Air hockey over a distance [12] and TacTowers [9] among many others. In research, the idea of combining physical elements from sports with computer games, exists under various headings, from Mueller and colleagues' [10] definition of exertion interfaces, to exergames[16], kinaesthetic empathy interaction [5], interactive training equipment [9], everyday fitness applications [2] and Computer-Supported Collaborative Sport [22]. Despite the rise of computer-supported physical games, only few game mechanic frameworks have appeared, targeting the qualities added to

J.C. Anacleto et al. (Eds.): ICEC 2013, LNCS 8215 , pp. 48–60, 2013.

games by making them physical. As an example, Fogtmann [6] has explored and reflected upon the impact of the spatial setup of players competing through technology, as well as the players ability for kinaesthetic empathy within computer-supported physical games. Thus, when designing computer-supported physical games, it is important to be mindful about the way players physically compete and how it impacts a game. Often computer-supported games relies on sports as source of inspiration, however, when bringing elements of sports into a new context, it is important to rethink how players compete, relate and interact, and consider the impact it has on a game in order to utilise it in the creation of new games. This paper initiates the investigation of game mechanics for computer-supported physical games, by focusing on the aspect of opponent format and the impact it has on a game. We define opponent format as the rules, game elements and spatial setup that facilitates a competition between the participants of a game. Examining for example the opponent format of the 100-metre sprint, the high jump, football and curling, each of the games present different ways to be opponents, which ultimately affects the competition, e.g. whether competitors have the ability to encumber each other's actions, whether the competitors compete concurrently or subsequently and how competitors can physically and mentally pressure one another.

In this paper we explore the impact of the choice of opponent format, when designing computer-supported physical games, and in what manner it influences how players perceive the game and their opponents. We investigate existing classifications of sports and computer-supported physical games (Section 2), present and discuss an opponent format framework, based on two format distinctions: Encumbered versus unencumbered, and subsequent versus concurrent (Section 3). Furthermore, we present an interactive football-training platform and apply the framework in the development of three new computer-supported physical games with diverse opponent formats for the platform. We evaluate the games through a qualitative test and attempt to extract some general qualities within each of these three types of opponent formats (Section 4). We conclude by presenting initial findings on qualities inherent in different opponent formats and suggest how this can be utilised, when designing new exergames, interactive training equipment or even physical competitive games in general.

2   Analysing Existing Classifications of Sports and Computer-Supported Physical Games

Prior work, within sports science as well as HCI, has produced a number of frameworks and classifications, seeking to identify different types of games. The frameworks and classifications presented in this section do not build on an identical frame of reference, but form their distinctions on either the basis of competitions [4, 6, 13, 17], or a broader definition of games encompassing both competitive as well as non-competitive games [21]. Beyond the work presented here, classifications of games, dealing with sports, can be found within e.g. [14, 18].

Skultety's [17] classification of competitions builds upon four points, often used to outline a competitive event or 'format' within sports philosophy: *"(1) multiple participants engage in behaviours, (2) the quality of which is then assessed, compared and ranked (3) in accordance with rules (4) that do not determine the results ahead of time"* (p.440 [17]). Skultety adheres to these four competitive conditions, but criticises their neutrality as well as the absence of human agents. Considering the four points, Skultety adds additional distinctions, dividing competition into four competitive formats based on two distinctions: Vis-à-vis versus standardised, dealing with how the competition is judged; and encumbered versus unencumbered, concerning the manner in which the competitors interact.

Vossen's [21] classification of games is firmly grounded in Suits' [20] game definition, which considers play an attitude rather than an activity. Vossen's classification includes three distinctions: competitive versus non-competitive games, interactive versus non-interactive games, and physical versus non-physical games. According to Vossen the difference between competitive and non-competitive games is based on involvement of one or more opponents, pursuing the predefined goals of a game. Interactive and non-interactive games are distinguished by, *"[...] interactive games involve aspects of offence and defence, while non-interactive games do not"*. Thus, all competitive games are also interactive and all non-interactive games are non-competitive in nature [21]. With regard to physical competitive games, Vossen, divides these into two: Physical non-interactive competitive games and physical interactive competitive games, or respectively parallel sports and interactive sports [21].

Focusing on computer-supported games that require physical activity of the user, also known as exertion games, Mueller and colleagues [13] present a taxonomy drawing extensively on Vossen's [21] classification. The taxonomy predominantly relies on the same categorisations and terminology as Vossen, but focuses solely on what in Vossen's terminology would be termed physically competitive games. Mueller and colleagues [13] add an additional distinction within interactive sports, dividing it into combat versus object games. Combat games are defined as games wherein the player tries to control the opponent, whereas in object games, the player attempts to control an object in direct competition with the opponent [13].

Fogtmann [4] further elaborates on the framework proposed by Mueller, through adding a third aspect to Mueller's combat and object categorisation, namely that of grappling. Grappling refers to techniques used in games, in order to gain a physical advantage over an opponent. In [6], Fogtmann further examines the competitive roles, through comparing different physical setups of interactive training equipment. Four different types of physical setup are described: Individual, side-by-side, 'in front remote' and 'in front collocated', distinguished by their different possibilities for kinaesthetic empathy interaction.

2.1   Opponent Format in the Classifications

The classifications proposed by Skultety [17], Vossen [21], Mueller [13] and Fogtmann [4, 6], all, to some degree, deal with the opponent format within physical competitive games, however, the specific aim of these taxonomies and classifications is not to describe the opponent format. If we compare the 100-metre sprint and the high jump, then participants in the 100-metre sprint compete simultaneously along the track side-by-side. The physical setup enables the participants to read and decode their opponent's actions and push themselves harder, while they run, if their competitors are doing well. Contrary, in the high jump the competitors compete one after another, taking turn in getting over the highest bar, and if an opponent clears a height, it increases the pressure on the subsequent competitors. Despite their obvious differences in opponent format, both Skultety [17], Vossen [21] and Mueller [13] place these games within the same category. The importance of making a distinction between different opponent formats, is supported by Fogtmann's [5, 6] notion of kinaesthetic empathy. Comparing the possibility for kinaesthetic empathy in the two games, then in the 100-metre sprint the participants compete simultaneously, enabling kinaesthetic relations, which allow them to decode and react directly and continuously upon their opponent actions, whereas the competitors in the high jump exclusively react upon the static result of the previous participants.

3 Towards an Opponent Format Framework

Building on the existing work by Skultety [17] and Vossen [21], we propose a framework classifying physical competitive games based upon the opponent format (a visual representation of the framework can be seen in figure 1). In order to capture and define the relationship of the opponents in a physical competitive game, we present two opposing distinctions; Encumbered versus unencumbered, dealing with the physicality of the competition; and subsequent versus concurrent, dealing with the temporality of the competition. In the following sections we, firstly, discuss the two distinctions and reflect upon them in relation to existing frameworks and classifications. Secondly, we present the opponent format framework, and describe each of the four opponent formats derived from the two-fold distinctions.

3.1 Encumbered versus Unencumbered

Both Skultety [17] and Vossen [21], touch upon the notion of opponent format, through classifying games based upon whether or not the opponents can hinder each others actions. Albeit, dealing with the same aspect of competitive games, they do not base the distinction upon the same criterions. Skultety makes a distinction between whether or not competitors can affect one another's behaviour, defining games as being either encumbered or unencumbered. Vossen on the other hand, draws the line between whether or not the game is interactive, defining interactive games as games with aspects of offence and defence, where game participants serve as obstacles to be overcome by opponents [21]. Examining the two classifications, then Vossen's distinction provides a clearer definition, however the distinction, in our opinion, holds two difficulties in relation to defining opponent format, as well as applying it within HCI. Firstly, the term 'interactive', as Mueller and colleagues [13] have pointed out, hold a different connotation, in the realm of HCI, as opposed to sports science, thereby convoluting its meaning. Secondly, and more importantly, Vossen limits offensive and defensive moves to interactive games. Surveying for example running races, then although direct physical interaction is not allowed, the game is not devoid of tactics, strategy as well as offensive and defensive moves. The runners do not run individual races, but run simultaneously enabling them to hide behind a frontrunner, who is breaking the wind, or take the lead to push up the pace early in the race. The example shows that although the opponents do not go head to head in combat for the same objective and interact directly, it is not devoid of offensive and defensive strategies.

Based on the deliberations above, we have chosen to base our framework on Skultety's terms, dividing competitions with regard to whether or not the actions of a competitor are encumbered or unencumbered by their opponents. However, in choosing Skultety's terms we are aware of the vagueness of his definition and of the critique posed by Royce [15]. Skultety defines the distinction between encumbered or unencumbered, as *"...differences between not directly interfering with one another (unencumbered) and affecting one another's behaviour (encumbered)"* [15]. To which Royce [15] poses the question, *"when in sport is one's behaviour not affecting others?"*[15]. We agree with Royce, in his critique of Skultety's unclear definition, however, we still find the terms useful, as a way to classify different types of opponent formats within physical competitive games. We seek to clarify the distinction from Skultety, defining encumbered games as games, where players can directly interfere with each other's objective, by engaging in physical interaction or interacting with one or more shared objects, e.g. football, tennis or curling. On the other hand, unencumbered games are games, where physical contact is not allowed between the player and no objects are shared between them e.g. high jump, 100-meter sprint and synchronised swimming, where the only affect the participants have on each other is the pressure derived as a result of their performances.

3.2   Subsequent versus Concurrent

The temporal aspect of competitions is absent in the frameworks and classifications presented by both Vossen [21], Skultety [17] and Mueller and colleagues [13]. However, we believe that the temporality in a competition has a significant impact on the opponent format and how the competition is perceived, i.e. the participants' actions and their perception of a competition differs if participants compete concurrently in contrast to competing subsequently. Thus, we introduce a new distinction between concurrent and subsequent games. We define concurrent games as games, where participants compete at the same time, e.g. football, tennis and 100-meter sprint. It is our claim that a concurrent games intensifies participants' relations to one another, creating a more direct competitive atmosphere between them. In relation to Fogtmann's [6], concurrent games enable participants to utilise their innate kinaesthetic empathy to read and react upon their opponents actions. We define subsequent games, as games, where participants take turns competing, e.g. curling, the high jump and synchronised swimming. In subsequent games, the competitors compete against a static pre-determined goal, generally decided by previous opponents' performances, whereas the goal in concurrent games changes continuously during the game, allowing the competitors to adjust their performance accordingly. For example, in curling the field is static when a player is about to make a play, whereas in tennis a player is aware of the opponent's concurrent actions and position, which affects how the ball is played.

3.3   Four Types of Opponent Formats

In the following section each of the four opponent formats is in turn described, and exemplified through familiar sport disciplines as well as computer–supported physical games. The illustration below visualises the interactions of the opponents in each of the four types of opponent format categories.

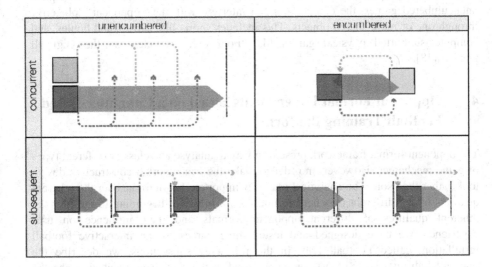

Fig. 1. Opponent format framework, showing how opponents, either individually or as a team (squares), can physically interfere (broad arrows), directly or through objects, as well as how mental pressure (dotted arrows) affects the performance of the opponent.

Concurrent unencumbered (top left): We define concurrent unencumbered games as games wherein the participants compete simultaneously, while not directly physically interfering with the objective of their opponents. This category includes sports such as 100-metre sprint, rowing and cycling races, as well as computer-supported physical games such as Dance Dance Revolution [23], Kinect Adventures Reflex Ridge 2 player game [24] and Jaw [7] developed by Kiili and Merilampi.

Subsequent unencumbered (bottom left): Subsequent unencumbered games, hold that participants take turns competing, thereby having no contact with their opponent and the only affect the participants' actions have on each other is the pressure derived as a result of their performances. Sports such as the high jump, bowling, golf and dressage are examples of this category, alongside examples of computer-supported physical games, such as Hanging of a bar [11] and Sports wall [26].

Concurrent encumbered (top right): We define concurrent encumbered games, as games where the participants compete simultaneously, in a manner where they can directly interfere with each other's objective, allowing them to engage in physical interaction or to interact with one or more shared objects. Examples of concurrent encumbered games can be found within sports such as: tennis, handball, basketball or karate, as well as computer-supported physical games such as Shootball [19], TacTowers [6], BodyQuake [4] or Airhockey over a distance [12].

Subsequent encumbered (bottom right): In subsequent encumbered games participants compete through turn taking, however opposed to subsequent unencumbered games, the competitors can interfere with their opponent's objective through one or more shared objects. This includes sports like curling and boules, and computer-supported physical games like 'Follow My Leader' on the Digiwall platform [8].

4 Opponent Format Experiments Based on a Computer-Based Football Training Platform

The opponent format framework presents a way to analyse and classify different types of game mechanics. However, in order to make the framework a constructive design tool, rather than solely an analytical one, it is important begin to uncover the inherent qualities of the different opponent formats. As a basis for beginning to uncover the inherent qualities of different opponent formats and their influence on user experience, we have designed and tested three games for an interactive football installation, called Football Lab. In the following subsections, we describe the Football Lab installation, the three games used in the user experiment, describe the user experiment setup and reflect upon the result from it.

4.1 Football Lab Installation

The computer-based game platform, we used for the experiment, is called Football-lab. It is a 12*12 m square artificial grass football field with 4 rebound surfaces (M-stations [25]) (see fig 2.). The rebound surfaces are wired with piezo sensors enabling measurement of where balls hit the surface.

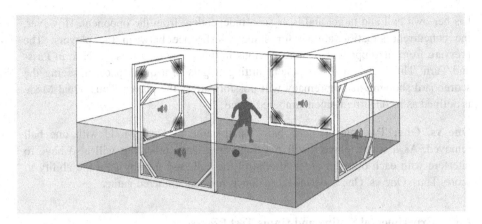

Fig. 2. Football Lab game space

Light and sound signals controlled by the games, guide the players to which rebound surface they are supposed to hit. The sounds played are recorded voices saying, "Play me!", "I'm free!", "Here!", similar to football lingo for co-players calling for the ball.

The facility has been running 24/7/365 since June 2011 as part of a large football training ground in Herning, Denmark.

Users have played more than 20.000 games (an average of 1000 per month) on the facility according to the log files, thus the existing games are considered a success.

4.2   Games Illuminating a Variety of Opponent Formats

In order to compare the qualities of different types of opponent formats, we designed three games, covering three of the four quadrants presented in the framework. The games are intended to be as similar as possible, only distinguished in terms of interaction between and presence of opponents. Below we describe each of the three games in turn. The fourth category, subsequent encumbered games, is not included in the study, as the platform does not hold natural options for creating such a game.

Pass-and-Turn: One player, one ball. One minute in the Football Lab trying to hit as many targets as possible. To keep a high level of transparency, one target hit results in one point. Players competing in this game will try subsequently to get the highest score. Thus, opponents are not able to interfere or intervene directly in the performance of opposing players. The only influence opponents have on the game is the pressure put upon a player from the current highest score. Thus, Pass-and-Turn is defined as a subsequent, unencumbered game.

Dual Mode: Two players, two balls. Same game as Pass-and-Turn but two players are playing concurrently on the same field. LED-lights flash in different colours indicating which M-station should be hit by which player. In other words, each player has her own ball and target and is as such independent from the opponent. However, the concurrent situation allows for some interference between the players. The pressure from the opponent is more obvious in this game than it is the case in Pass-and-Turn. The sound of the opponent hitting targets in a quick pace or seeing the scoreboard showing her supremacy will possibly stress the player. Thus, Dual Mode is defined as a concurrent, unencumbered game.

One vs. One: Two players, one ball. Same game as Dual Mode with one ball removed. As a result, players will not only stress each other but will also have to interfere with each other in order to control the ball, and thereby gain the ability to score. Thus, One vs. One is defined as a concurrent, encumbered game.

4.3   Experimental Setting and Game Test Process

The experiment was conducted at the football club, where the Football Lab is installed. The study was conducted with 12 participants, aged 11-15, which were recruited from two different youth teams, and more than half of them had prior experience with Football Lab, as the Pass-and-Turn game has been part of the installation since 2011. The 12 participants were divided into three groups, where each group was introduced to one game at a time, whereupon each participant played the game three times. After all participants had had their three attempts, an overall winner of the specific game was announced. The order in which the three games were played was altered for the three groups. In Pass-and-Turn the participants took turns competing, whereas they in both Dual Mode and One vs. One played one game against each participant in the group. After a group had played the three different games, a 15-minute semi-structured interview was conducted, focusing on the qualities of the different types of competition. It is relevant to note that group members not competing were spectators, and the entire experiment was videotaped.

Fig. 3. The three games, left: Pass-and-Turn, middle: Dual Mode, right: One vs. One

4.4   Results from Test of the Experimental Games

Findings from the experiment were centred on three different topics: Perception of competition, pressure during a game and spectator excitement. The three topics point to different qualities of the opponent formats exhibited in the games.

The majority of the participants perceived One vs. One as more competitive, as well as giving a stronger impression of winning, than the other two games. The participants stated that, *"it's like there is more competition in it"*, and, *"you were against someone, where you can show that 'okay, I won'"*. As a group of players went from playing One vs. One to Dual Mode a player said, *"Come on, Jens. Now we are not against each other anymore"*, indicating that perception of the competition changed. Considering the perception of the opponent, in Dual Mode the participants generally stated the objective as conquering the opponent, whereas in Pass-and-Turn, the objective was conquering the high score. This difference was emphasised in comments, remarking that in Dual Mode: *"It's like you have someone you can beat"*, and, *"there you also compete against someone"*, whereas in Pass-and-Turn one participant even remarked that *"there was no opponent"*, indicating a focus on beating the score rather than the opponents.

Surveying the pressure, the participants felt from their opponent, it is noteworthy that One vs. One displayed the highest degree of physical intensity, shown by the players frequently yelled at themselves and their opponents, threw themselves on the ground in attempt to score a final goal as well as from fatigue after a match. However, despite the more intense and direct competition, the majority of the participants did not consider it the game, where the pressure from the opponent was greatest. Instead they pointed to Dual Mode, due to the uncertainty of the opponent's score as well as the continuous peripheral auditory feedback from the opponent's game progress. One of the participants described it as: *"in the duels (One vs. One) you knew where you had the opponent most of the time and you noticed when he scored and you knew reasonably well what the score was, but in Dual Mode, you could just hear when your opponent kept scoring, which forced you to make harder passes"*. In Pass-and-Turn participants remarked that time was the main source of pressure, however, the high score also provided a source of pressure, especially if one of the opponents made a significantly higher score, appearing impossible to beat. As one of the participants remarked, *"if one gets a high score, then you think that he has probably won"*, despite there being games left to play. The participants also exhibited different degrees of dedication to the three games. Some indicated that they tended to give up early in Pass-and-Turn games if they made a significant mistake. They stated both the lack of impact on the opponent's actions, as well as a bad start to a game, as reasons for giving up, *"it was important to get a good start, otherwise it could all fail, and then you lose faith in it"*. Others argued that they quickly gave up in One vs. One, if the opponent had a significant lead, because the tactical element made it possible for the opponent to protect the ball and make a comeback an immense mission. However, in Dual Mode the players kept competing because, as the players said, *"they (the others) could still make mistakes"* and *"you feel that you can still come back"*.

In addition to the perception of competition and pressure between opponents, the reactions of the spectators revealed differences between the opponent formats. In the Pass- and-Turn games, the spectators typically were quiet throughout the game, until the last ten seconds, where they started yelling the score and counting down the clock, increasing the intensity of the game. However, the yelling only appeared when a player was close to the high score, which indicates the difficulty in evaluating, how a player is performing during a game. A player recognised this issue and stated that the game would be 'better' if intermediate milestones were announced during a game, which potentially could create intensity peaks, increasing excitement for players and spectators. Furthermore, in Pass-and-Turn player and spectators knew the score to beat in advance, whereas in Dual Mode and One vs. One the score to beat depended entirely on the concurrent opponent's performance. This dynamic objective seems to influence the perception of the level of direct competition for players as well as spectators, indicated by observations where spectators of Pass-and-Turn shouted the number of targets hit, whereas in the other games they shouted the relative score.

5   Conclusion

We have argued that there is a need for systematic development of game mechanics for computer supported physical games. In this paper we have taken steps towards the development of guidelines and theories for such game mechanics by exploring the variety of opponent formats and illustrated how the variations in opponent formats can impact game development. The main contribution of this paper is the proposal of a framework for design of computer-supported physical games, which seeks to unfold different opponent formats, derived from the two distinctions: Encumbered versus unencumbered, and concurrent versus subsequent, which in combination forms four types of opponent formats. Furthermore, based on an interactive football-training platform, we have utilised the framework to design three new computer-supported physical games with different opponent formats, which constitute the paper's secondary contribution. We have attempted to begin initial investigations into the inherent qualities of the opponent formats through a user experiment. The experiment conducted, was a small-scale qualitative study, thus, there is a need to further explore the four opponent formats, with regards to both a larger volume of opinions, as well as within different contexts. However, based on the experiment, we begin to identify qualities related to the different opponent formats. We point to each format possessing different qualities with regard to; Perception of competition, pressure during a game and spectator excitement. For example, concurrent encumbered games are perceived as exceedingly competitive, however, they lack the constant pressure, which is present in unencumbered concurrent games. Additionally, concurrent games in general seems to excite spectators constantly throughout a game, whereas the spectators' excitement is concentrated towards the end of unencumbered subsequent games. The work contributes to a better understanding of how the opponent format influences the game and the participant's perception of it, and that it can form the basis for reflection when designing new computer-supported physical games, exergames, interactive training equipment or even physical competitive games in general. However, in order to get clearer knowledge about the qualities within different formats presented in the framework, more widespread quantitative evaluations are necessary. Furthermore, future work should include examination of qualities within subsequent encumbered games, since this format has not been covered by our work.

Acknowledgements. We thank Jacob Andersen and Jesper Nielsen, Alexandra Institute, and Nikolaj Thomassen, Munin Sports, for establishing the Football Lab platform. We also thank players and coaches of Herning Fremad for their participation in the test.

References

1. Björk, S., et al.: Game Design Patterns. in level up. In: Level Up: Digtal Games Research Conference, pp. 4–6 (2003)
2. Campbell, T., et al.: Game design principles in everyday fitness applications. In: Proceedings of the 2008 ACM Conference on Computer Supported Cooperative Work, pp. 249–252. ACM, New York (2008)
3. Egenfeldt-Nielsen, S., et al.: Understanding Video Games: The Essential Introduction. Routledge (2008)
4. Fogtmann, M.H.: Designing bodily engaging games: learning from sports. In: Proceedings of the 12th Annual Conference of the New Zealand Chapter of the ACM Special Interest Group on Computer-Human Interaction, pp. 89–96. ACM, New York (2011)
5. Fogtmann, M.H.: Designing With The Body in Mind - Kinesthetic Empathy Interaction (2011)
6. Fogtmann, M.H., et al.: Interaction technology for collective and psychomotor training in sports. In: Proceedings of the 8th International Conference on Advances in Computer Enter-tainment Technology, pp. 13:1-13:8. ACM, New York (2011)
7. Kiili, K., Merilampi, S.: Developing engaging exergames with simple motion detection. In: Proceedings of the 14th International Academic MindTrek Conference: Envisioning Future Media Environments, pp. 103–110. ACM, New York (2010)
8. Liljedahl, M., Lindberg, S.: DigiWall - an audio mostly game. In: ICAD, London, UK (2006)
9. Ludvigsen, M., et al.: TacTowers: an interactive training equipment for elite athletes. In: Proceedings of the 8th ACM Conference on Designing Interactive Systems, pp. 412–415. ACM, New York (2010)
10. Mueller, F., et al.: Exertion interfaces: sports over a distance for social bonding and fun. In: Proceedings of the SIGCHI Conference on Human Factors in Computing Systems, pp. 561–568. ACM, New York (2003)
11. Mueller, F., et al.: Hanging off a bar. In: Proceedings of the 2012 ACM Annual Conference Extended Abstracts on Human Factors in Computing Systems Extended Abstracts, pp. 1055–1058. ACM, New York (2012)
12. Mueller, F., et al.: Airhockey over a distance. In: CHI 2006 Extended Abstracts on Human Factors in Computing Systems, pp. 1133–1138. ACM, New York (2006)
13. Mueller, F., et al.: Taxonomy of exertion games. In: Proceedings of the 20th Australasian Conference on Computer-Human Interaction: Designing for Habitus and Habitat, pp. 263–266. ACM, New York (2008)
14. Reilly, S. et al.: A General-Purpose Taxonomy of Computer-Augmented Sports Systems. Digital Sport for Performance Enhancement and Competitive Evolution. IGI Global (2009).
15. Royce, R.: Skultety's Categories of Competition A Competing Conceptualisation? Sport, Ethics and Philosophy, 1–14 (2012)

16. Sinclair, J., et al.: Considerations for the design of exergames. In: Proceedings of the 5th International Conference on Computer Graphics and Interactive Techniques in Australia and Southeast Asia, pp. 289–295. ACM, New York (2007)
17. Skultety, S.: Categories of Competition. Sport, Ethics and Philosophy 5(4), 433–446 (2011)
18. Stefani, R.T.: A taxonomy of sports rating systems. IEEE Transactions on Systems, Man and Cybernetics, Part A: Systems and Humans 29(1), 116–120 (1999)
19. Sugano, Y., et al.: Shootball: the tangible ball sport in ubiquitous computing. In: Proceedings of the 2006 ACM SIGCHI International Conference on Advances in Computer Entertainment Technology. ACM, New York (2006)
20. Suits, B.: The Grasshopper: Games, Life and Utopia. Broadview Press (2005)
21. Vossen, D.P.: The Nature and Classification of Games. Avante 10(1), 53–68 (2004)
22. Wulf, V., Moritz, E.F., Henneke, C., Al-Zubaidi, K., Stevens, G.: Computer Supported Collaborative Sports: Creating Social Spaces Filled with Sports Activities. In: Rauterberg, M. (ed.) ICEC 2004. LNCS, vol. 3166, pp. 80–89. Springer, Heidelberg (2004)
23. Dance Dance Revolution, http://www.ddrgame.com/
24. Kinect Adventures!, http://en.wikipedia.org/wiki/Kinect_Adventures
25. Munin Sports, http://www.muninsports.com/en/
26. XerGames, http://xergames.com/

Investigating the Role of Composition Conventions in Three-Move Mate Problems

Azlan Iqbal

College of Information Technology, Universiti Tenaga Nasional, Kampus Putrajaya,
Jalan IKRAM-UNITEN, 43000 Kajang, Selangor, Malaysia
azlan@uniten.edu.my

Abstract. In improving the quality of their chess problems or compositions for tournaments and possibly publication in magazines, composers usually rely on 'good practice' rules which are known as 'conventions'. These might include, *contain no unnecessary moves to illustrate a theme* and *avoid castling moves because it cannot be proved legal*. Often, conventions are thought to increase the perceived beauty or aesthetics of a problem. We used a computer program that incorporated a previously validated computational aesthetics model to analyze three sets of compositions and one set of comparable three-move sequences taken from actual games. Each of these varied in terms of their typical adherence to conventions. We found evidence that adherence to conventions, in principle, contributes to aesthetics in chess problems – as perceived by the majority of players and composers with sufficient domain knowledge – but only to a limited degree. Furthermore, it is likely that not all conventions contribute equally to beauty and some might even have an inverse effect. These findings suggest two main things. First, composers need not concern themselves too much with conventions if their intention is simply to make their compositions appear more beautiful to most solvers and observers. Second, should they decide to adhere to conventions, they should be highly selective of the ones that appeal to their target audience, i.e. those with esoteric knowledge of the domain or 'outsiders' who likely understand beauty in chess as something quite different.

Keywords: Chess, problem, convention, beauty, composer.

1 Introduction

A chess problem or composition presents potential solvers with a stipulation. For example, *White to play and mate in 2 moves*. They are typically considered works of art and therefore often described as 'beautiful' [1-5]. Composers usually adhere to many 'composition conventions' when competing in tournaments (or 'tourneys') in order to improve the quality of their problems. Examples include, *contain no unnecessary moves to illustrate a theme, avoid castling moves because it cannot be proved legal, possess more moves in the solution that are also of the 'quiet' type and create a deceptive setting for the solver*. A longer list is available in section 3.3.1 of [6].

J.C. Anacleto et al. (Eds.): ICEC 2013, LNCS 8215, pp. 61–68, 2013.
© IFIP International Federation for Information Processing 2013

Conventions are also useful as a kind of standard so that *"like is compared with like"* [7]. A case has been made for how not all conventions are actually prerequisites for beauty; see section 3.2 of [6].Regardless, many composers and players tend to conflate or confuse convention with aesthetics such that a 'good' composition (one that adheres to conventions) is a more *beautiful* one. Award-winning compositions are therefore considered the most *beautiful*. We put this assumption to the test as it tends to lead to confusion in the world of composition and how others perceive their works. A selection of relevant material relating to computational aesthetics in chess can be found in chapter 2 of [6]. In the next section, we present our approach or methodology for this research. Section 3 contains details about the experiment and results. In section 4 we discuss these results. Finally we conclude the article in section 5 by presenting some closing statements and directions for further work.

2   Approach

In this research, we investigated three-move mate problems which are essentially positions where White is to play and can force mate in three moves against any defense by Black. We applied an experimentally-validated computational aesthetics model [8] to evaluate their beauty. The model has been demonstrated to be able to evaluate and rank this quality in chess problems in a way that correlates positively and well with domain-competent human assessment (not necessarily experts in the domain). It uses mathematical formulas as representations for well-known aesthetic principles and themes in chess. It also incorporates stochastic technology, i.e. the inclusion of some randomness. This means that the next time it evaluates the same composition the score could be *slightly* different. This is why for our experimental purposes, each composition was evaluated three times and the average score used. Additional information can be found in [8].

The model assesses primarily 'visual appeal' (ibid.) which is what the majority of chess players and composers with sufficient domain competence (e.g. the club-player level or higher) understand by 'beauty' in the game. This includes, for instance, tactical maneuvers like sacrifices or combinations with a clear objective such as delivering checkmate. These are relatively straightforward and easy to understand. 'Depth appeal', on the other hand, is associated more with strategic or long-term maneuvers that require more specialized or esoteric knowledge of the game, particularly in relation to chess problems. It is an open philosophical question which has more 'right' to the term 'beauty'.

A chess problem is expected to be legal (possible in a real game, however unlikely), sound (has a unique solution) and 'original' [9]. The first two are 'technical' issues that, if in doubt, can be determined quite reliably using retrograde analysis and a good mate solver engine. The third typically depends on the experience of the human judge. Computationally, it is virtually impossible to account for unless a database of all previous compositions is made available. Since originality can only be determined *ex post facto*, if at all, and has little to do with the 'inherent' beauty of the problem itself, its aesthetic consequences are considered minimal given our experimental purposes. In addition to these three factors, 'economy' and 'aesthetics' are emphasized in the creation of chess problems (ibid.). The aesthetics model used takes into account all of them to varying degrees except for originality. There are conventions that relate to each of these five factors. In section 3.3.1 of [6], for instance, there are over 20 conventions listed. They therefore cover the spectrum of what makes a problem a 'good' one and it should be clearer now why simple adherence to them is often confused with what makes a problem 'beautiful' to human observers.

Chess problems composed by human composers for tournament or publication purposes can therefore safely be assumed to abide by the most number of conventions. Those composed by computer can be controlled to follow fewer or even no particular conventions at all. Forced three-move sequences taken from actual games – which technically 'resemble' chess problems – can be assumed to abide by few, if any, conventions since the players have no such concerns during the game. This provides a reasonable basis of comparison for the role of conventions when it comes to beauty in the game.

CHESTHETICA, a computer program which incorporates the model, was used to compose, as required, three-move mate problems [10] and also evaluate the aesthetics of such sequences. Computer-generated compositions tend to feature just one forced line and fewer, more easily identifiable conventions. The composing module of the program is separate from the aesthetics-evaluating one. One might suppose that the latter should be usable to aid the former but doing so has proven to be exceedingly difficult. The ability to rank beautiful pieces of art does not easily translate into the ability to *create* beautiful pieces of art.

3   Experiment and Results

For our experiment, we tested four sets of chess positions and their move sequences, i.e. three sets of compositions and one set of forced three-movers taken from actual games. The first set consisted of 145 compositions by human composers taken from the 'FIDE Album 2001-2003' [11]. This is all that was available for our purposes. The second set contained 145 compositions generated by CHESTHETICA using both a 'random' and 'experience' approach. The latter approach relies on a database of human compositions to determine piece-placement probability. Further details are available in [10].

These computer-generated compositions were constrained into adhering (randomly) to two, three or four conventions from a list of five namely, *no 'cooked' problems, no dual in the solution, no 'check' in the key move, no captures in the key move* and *no key move that restricts the enemy king's movement*. A chess problem is 'cooked' when there is a second 'key move' (i.e. first move) not intended by the composer. A 'dual' occurs when White has more than one valid continuation after the key move. These conventions were all treated as equal and are among those more reliably detectable using a computer. Manual detection would have been too tedious, inconsistent and prone to error.

The third set consisted of 145 forced three-move sequences taken from real games between two chess engines (Rybka 3 vs. Fritz 8) under 1-minute time controls, known as blitz chess. The first engine, always having the white pieces, is the stronger of the two and they were configured to play until checkmate took place. These are therefore sequences that resemble composed chess problems but lack their typical qualities. The fourth and final set is the same as the second set except that the composing approach was entirely random (no 'experience') and there were no convention filters, meaning that the compositions generated need not conform to any of the five listed earlier. The number of compositions evaluated in all four sets was kept consistent to minimize potential statistical issues due to different sample sizes.

The compositions in the first set can safely be assumed to adhere to the most number of conventions because they were created for 'official' purposes such as competition and publication. It does not matter if the conventions they adhere to are the same as those generated by the computer because there is no known hierarchy of importance with regard to convention. The compositions in the second set adhered to anywhere between at least two and at least four conventions. This is because there may have been conventions other than the five listed earlier that were not tested for but happened to occur by chance, however unlikely. In any case, this second set can be assumed to contain fewer conventions than the first set. The third set in all likelihood contained the fewest conventions because there is no motive to compose anything of beauty in a real game, especially in a blitz match between two chess engines. The fourth set contained logically fewer conventions than the second and lacked 'human' composing knowledge. Table 1 shows the results.

Table 1. Mean aesthetics scores of the different sets of compositions and sequences

	Set 1	Set 2	Set 3	Set 4
Type	Human	Computer (2-4 conv.)	Real Games	Computer (0 conv.)
Typical Adherence to Conventions	High	Moderate	Low	Low
Mean Aesthetics Score	2.265	2.190	1.962	2.209
Standard Deviation	0.48	0.46	0.40	0.43

In comparing just the first three sets, the mean aesthetics scores were all different to a statistically significant degree using a single-factor ANOVA (analysis of variance) test; $F(2, 432) = 17.9$, $P < 0.001$. Given the reducing mean aesthetics scores across sets 1 through 3, this suggested that adherence to conventions did contribute positively to the perceived aesthetics of compositions or sequences in the game. However, using a two-sample t-test assuming equal variances to compare sets 1 and 2, and a two-sample t-test assuming unequal variances to compare sets 2 and 3, only the latter showed a statistically significant difference;

t(282) = 4.47, P < 0.001. This suggested that there was a limit to the role of convention when it came to beauty.

Set 4 (in contrast to set 2) came into play to provide a more realistic basis of comparison by using similar computer-generated compositions and 'machine-adherence' to convention. We found no statistically significant difference between the means of sets 2 and 4. This seemed to contradict the idea that conventions contributed positively to aesthetics. In the next section, we discuss these results in more detail.

4 Discussion

If we can accept that human compositions intended for competition or publication (set 1) adhere most to conventions, then it comes as no surprise that, on average, they are aesthetically superior assuming conventions do indeed improve the aesthetics of a problem. Using the same logic, computer-generated compositions that adhere to fewer conventions (set 2) should average lower, aesthetically. Even lower would therefore be sequences taken from real games (between chess engines, to boot) where conventions do not come into play at all (set 3). In comparing three such sets together, we find statistical evidence that this is all true.

However, in comparing them in pairs, we find that applying some conventions help [1]. This is because the difference between sets 1 and 2 does not appear to be statistically significant yet the difference between sets 2 and 3 is. The increment in the number of typical conventions applied going from none (set 3) to some (set 2) is apparently significant aesthetically but from some (set 2) to many (set 1) is apparently not. On the other hand, if we contrast set 4 (also none) against set 2 (some), we find that the use of some conventions is also irrelevant. Sets 2 and 4 have more in common than any of the first three sets do with each other so the result here should not be ignored.

In order to reconcile the last finding with the rest, we need to assume that there is, in fact, a hierarchy to the many different composition conventions, especially with regard to aesthetics. In other words, some matter and some do not. Furthermore, among those that do matter, some are likely more important than others. This is why the five conventions that applied to sets 2 and 4 had little aesthetic effect. Yet, this little effect was sufficient in contrasting the aesthetic difference between sets 2 and 3 even though in the case of the latter, the relatively crowded board and lack of planned economy in the real game sequences probably worked against whatever aesthetic content they had that might have compensated for those five conventions.

Set 1, having the most in terms of convention, suffered an inverse effect. This means that there were probably some conventions that had little to do with aesthetics and others that had more; these cancelled each other out aesthetically which is why there was no difference in comparing sets 1 and 2. While we acknowledge that there may be other explanations or ways of interpreting the

---

[1] By 'some' we mean both 'a few' and 'the right ones' [12].

66   A. Iqbal

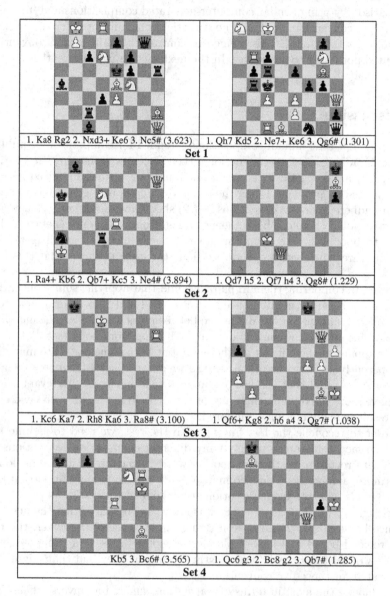

Fig. 1. The highest (left) and lowest (right) scoring compositions/sequences from each set

results, the explanation provided above is what we believe is most likely the case and consistent with all the findings in this research. For the interested reader, Fig. 1 shows the aesthetically highest-scoring and lowest-scoring three-movers from all the four sets. Only the main lines and scores (in brackets) are given here.

Readers should not read too deeply into the precision of the scores because they are used primarily as ordinal data, i.e. for ranking purposes within a particular database of compositions or sequences. However, the aesthetics contrast between the highest and lowest scoring compositions and sequences should be evident to those with sufficient knowledge of the game.

5 Conclusion

Composition conventions are important in chess problems because they generally help composers create better works of art. However, the experimental work presented in this article suggests that not all conventions should be treated equally, especially when it comes to aesthetics or beauty as perceived by the larger community of domain-competent chess players and composers. These are people who need not be experts or possess esoteric knowledge of problems. Some conventions might even work against the typical conception of aesthetics in the game. The establishment of a standardized and recognized classification and 'hierarchy' of conventions with regard to their specific roles in chess problems would therefore be both practical and helpful. This would be useful to composers in tailoring their artworks to better suit their intended audience.

It is perhaps pertinent for experienced composers to realize that the term 'beauty', which they often use, actually carries different connotations outside the world of composition. This would help minimize confusion and frustration on both sides when trying to communicate chess problems as works of art. Any casual player – even with sufficient knowledge to recognize beauty in the game – who has bothered to go through the detailed analysis of an award-winning chess problem, would be able to relate to this. Just as any experienced composer who has had to explain clearly why such a problem is 'beautiful' would as well.

One direction for further work in this area would be a replication of the experiment but using instead endgame studies which are compositions of a different class. This would be to see if the findings are similar. Another direction worth pursuing would be the development of a formalized, objective method of classifying and ranking conventions with regard to their roles in compositions. The knowledge and possibly technology gained from all this would likely improve the quality of automatic chess problem composition [10] and add significantly to the wealth of artworks available to us [13].

Acknowledgement. This research is sponsored in part by the Ministry of Science, Technology and Innovation (MOSTI) in Malaysia under their eScienceFund research grant (01-02-03-SF0240).

References

1. Osborne, H.: Notes on the Aesthetics of Chess and the Concept of Intellectual Beauty. British Journal of Aesthetics 4, 160–163 (1964)
2. Humble, P.N.: Chess as an Art Form. British Journal of Aesthetics 33, 59–66 (1993)
3. Troyer, J.G.: Truth and Beauty: The Aesthetics of Chess Problems. In: Haller (ed.) Aesthetics, Holder-Pichler-Tempsky, Vienna, pp. 126–130 (1983)
4. Walls, B.P.: Beautiful Mates: Applying Principles of Beauty to Computer Chess Heuristics. Dissertation.com, 1st edn. (1997)
5. Levitt, J., Friedgood, D.: Secrets of Spectacular Chess, 2nd edn. Everyman Chess, London (2008)
6. Iqbal, M.A.M.: A Discrete Computational Aesthetics Model for a Zero-sum Perfect Information Game. Ph.D. Thesis, Faculty of Computer Science and Information Technology, University of Malaya, Kuala Lumpur, Malaysia (2008), http://metalab.uniten.edu.my/~azlan/Research/pdfs/phd_thesis_azlan.pdf
7. Albrecht, H.: How Should the Role of a (Chess) Tourney Judge Be Interpreted? The Problemist, 217–218 (July 1993); Originally published as Über Die Auffassung Des Richteramtes in Problemturnieren, Problem, 107–109 (January 1959)
8. Iqbal, A., van der Heijden, H., Guid, M., Makhmali, A.: Evaluating the Aesthetics of Endgame Studies: A Computational Model of Human Aesthetic Perception. IEEE Transactions on Computational Intelligence and AI in Games: Special Issue on Computational Aesthetics in Games 4(3), 178–191 (2012)
9. Velimirovic, M., Valtonen, K.: Encyclopedia of Chess Problems. Chess Informant, Serbia (2012) ISBN 978-86-7297-064-7
10. Iqbal, A.: Increasing Efficiency and Quality in the Automatic Composition of Three-move Mate Problems. In: Anacleto, J.C., Fels, S., Graham, N., Kapralos, B., Saif El-Nasr, M., Stanley, K. (eds.) ICEC 2011. LNCS, vol. 6972, pp. 186–197. Springer, Heidelberg (2011)
11. Fougiaxis, H., Harkola, H.: World Federation for Chess Composition. FIDE Albums (June 2013), http://www.saunalahti.fi/~stniekat/pccc/fa.htm
12. Iqbal, A., Rashid, A.: Intended Multiple Interpretations. In: Proceedings of the 4th Malaysian International Conference on Academic Strategies in English Language Teaching, Shah Alam, Malaysia, November 27-28, pp. 97–101 (2012), http://metalab.uniten.edu.my/%7Eazlan/Research/pdfs/imi_azlan_aishah.pdf
13. Myers, D.: What Chess Games and Chess Problems Tell Us About Digital Games and Art. Digital Creativity 23(3-4), 260–271 (2012)

Mappets: An Interactive Plugin
for Transmedia Machinima on Unity3D

Rafael Kuffner dos Anjos, Eugenio Di Tullio, and Rui Prada

Inteligent Agents and Synthetic Characters Group,
Instituto Superior Técnico, UTL, INESC-ID, Lisbon, Portugal
{rkuffner,etullio,rui.prada}@gaips.inesc-id.pt
http://gaips.inesc-id.pt

Abstract. The popularity of Machinima movies has increased greatly
in the recent years. From a transmedia point of view, there was little development regarding tools to assist the production of Machinima.
These are still mainly focused on the gaming community, and 3D anima-
tors. The developed tool aims to bring the typical workflow present on
a normal movie set, into a machinima creation environment, expanding
possibilities for transmedia productions. With Mappets as a plugin for
the Unity3D game engine, we allow a translation from the typical movie
dimension to a virtual one. This work evaluates the current state of art
of machinima development tools and presents a working solution more
adequate for transmedia productions and non-expert users interested in
the production of machinima.

Keywords: TransMedia, Entertainment, Machinima, Narratives, Authoring System, Digital Entretainment, Entretainment Technology,
Artificial Inteligence.

1 Introduction

When thinking about Transmedia [1], movies come up naturally as an alternative
medium to tell a story that is written on a book or comic, or just passed by orally.
While anyone can create the story, communicating it through a certain medium
requires access to tools that might not be available to everyone, or require a
certain skillset that has to be learned. Also, producing a high quality movie still
require a big array of assets such as actors, locations, lights or cameras. The
production of animated movies in the form of Machinima is a viable alternative
to a casual filmmaker.

Although tools that support the creation of these movies exist, they still require a certain skillset to be used. There is still a gap between the concepts
involved in filmmaking, and machinima, thus hampering the progress of transmedia attempts in this field. There is the need for more specific tools that shorten
the distance between this two realities, so that more people can have access to
the fast production capabilities of machinima. This article will provide insight
into the existing tools to produce Machinima, comparing and evaluating them

J.C. Anacleto et al. (Eds.): ICEC 2013, LNCS 8215, pp. 69–74, 2013.

under the Transmedia perspective. A description of our approach follows, arguing why we feel our system is more adequate to transmedia productions, followed by future work and how the tool will be expanded.

2   Related Work

As Machinima is a new kind of media, there are but a few efforts into developing tools that aid the production of these movies. Series such as Red vs. Blue from *Halo* or the first Machinima *Diary of a Camper* were not assisted by tools, but simple recordings of gameplay, sometimes aided by mods that would give better camera options or change some game rules to allow for more interactions. Nowadays, some in-game tools exist to support these mods, not requiring the user to change his game code. One good example is *WoW Machinima Tool*[1] for the World of Warcraft game client. Other games that show similar tools are *League of Legends*, *The Sims*, *Half Life 2*, *Minecraft* and *Eve Online*.

Regarding standalone tools, all of them provide control over lights and camera and the basic workflow: scripting the story, gathering the visual assets needed, casting the actors, preparing the location, and finally playing and recording the scene; but some brought up new features. *Machinima Studio*[2] allows one to get assets from more than just one game and use on the same production. *Xtranormal*[3] is a similar tool that adds features such as staring, gestures and facial expressions to the characters to the usual ones. *Matinee*[4] is the cinematic tool from *Unreal Development Kit*, mor focused on games. *Source Filmaker*[5] uses *Valve's Source Engine*[6] to perform similar tasks, but not integrated in a Game SDK as Matine. *Moviestorm*[7] is probably one of the best machinima tools on the scene, regarding workflow and ease-to use, Although being behind graphics-wise when compared to the previous two.

3   Mappets Overview

Some state of the art machinima tools described on Section 2 solve one of the problems described in Section 1, that is the high entry point for machinimists without gaming or modding experience, but they still lack the support for transmedia productions. After the evaluation of these tools and direct contact with members of BeActive[8], a company dedicated to Transmedia Storytelling, we gathered a small list of basic requirements that a Machinima tool that could be used on Transmedia production should have, besides the ones already referred in

---

[1] http://pxr.dk/wmt/

[2] http://www.machinimadev.com/

[3] http://www.xtranormal.com/

[4] http://www.unrealengine.com/features/cinematics/

[5] http://www.sourcefilmmaker.com/

[6] http://source.valvesoftware.com/

[7] http://www.moviestorm.co.uk

[8] http://www.beactivemedia.com

Section 2. Although some of these are supported by the best available tools (Matine and Moviestorm), none of the evaluated tools provide all of them. The new requirements for transmedia productions fulfilled by our tool are the following:

1. Capability to import an external script written in the most used scriptwriting tool worldwide, Final Draft[9]
2. Adaptability to different assets and sceneries, to support different stories.
3. Reusability of assets and possibly content into a different media like a game.
4. Expansibility of the tool to support new assets for subsequent productions.
5. Enabling the division of tasks among a filmmaking team, not concentrating all the tasks in one single user.

3.1   Architecture

We decided to develop a tool over Unity3D, one of the most popular Game Developing Kits nowadays. Not only we are able to develop a generic game to be used as a base for the produced machinima, the tool already fulfills some of the requirements by itself such as character importing, map or scene creation Above all, Unity3D allows us to develop plugins to it's existing editor, a feature not offered by any other Game Development Kit. Figure 1 shows the current architecture for the developed tool that was divided in three main components: The Asset Manager, Director and Player.

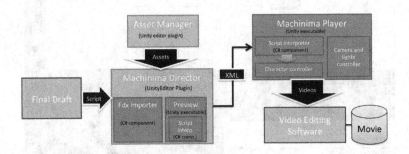

Fig. 1. Overview of our system. Final Draft and the video editing software are external tools.

In analogy to the real life, the assets used in a movie production are Actors, physical locations, and props .On the *Asset Manager* Actors are defined by combining a 3D model to character motion to define it's acting capabilities. By using SmartBody [10] as our character controller, we can remap an animation set used by one model into another, decoupling the playstyle from the looks of the character. The 3D locations can be created on unity or an external tool, and filled with the needed props for one specific scene. Props are also defined on the Asset manager as a combination of a 3D model, and metainformation

---
[9] http://www.finaldraft.com

for interaction with the actors. These assets are packed into a bundle so they can be imported on the director across different projects, maintaining the tool's modularity.

By importing a script wrote in *Final Draft* on the *Machinima Director*, the tool creates a list of characters and locations from the script, and divides the scenes defined on the script, with each scene containing a list of characters that play it, and a location assigned to it. Since dialog actions are annotated, those can be automatically placed on a timeline and assigned to the correct character. All the other actions that do not have a defined structure are manually translated through a simple actor/action interface (Figure 2), and placed on the same timeline, where their sequence and parameters can be defined. A small preview module is available through UnityEditor, where the assets and actions can be checked. An XML description of everything is then exported to be played on the *Machinima Player* to be recorded as a complete machinima. Camera settings such as focus, field of view and aperture can be controlled and saved on a timeline, and also light settings. The script interpreter module will read the XML action definition and forward it to SmartBody, the character controller, which tells the characters what to do at each moment.

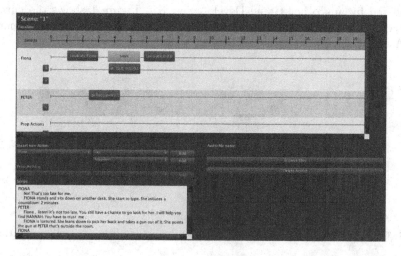

Fig. 2. Mappets plugin interface example. Window on the Director component where the actions are translated from the script to a timeline.

3.2   Early Results

At this stage, our tool is on par with the most recent available options reffered on Section 2. Most of the basic requirements are already included in Unity3D, therefore also in our tool. Other functions such as lipsync, text-to-speech, emotions, can be found on SmartBody, our character controller. We currently do not have a character creator on our tool, but we believe importing any 3D model from Unity3D assets store or other source, and applying different animation sets to it results in a more natural and varied array of characters. Regarding visual quality, Unity3D is very powerful, but the quality of the produced machinima will most likely depend on the detail of the used assets. On the transmedia point of view, our tool has the upper hand among the contestants, making it incredibly faster to jump from a written script to the skeleton of a full movie. By being integrated in a gaming platform, code and content can be reused if a game is to be developed. And as a plugin to Unity Editor, a user experienced with the platform is also able to expand and adapt the tool to his own needs.

3.3   The Role of the AI

Altough the current machinima tools are able to speed up and provide functions that facilitate the production of machinima, they are still a step behind real movie productions. The lack of social presence [11], is a problem seen in several machinima production nowadays. Trying to create it through manual instructions is not practical. By using intelligent agents as our actors, we aim to achieve the desired social presence, acting quality and diversity. Figure 3 shows the proposed change to Machinima Player, including two new components that aim to fulfill this.

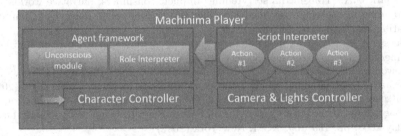

Fig. 3. Proposed changes on Machinima Player. The extended agent framework will provide unconscious behavior and a Role interpreter module.

The *Unconscious Module* (Figure 3) will include unscripted non-verbal communication such as reactions to other actor's presence and actions. The *Role Interpreter* (Figure 3) will add the diversity needed on machinima actors, allowing a director not only to define and change a playstyle for a specific character, but also will allow him to communicate and instruct these agents regarding their acting style, pacing, intensity, and other important aspects of a *Good acting*. We argue that specially on a transmedia setting, a film director will be more at ease, and will be able to employ his skills in a better fashion, if he is not burdened with keyframing and specifying action details.

4 Conclusion and Future Work

We presented a new tool for producing machinima in a transmedia environment. Our tool shortens the distance between a movie production and a Machinima by allowing a director to work with concepts used on a classical production, and a similar workflow. Even though it is still in an early stage, the tool is able to recreate an environment that looked familiar and easy to understand to the experts we are in contact with. Future work on this tool will follow the path described in Section 3.3, developing AI into our virtual actors, so the director can communicate with them as he does with human actors. We believe this will be the next big step taken by these tools, making the workflow and the results closer to real life productions.

Acknowledgments. This work was supported by national funds through FCT Fundação para a Ciência e a Tecnologia, under project PEst-OE/EEI/LA0021/ 2013 and the bilateral contract with BeActive Media. We also thank Cat Kutay, António Brisson, and Nuno Bernardo for cooperating in the development of this Tool.

References

1. Scolari, C.A.: Transmedia storytelling: Implicit consumers, narrative worlds, and branding in contemporary media production. International Journal of Communication 3(4), 586–606 (2009)
2. Berkeley, L.: Situating machinima in the new mediascape. Australian Journal of Emerging Technologies and Society 4(2), 65–80 (2006)
3. Lowood, H.E., Nitsche, M.: The Machinima Reader. MIT Press (2011)
4. Picard, M.: Machinima: Video game as an art form. In: Proc. CGSA 2006 (2006)
5. Nitsche, M.: Experiments in the use of game technology for pre-visualization. In: Proceedings of the 2008 Conference on Future Play: Research, Play, Share. Future Play 2008, pp. 160–165. ACM, New York (2008)
6. Numminen, E., Wrenne, A.: Uncertainty reduction in software development by the use of a platform based development strategy. In: The Proceedings of the 3rd European Conference on Information Management and Evaluation, University of Gothenburg, Sweden, September 17-18, p. 356. Academic Conf. Limited (2009)
7. Elson, D.K., Riedl, M.O.: A lightweight intelligent virtual cinematography system for machinima production. Defense Technical Information Center (2007)
8. Jhala, A., Rawls, C., Munilla, S., Young, R.M.: Longboard: A sketch based intelligent storyboarding tool for creating machinima. In: Proceedings of the Florida Artificial Intelligence Research Society Conference, FLAIRS (2008)
9. Kirschner, F.: 4 toward a machinima studio. The Machinima Reader, 53 (2011)
10. Thiebaux, M., Marsella, S., Marshall, A.N., Kallmann, M.: Smartbody: behavior realization for embodied conversational agents. In: Proceedings of the 7th International Joint Conference on Autonomous agents and Multiagent Systems, AAMAS 2008, vol. 1, pp. 151–158. International Foundation for Autonomous Agents and Multiagent Systems, Richland (2008)
11. Mennecke, B., Triplett, J., Hassall, L., Conde, Z.: Embodied social presence theory. In: 2010 43rd Hawaii Intern. Conf. System Sciences (HICSS), pp. 1–10 (2010)

MobileWars: A Mobile GPGPU Game

Mark Joselli[1], Jose Ricardo Silva Jr.[2], Esteban Clua, and Eduardo Soluri[3]

[1] PUC-PR
mejoselli@gmail.com
[2] MediaLab - UFF
{jricardo,esteban}@ic.uff.br
[3] Nullpointer Tecnologia
esoluri@nullpointer.com.br
http://www.nullpointer.com.br

Abstract. Nowadays mobile phones, especially smartphones, are equipped with advanced computing capabilities. Most of these devices have multicore processors such as dual-core CPUs and many-core GPUs. These processors are designed for both low power consumption and high performance computation. Moreover, most devices still lack libraries for generic multicore computing usage, such as CUDA or OpenCL. However, computing certain kind of tasks in these mobile GPUs, and other available multicores processors, may be faster and much more efficient than their single threaded CPU counterparts. This advantage can be used in game development to optimize some aspects of a game loop and also include new features. This work presents an architecture designed to process most of the game loop inside a mobile GPU using the Android Renderscript API. As an illustrated test case for the proposed architecture, this work presents a game prototype called "MobileWars", completely developed using the proposed architecture.

Keywords: Mobile, Mobile Multicore Computing, Game Architecture, GPGPU, Game Physics, Game AI, RenderScript API, Android.

1 Introduction

Digital games are defined as real-time multimedia applications that have a time constraints to run their tasks [1]. If the game is not able to execute its processing under some time threshold, it will fail [2], as its immersion will be lost. Mobile games are also real-time multimedia application that run on mobile phones, having the same time constraints. However, many others characteristics are different [3], when compared to PC or console games: hardware (processing power and screen size); user input, (buttons, voice, touch screen and accelerometers); and a big diversity of operating systems, such as Android, iOS, Symbian and Windows Mobile[4].

The market of mobile devices is growing [5]. Devices powered with Android have 60% of the sale market share in the first quarter of this year in the USA, according to [6]. Also the usage of the internet on such devices are gaining

J.C. Anacleto et al. (Eds.): ICEC 2013, LNCS 8215, pp. 75–86, 2013.

importance, since its has been doubling every year [7]. These are important motivations for game developers and designer to create blockbusters and high end mobile games.

Google introduced in the Honeycomb version of Android the Renderscript API (application programming interface) [8]. Renderscript is an API for achieving better performance on Android phones and tablets. Using this API, developers can use the same code to process on different hardware architectures such as different CPUs (Central Processing Unity), ARM (Advanced RISC Machine) v5, ARM v7, and X86, GPUs (Graphic Processing Unit) and DSPs (Digital Signal Processors). The API decides which processor will run the code on the device at runtime, choosing the best processor for the available code. This work presents a novel game architecture suitable for this new architecture, which extends previous work that were applied in a desktop hardware [2]. As far as the authors knows, this is the first mobile game that uses this kind of architecture.

Summarizing, this work has following contributions: Modeling of a game architecture for mobile device; Adaptation of the architecture and data structures for Renderscript API; and Implementation of a state machine on the mobile GPU.

The paper is organized as follows: Section 2 presents related works on mobile multicore processing and the Renderscript API. Section 3 presents the related work on GPGPU on mobile devices while Section 4 the game design of Mobile-Wars is presented. Section 5 presents the game architecture used in this work and Section 6 presents the results. Finally Section 7 presents the conclusion of this paper.

2   Mobile Multicore Processing

Multicore architecture are, nowadays, found in home PCs and mobile phone, available as multicore CPUs and GPUs. GPUs are powerful processors originally dedicated to graphics computation [9]. GPUs for PCs are composed by hundreds of parallel processors, achieving much better performance then modern CPUs for several specific applications scenarios. The GPU can be used on the PC as a generic processor to process data and deal with computationally intensive tasks, through development of elaborate architectures such as CUDA (Compute Unified Device Architecture) and OpenCL.

On mobile devices, the GPU is much less capable and powerful [10], and is typically integrated into the mobile processor system-on-a-chip (SoC), which also consists of one or several CPUs, DSP (digital system processor), and other available mobile-specific accelerators. This embedded GPU does not have a dedicated memory, having to share the system bus with others processors for accessing the memory. Consequently the memory bandwidth is also much lower when compared to desktops GPUs [11]. Currently, mobile GPUs emphasis more on lower power consumption [12] than performance. Some of these currently available GPUs devices are the Qualcomm's Adreno 200, the TI's PowerVR SGX 530/535 and the nVidia Tegra3.

Normally, most works that uses mobile for parallel processing deals with the use of GPU for generic processing with the OpenGL ES programable shaders, the vertex and fragment shader, as the programming interface [13]. The disadvantage found in some approaches is the traditional shader languages limitations (such as scatter memory operations, i.e. out-of-order indexed write array operations), and features that are not even implemented on those languages (such as integer data operands like bit-wise logical operations AND, OR, XOR, NOT and bit-shifts). Some of these disadvantages are also presented in the Rendersript API, as the limitation of scatter memory operations.

2.1 The Renderscript API

Renderscript is a new software development kit and API for Android firstly introduced by Google in the Honeycomb version of Android. Renderscript is an API for high-performance graphics processing on Android phones and tablets. It is used for fast 3D rendering and computing processing, having similar paradigm as GPU computing libraries and frameworks [14]. The main goal of Renderscript API is to bring a lower level, higher performance API to Android developers, in order to achieve better performance on visual animations and simulations [15].

Renderscript code is compiled at runtime on the device, avoiding the necessity of application recompilation for different processor types. This fact makes its usage more easily for the developer. Its language is an extension of the C99 language that is translated to an intermediate bytecode at compile time and then to machine code at runtime. The API scales the generated code to the amount of processing cores available on the device, being it CPUs, GPUs or DSPs. The decision of choosing which processor is going to run the code is made on the device at runtime, being completely transparent for the developer. Normally simple scripts will be able to run on the available GPUs, while more complex scripts will run on the CPU. The CPU is also a fallback, running the code in case there is no available suitable device.

All the tasks implemented in Renderscript are automatically portable for parallel processing on the available processors of the device, such as the CPU, GPU and even DSP. Renderscript is specially useful for apps that do image processing, mathematical modeling, or any other operation that requires lots of mathematical computation, similar to GPU computing paradigm. The main use of Renderscript is to gain performance in critical code where the traditional Android framework and OpenGL ES APIs are not fast enough.

3   Related Work

There are few works on literature about approaches that deals with the use of the mobile on multicore processors, especially dealing with games. Most of the work deals with image processing, using the GPU for generic processing. In [16] some image processing algorithms are designed and implemented on handheld device using OpenGL ES 2.0. In [17] a mobile-GPU implementation of Local

Binary Pattern feature extraction is presented, showing a better performance and power consumption when used the CPU together with the GPU.

Also using OpenGL 2.0 for image processing [11] shows a face recognition algorithm, with a 4.25x speedup and a 3.88x reduction on the total energy consumption. [18] presents an implementation of GPU-based window system on top of EGL and OpenVG. Also the openCV [19] is a library for computer vision, which includes some new and experimental features for the mobile devices. These works are particularly important since they show that the use of the mobile GPU is faster and have low power consumption.

Nah et al. [20] shows OpenGL ES-based CPU-GPU hybrid ray tracer for mobile devices, using Kd-trees. In [21], a system for building document mosaic images from selected video frames on mobile phones using the GPU for accelerating its processing is presented. Also a image deformation implementation with a misc of ARM-Linux and OpenGL ES for mobile device is presented in [22].

There are also some works [23,24,25,26] that uses cloud-computing for distribution of the processing over the cloud for mobile in real time simulation and games. These approaches tend to rely on the network for these distribution, which can be very unreliable and slow using the mobile phones carrier.

Unfortunately, there is nothing in literature that deals with game tasks processed on the mobile GPGPU such as proposed in this work. The only similar work is the previous one [27], where a flocking boids is implemented in the mobile GPU using the Renderscript. This work also takes some concepts from [2], where a PC game were fully implemented in the GPU using CUDA.

4   Design of the Game

The MobileWars game prototype is a massive 2D prototype shooter with a top-down perspective. The game is similar to games like Geometric Wars and E4. The main enhancements of MobileWars is that it uses the mobile GPU to process its calculations, allowing to process and render thousands of enemies, while similar games only process hundreds.

The game play is very simple: the player plays as a mobile phone (which is called "mShip") inside the "computer universe", where the main task is to process (by shooting them) polygons, shaders and data (the enemies) from a game. Every time the "mShip" make physical contact with a enemy it looses time and in consequence it looses FPS. The objective is to process the maximum number of data in the smaller amount of time, at the same time keeping the game interactive with a minimum 12 frames per second. The MobileWars uses the multi-touch screen as the input device of the game, controlling the movement of the "mShip", and the direction of the shots.

5   Proposed Architecture

Computer games are multimedia applications that employ knowledge of many different subjects, such as Computer Graphics, Artificial Intelligence, Physics,

Network and others [28]. Additionally, computer games are also interactive applications that exhibit three general classes of tasks: data acquisition, data processing, and data presentation. Data acquisition in games is related to gathering data from input devices like touch, mice and accelerometers. Data processing consist on applying game rules in order to responding user commands, simulating Physics and Artificial Intelligence behaviors. Data presentation is relate to provides feedback to the player about the current game state, usually through image, audio, and force feedback. In the proposed architecture, all game logic is processed in GPU, i.e., all the data processing tasks. The CPU is only used for tasks that cannot be archived in a parallel manner, such as data acquisition.

In order to fully work on the mobile device, the simulation architecture is divided into four different ambients: the Android framework, where the application is created together with the renderscript context. Also, this ambient is responsible for gathering inputs and to sends them to computing renderscript; the computing renderscript is where the variables for the simulation are created, the call for the renderscript computing engine are made and the maintenance of the NGrid, which is a data structure for neighborhood gathering, which will be explained in the next subsection. The renderscript computing engine process the behavior of the scene, distributing its process among the available processors. OpenGL is responsible to render all the objects, applying shaders and visual effects on them. This architecture is illustrated in Figure 1.

The execution of the MobileWars work as follows. First the Activity create all the context in order to use the RenderScript API. Then the compute Renderscript initialize all the necessary variables and creates the player and enemies. After this initialization, the game loop starts by gathering the user input throughout the Activity and sending it to the Compute Renderscript for further processing. The Compute Renderscript make the calls to the Renderscript Compute Engine for the processing of the game physics and game AI in all entities of the game. The Compute Renderscript does a process based on the rules of the NGrid data structure. All these updates are stored on a VBO (Vertex Buffer Object) and sent to the shaders for its rendering. The GPU also share variables with CPU in order to tell whether it should terminate the application or play sounds effects.

Renderscript programs are divided in threads. In order to process the main game logic, which needs to be executed sequentially, the proposed architecture have a special thread which is responsible for it. This thread is also responsible to treat the "mShip" data and inputs. In this process, the following tasks are included: update the position of the "mShip" accordingly to the input; creation of shots, which are made by other threads; computing the scores; checks the game over; and check for the creation of new enemies. The others threads are responsible for updating the enemies (as a physisical-behavior entity), the shots (as a physical entity) and some particles animations, like explosions (as a behavior entity). The positions and type are put in a VBO and sent to a vertex shader in order to render the individuals without using the Activity.

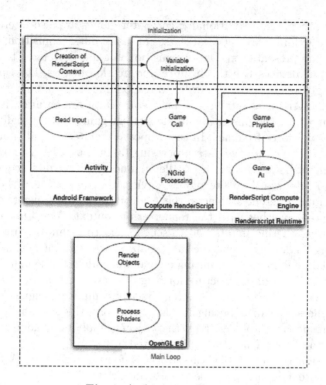

Fig. 1. Architecture Overview

Since all the entities are being updated and executed using the GPU, which has some limitation. It is important to have a data structure that is efficient and capable of adapting in such hardware. In order to fulfill this need this work uses the NGrid, which is presented in the next subsection.

5.1   The NGrid

In order to process the physics and AI, some sort of neighborhood gathering is needed. Most of the games tries to avoid the high complexity of proximity queries by applying some kind of spatial subdivision to the environment and classifying entities among the cells based on their position. To accelerate data fetching, the entities list must be sorted in such a way that all entities on the same cells are grouped together. This approach helps lowering the number of proximity queries but is very sensible to the maximum number of entities that can fit in a single cell. The proposed architecture implements a novel simulation data structure that maintains entities into another kind of proximity based structure, which is called NGrid. In this data structure, each cell now fits only one entity and does not directly represent a discrete spatial subdivision. The NGrid is an approximate representation of the system of neighborhoods in the environment that maps the N-dimensional environment to a discrete map (lattice) with N

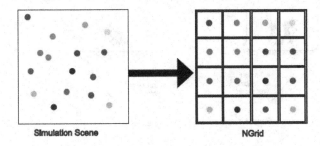

Simulation Scene   NGrid

Fig. 2. Construction of the NGrid in a top-down camera

dimensions. This way, entities that are close in a neighborhood sense appear close to each other in the map. Thus can be also seen as a multi-dimensional compression of the environment that still keeps the original position information of all entities. Figure 2 shows the contraction of the NGrid.

In order to keep entities that are close in a neighborhood sense to appear close to each other in the NGrid, a sorting mechanism is used. Since the entities moves at each frame, the neighborhood grid becomes misaligned. In order to maintain the neighborhood grid in such a way that neighbors in geometric space are stored in cells close to each other, the sorting needs to be done at every step. For this work a odd-even sort data structure is used. More on this data structure can be seen on [29,30].

5.2 Physics Processing

The Physics processing is responsible for the update of physical behavior, i.e, how the entities process and resolve all collisions and forces responses. The Physics of this architecture is based on the one found for particle systems [31] and a hybrid physics engine [28].

Collision detection is a complex operation. For n entities in a system, there must be a collision check between the $O(n^2)$ pairs of entities. Normally, to reduce this computation cost, this process is performed in two steps: first, the broad phase, and second, the narrow phase. In the broad phase, the collision library detects which bodies have a chance of collision among themselves, where the NGrid is being used. In the narrow phase, a more refined algorithm to do the collisions tests are performed between the pairs of bodies that had passed in the broad phase.

The Physics step is responsible for making the broad phase of the collision detection; it also executes the narrow phase of the collision detection, i.e, apply the collision in each body; forwarding the simulation step for each body by computing the new position and velocities according to the their forces and the time step by integrating the equations of motion.

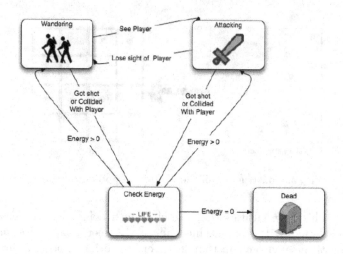

Fig. 3. A Example of State Machine

5.3 Game AI and Login

Game AI is used to produce the illusion of intelligence in the behavior of non-player characters (NPC) which is applied for enemies, in most games. There are a collection of techniques used to implement the game AI such as finite state machines, fuzzy logic, neural networks, and many others. This work uses finite state machine (FSM), which are powerful tools used in many computer game implementations [32], like the NPC behavior, the characters animation states and the game menu states. A finite state machine is a model of behavior composed of states, transitions between those states, and the actions.

The behaviors are affected by the size of vision (which uses the NGrid), velocity and energy, being variables available for each type of enemy. With the modification of these values, this work implements different types of enemies, all based on state machines, as detailed in the following subsections. The following behaviors are proof of concepts, which could be changed or customized in order to the specific game project.

Kamikaze Behavior. The kamikaze approach is a behavior that simulates suicidal attacks. It wanders until the "mShip" is saw, which attacking it by throwing itself against it. This approach is well suited for a parallel architectures, since few information about the scene is necessary. It uses a state machine that has only four state, wandering, attacking, checking energy and dead. This state machine can be seen can be seen on Figure 3.

Group Behavior. The group behavior is a behavior that make groups, avoid bullets and attacks. The individual wanders try to find similar individuals, i.e, individuals of the same type, and the "mShip". If it sees a similar individual, it goes close to it and make a group. And if it can see the player, it attacks the player by throwing itself against it. If the individual sees a bullet coming in its direction it tries to avoid. It has a state machine that has six state, wandering, grouping, attacking, checking energy, avoiding bullets and dead.

Tricky Behavior. The tricky behavior is the most complex one found in the game. This behavior, besides trying to group similar individuals, it also is the only that recover energy. At first, the enemy wanders trying to find the "mShip" or similar individuals. If it sees a similar individual, it goes close to it and make a group. In case it sees the player, it throws itself against it. Additionally, if the individual sees a bullet coming in its direction, it tries to avoid it. Finally, in case of low energy, it tries to scape to recover the lost energy. Their state machine has seven states: wandering, grouping, attacking, avoiding bullets, checking energy, escaping, and dead.

6 Results

For the tests, we have used an Asus Tranformers TF101, which is a 10.1 inches tablet with Android 4.1.1 as operating system. Also, it has a Nvidia Tegra 2 T20 chipset with a Dual-core 1 GHz Cortex-A9 CPU and a ULP (ultra-low power) GeForce GPU, with 8 cores and 1GB of RAM memory. Simulations tests with different configurations were performed. The rendering is done in screen space, through applying a bilateral filter in sphere's normal. To assure that results are consistent, each test was repeated 10 times and the standard deviation of the average times was confirmed to be within 5%.

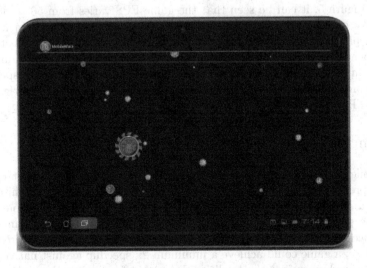

Fig. 4. A screenshot of the game in execution

The number of enemies determines the performance of the game. This work has decided to have a maximum bound of 8192 enemies. A screenshot of the game can be seen in Figure 4.

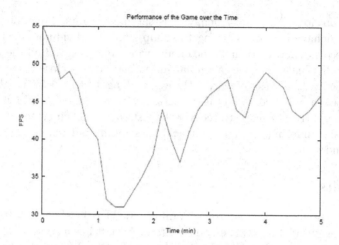

Fig. 5. Measured performance of the game

Similar to others game of the same type, the game has waves of enemies, where a huge amount of enemies appear in a short period of time. Figure 5 show a graph presenting the performance, in FPS, of the game in 5 minutes execution, where a huge wave of 8k enemies appeared during the first minute of the test.

From Figure 5, it can be seen that the game FPS varies from 50 to 30 FPS during the game. The achieved performance is considered optimal in a game [33]. The proposed game prototype has been tested without the architecture in two ambients: using the Android framework and the native code. The game FPS varies from 17 to 5 FPS (the presented architecture has at least 3x speedup) with the android framework. Using the native code, the game FPS varies from 13 to 27 FPS (the presented architecture has a minimum of 2x speedup).

7   Conclusions

The mobile phones have evolved to high end devices with GPUs that can be used to process different tasks of the game loops. The proposed architecture presents a game that uses this kind of devices for processing the whole game loop. The presented results can make a new trend on game development, as more processing can be done in the same period of time. Using the presented architecture, a game could achieve a minimum 2x speedup against native code, and a 3x speedup against the traditional Android framework. As future work, we are focusing on creating a more generic framework in order to be used in others game types.

References

1. Joselli, M., Zamith, M., Clua, E., Leal-Toledo, R., Montenegro, A., Valente, L., Feijo, B., Pagliosa, P.: An architeture with automatic load balancing for real-time simulation and visualization systems. JCIS - Journal of Computational Interdisciplinary Sciences, 207–224 (2010)
2. Joselli, M., Clua, E.: Gpuwars: Design and implementation of a gpgpu game. In: Brazilian Symposium on Games and Digital Entertainment, pp. 132–140 (2009)
3. Joselli, M., Silva Jr., J.R., Zamith, M., Soluri, E., Mendonca, E., Pelegrino, M., Clua, E.W.G.: An architecture for game interaction using mobile. In: 2012 IEEE International Games Innovation Conference (IGIC), pp. 73–77 (August 2012)
4. Joselli, M., Clua, E.: Grmobile: A framework for touch and accelerometer gesture recognition for mobile games. In: Proceedings of the 2009 VIII Brazilian Symposium on Games and Digital Entertainment, SBGAMES 2009, pp. 141–150. IEEE Computer Society, Washington, DC (2009)
5. Koivisto, E.M.I.: Mobile games 2010. In: CyberGames 2006: Proceedings of the 2006 International Conference on Game Research and Development, pp. 1–2. Murdoch University, Australia (2006)
6. CNET: Android reclaims 61 percent of all u.s. smartphone sales (2012), http://tinyurl.com/cgsszfc
7. GlobalStats: Mobile internet usage is doubling year on year (2012), http://gs.statcounter.com/press/mobile-internet-usage-is-doubling-year-on-year
8. Android, G.: Android renderscript (2012), http://developer.android.com/guide/topics/renderscript/index.html
9. Joselli, M., Silva Jr., J.R., Zamith, M., Soluri, E., Mendonca, E., Pelegrino, M., Clua, E.W.G.: Techniques for designing gpgpu games. In: 2012 IEEE International Games Innovation Conference (IGIC), pp. 78–82 (August 2012)
10. Akenine-Moller, T., Strom, J.: Graphics processing units for handhelds. Proceedings of the IEEE 96, 779–789 (2008)
11. Cheng, K.T., Wang, Y.C.: Using mobile gpu for general-purpose computing a case study of face recognition on smartphones. In: 2011 International Symposium on VLSI Design, Automation and Test (VLSI-DAT), pp. 1–4 (2011)
12. Therdsteerasukdi, K., Byun, G., Cong, J., Chang, M.F., Reinman, G.: Utilizing rf-i and intelligent scheduling for better throughput/watt in a mobile gpu memory system. ACM Trans. Archit. Code Optim. 8, 51:1–51:19 (2012)
13. Kim, T.-Y., Kim, J.-H., Hur, H.: A unified shader based on the openGL ES 2.0 for 3D mobile game development. In: Hui, K.-c., Pan, Z., Chung, R.C.-k., Wang, C.C.L., Jin, X., Göbel, S., Li, E.C.-L. (eds.) EDUTAINMENT 2007. LNCS, vol. 4469, pp. 898–903. Springer, Heidelberg (2007)
14. Huang, Y., Chapman, P., Evans, D.: Privacy-preserving applications on smartphones. In: Proceedings of the 6th USENIX Conference on Hot Topics in Security, HotSec 2011, p. 4. USENIX Association, Berkeley (2011)
15. Guihot, H.: Pro Android Apps Performance Optimization. Apress (2012)
16. Singhal, N., Yoo, J.W., Choi, H.Y., Park, I.K.: Design and optimization of image processing algorithms on mobile gpu. SIGGRAPH Posters, 21 (2011)
17. Lopez, M., Nykänen, H., Hannuksela, J., Silven, O., Vehviläinen, M.: Accelerating image recognition on mobile devices using gpgpu. In: Proceedings of SPIE, vol. 7872, p. 78720R (2011)

18. Jeong, D., Kamalneet, Kim, N., Lim, S.: Gpu-based x server on top of egl and openvg. In: International Conference on Computers in Education, pp. 1–2 (2009)
19. Pulli, K., Baksheev, A., Kornyakov, K., Eruhimov, V.: Real-time computer vision with opencv. Commun. ACM 55, 61–69 (2012)
20. Nah, J.-H., Kang, Y.-S., Lee, K.-J., Lee, S.-J., Han, T.-D., Yang, S.-B.: Mobirt: an implementation of opengl es-based cpu-gpu hybrid ray tracer for mobile devices. In: ACM SIGGRAPH ASIA 2010 Sketches, SA 2010, pp. 50:1–50:2. ACM, New York (2010)
21. López, M.B., Hannuksela, J., Silvén, O., Vehvilainen, M.: Graphics hardware accelerated panorama builder for mobile phones. In: Proc. SPIE Multimedia on Mobile Devices, vol. 7256 (2009) ISBN 9780819475060
22. Hu, X., Xia, Z., Yuan, Z.: Study on image deformation simulation based on arm linux and opengles. In: Proceedings of the 2011 International Conference on Intelligence Science and Information Engineering, ISIE 2011, pp. 303–306. IEEE Computer Society, Washington, DC (2011)
23. Barboza, D.C., Junior, H.L., Clua, E.W.G., Rebello, V.E.: A simple architecture for digital games on demand using low performance resources under a cloud computing paradigm. In: Brazilian Symposium on Games and Digital Entertainment, pp. 33–39 (2010)
24. Joselli, M., Zamith, M., Clua, E.W.G., Montenegro, A., Leal-Toledo, R.C.P., Valente, L., Feijó, B.: An architecture with automatic load balancing and distribution for digital games. In: 2010 Brazilian Symposium on Games and Digital Entertainment (SBGAMES), pp. 59–70. IEEE (2010)
25. Zamith, M., Valente, L., Joselli, M., Clua, E., Toledo, R., Montenegro, A., Feij, B.: Digital games based on cloud computing. In: SBGames 2011 - X Simpsio Brasileiro de Jogos Para Computador e Entretenimento Digital (2011)
26. OnLive (2012), http://www.onlive.com/
27. Joselli, M., Soluri, E., Passos, E., Junior, J.S., Zamith, M., Clua, E.: A flocking boids simulation and optimization structure for mobile multicore architectures. In: SBGames 2012 - Trilha de Computao, Braslia (2012)
28. Joselli, M., Clua, E., Montenegro, A., Conci, A., Pagliosa, P.: A new physics engine with automatic process distribution between cpu-gpu. In: Sandbox 2008: Proceedings of the 2008 ACM SIGGRAPH Symposium on Video Games, pp. 149–156 (2008)
29. Joselli, M., Passos, E.B., Zamith, M., Clua, E., Montenegro, A., Feijo, B.: A neighborhood grid data structure for massive 3d crowd simulation on gpu. In: Brazilian Symposium on Games and Digital Entertainment, pp. 121–131 (2009)
30. Passos, E.B., Joselli, M., Zamith, M., Clua, E.W.G., Montenegro, A., Conci, A., Feijo, B.: A bidimensional data structure and spatial optimization for supermassive crowd simulation on gpu. Comput. Entertain. 7, 60:1–60:15 (2010)
31. Joselli, M., Zamith, M.: A novel data structure for particle system simulation based on gpu with the use of neighborhood grids. In: Proceedings of the GPU Forum 2012 (CSBC), SBC (2012)
32. Li, F., Woodham, R.J.: Video analysis of hockey play in selected game situations. Image Vision Comput. 27, 45–58 (2009)
33. Joselli, M., Zamith, M., Valente, L., Clua, E.W.G., Montenegro, A., Conci, A., P., F.P.: An adaptative game loop architecture with automatic distribution of tasks between cpu and gpu. In: Proceedings of the VII Brazilian Symposium on Computer Games and Digital Entertainment, pp. 115–120 (2008)

StepByStep: Design of an Interactive Pictorial Activity Game for Teaching Generalization Skills to Children with Autism

Alberto Gruarin[1], Michel A. Westenberg[2], and Emilia I. Barakova[1]

[1] Industrial Design Department, Eindhoven University of Technology
[2] Department of Mathematics and Computer Science, Eindhoven University of Technology
a.gruarin@student.tue.nl, {m.a.westenberg,e.i.barakova}@tue.nl

Abstract. Translating acquired behavioral skills from training environments to daily-life situations is difficult for children with autism. This study introduces the StepByStep platform, in which pictorial activity schedules are implemented. Design decisions that increase the sameness in the environment and the comfort of the children were implemented to isolate the learning task and promote the training of generalization skills. Differently from existing visual scheduling systems, we use photographs of the child that is trained instead of general activity pictures. The design promotes the features of easy individualization of the training and of playfulness while learning. StepByStep was used by one participant in a pilot study, who showed behavior acquisition and translation to real life situations.

Keywords: Interactive game design, training generalization skills, assistive technology, pictorial activity, personalized training for children with ASD, visual scheduling.

1 Introduction

Generalization is the ability to transfer a learned behavior to another similar or related activity or situation, and is considered to be a difficult task for children with autism spectrum disorders (ASD). It is a complex task that can be divided in subtasks which include learning the right sequence of actions, understanding self-referential (emotionally non-neutral) concepts, and possibly imitation as a social learning mechanism.

The existing procedures for behavioral training of individuals with autism have been successful in structured and controlled environments [4,5]. In these situations, both the behavior and the stimulus that sets the occasion for learning are clearly presented to the child by an instructor. Moreover, the structured environment does not present other possible cues which can distract the child. In daily-life contexts, however, a child is usually exposed to various stimuli which can all set an occasion for social learning and generalization. Due to the difficulties these children have in dealing with multiple cues, isolating the stimulus that needs to be learned may help translating the learned behavior from training environments into real life. This design study implements a specific context for the behavior which should be learned by the child; the training is meant to present and teach a skill within the environment familiar to the child. In addition, we

J.C. Anacleto et al. (Eds.): ICEC 2013, LNCS 8215, pp. 87–92, 2013.

attempt to utilize the benefits of playfulness during training. The design is meant to give the child the impression that he/she is playing rather than learning, and it aims to decrease the perception of a starting and an ending time, usually associated with a therapy schedule. In particular, we propose an interactive game with physical objects which can be more engaging for the child. Behavioral training through interactive games has been used in the past years to reduce the stress of learning different skills [2,4].

Children with ASD generally tend to stick with sameness [8], which usually results in problematic behavioral responses to changes in daily routines. In this context, the literature shows that children with autism may benefit from visual support, especially when comprehending changes throughout the day [9]. Cihak [6] showed that both video modeling [4,11] and pictorial activity schedules provide benefits for autonomy and independence during the transition, reducing at the same time negative behavioral responses due to anxiety or aggressiveness. Activity schedules are visual support systems that combine photographs, images, or drawings in a sequential format to represent targeted sequences. Although they are an established and often used support for young people with autism, they mostly make use of paper sequences [12]. Creation and use of visual sequences that show the child's schedule can demand much time and it can be difficult to record data to track progress [10]. The design of vSked, a computerized visual scheduling system for interaction and collaboration, addresses these problems [10].

In the present study, we build on the concept of computerized activity schedules. However, we pursue different learning goals: teaching generalization skills to children with autism. We use the familiar home environment of the child, his/her mother as a trainer and an element that to our knowledge has not been used in other designs, namely pictures of the child himself/herself performing the actions of the behavioral sequence to be learned. These design decisions help to increase the familiarity of the child with the context and the event expressed in the pictures, and also to make the interpretation of the presented event unique. Since pictorial sequences are static, the child's attention can move from one image to another without losing any information at any time. This characteristic makes pictorial sequences also more effective for children who are easily distracted [1].

Regarding the content of the pictorial activity schedule, the child's personal representation in the images help him/her to interpret and acquire the meaning of the pictures. In general, autistic children show a lack of "theory of mind", i.e. they have difficulties in understanding others' mental states, beliefs and desires [3]. Corcoran & Frith [7] suggested that understanding others' thoughts relies partially on the ability to recall autobiographical memories. These studies inspired the decision to implement pictures of the children themselves and of their own activities into designed game sequences, avoiding translation of others' actions to an own schedule. In addition, the children are assisted by recognizing themselves in the sequences. Recalling personal memories would, then, help them to perform the acquired behavior in real life.

To summarize, the designed game StepByStep implements activity schedules into behavioral training, presenting behavior in known context and environment and through picture sequences of the particular child performing these actions. The expectation is that these recognizable features will help the child to more easily learn and generalize this behavior to a real-life situation.

2   Design and Proof-of-Concept Validation

Game Concept. StepByStep consists of two parts: a tangible carpet used as a controller, which interacts with the software game installed on a computer. The tangible carpet consists of 6 colorful pads with embedded buttons, on which the child can press or step (see Fig. 1(a)). The carpet is intentionally designed large sized to promote more physical activity. The game setting is as follows: pictorial activity sequences have to be reordered by the child. Every time a level starts, the sequence images are presented in a random order and assigned to a colored box at the top of the screen. By pressing the corresponding colored carpet button, the child is asked to construct the correct sequence order. If the answer is correct, an audio feedback will play a predefined tone once, and the software will move the image to the correct sequence position at the bottom of the screen (see Fig. 1(b)). In this way, visual feedback is provided to attract the child's attention both on the remaining images and on the already correct ones. If the answer is wrong, a different tone is continuously played until the child presses a button. The answer feedback is intentionally designed to avoid negative responses by the software.

The pictorial activity sequences are uploaded on the computer by the parents, perhaps together with a therapist, in order to direct the behavioral training to specific learning goals. In this way, the parents are able to control the amount of information provided to children with new sequences, balancing them with their child's abilities in integration and acquisition of new behaviors.

StepByStep Technical Specifications. StepByStep includes both hardware and software sections, which are designed on the Arduino microcontroller platform and Processing software, respectively.

The carpet is built with white eco-friendly leather onto which six eco-friendly leather colored sheets are sewn; inside this white folder, six pressure mats are positioned below the six colored sheets. These sensors, once pressed by the child, act as a switch for Arduino, which consequently is able to detect exactly which sensor is pressed. A threshold is set by Arduino in order to determine the minimum amount of pressure the child should apply to the sensor, to avoid that the carpet responds to small forces. When Arduino detects the signal from the pressure sensor, it sends this information to the software game controller for further handling.

The game controller is implemented in Processing to allow maximum platform independence and flexibility. The game resides on the computer, and the carpet merely acts as a game interface. This setup allows easy extensions to other input devices, such as keyboard or mouse, but also to touch interfaces as provided by tablet computers or smart phones. New image sequences can be added by the parents, simply by putting the corresponding pictures (minimally three and maximally six) in a pre-specified place and by providing a single text file that contains the filenames of the pictures in correct order. At the beginning of each level, the game presents a dialog box from which a desired training sequence can be chosen. The number of pictures in the sequence is communicated to Arduino, which initializes the sensors of the carpet, and disables the ones that are not involved in the sequence to avoid that the child receives feedback that is not meaningful. After loading the sequence, the images are permuted using a variant of the Fisher-Yates shuffling algorithm and linked to the carpet sensors.

 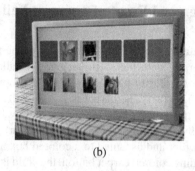

(a)   (b)

Fig. 1. (a) StepByStep design. (b) Screenshot during game play: [top] random image sequence and correspondence to the colored buttons; [bottom] partially ordered image sequence.

During game play, the child presses the sensors on the carpet. Arduino communicates the received input from this sensor to the game software, which checks if the child's answer is correct or wrong. This answer is sent back to Arduino which will play a sound depending on the outcome as described previously.

Experimental Procedure. The design and the proof-of-concept user test were performed with a Dutch female child aged 8. She was diagnosed to belong to the Pervasive Developmental Disorder Not Otherwise Specified (PDD-NOS) group, specifically to the high-functioning subgroup (whose symptoms largely overlap that of Asperger syndrome), but presenting language delays and mild cognitive impairments. The study took place at the child's home throughout the entire experimental period. Informed consent to take part to the test was obtained from the parents.

Two pictorial activity sequences were tested by the participant. Both sequences represented behaviors that the participant did not perform alone. Sequence 1 refers to coming back home from school, where she was required to open the front door, hang up the bag and then the jacket, take off the shoes and store them in a shoe rack. Sequence 2 represents what she should do if a nightmare occurs: turn on the room light, go up the stairs, and wake up her mother asking for help. The pictures for the two sequences were taken by the participant's mother, who involved the child and explained her the meaning and context of the pictures. The photographed environment was the participant's house, and the child and her personal objects appear in the image sequences.

During a three weeks span on regular intervals, the participant played StepByStep 7 times for 15 minutes. In each session, both sequences were presented to the child. The experimenter was present only in the first training together with the participant's mother, who was instructed how to observe the child's emotional state and behavior during the next trainings. An indirect observation method was chosen for this study; the participant's mother took on the observer role in the research due to her confidence with autistic children and her experience on understanding small emotional and behavioral changes of her child. Additionally, children with autism are largely affected by the presence of new individuals, which can lead to stress and anxiety and will affect their responses to the game. After all sessions, an interview with the participant's mother was held to collect data.

3 Results

The participant showed enjoyment and willingness to play with StepByStep during all sessions. Children with autism typically refuse activities which do not match their preferences, and they tend to abandon them after a certain time span. In this specific study, since repetitive use is crucial for acquiring behaviors and translating them into daily life, it would also be difficult to achieve any valuable results if the child did not like the game or felt forced to play with StepByStep. Furthermore, the participant showed enjoyment in experimenting with the carpet by finding new ways for moving on it, and she used the carpet as a means to express her emotional state (for example, she would step back from the carpet after a mistake and then slowly push the button corresponding to the new answer trial).

After the training period, the participant was able to wake up her mother for help when a nightmare occurred (Sequence 2). Hence, she showed the ability to translate the pictorial sequence learned during game play to a real-life situation. In addition, the mother reported a conversation between the child and her therapist, where the child told that, in total, three nightmares occurred during the training period and that, since she played with the game, she was aware of the correct behavior to show in that situation. She asked for help (i.e. performed the sequence of actions for real) only the first time when the nightmare occurred. The mother thinks that during the other two occurrences, being aware of the correct response to a nightmare was already enough to reduce fear and anxiety of the child without asking for her mother's help.

The child could not yet translate the behavior from Sequence 1 (coming back from school) to real life. Most of the training took place during Christmas holidays, however, which had very few opportunities for the child to perform the intended behavior.

4 Discussion

Pictorial activity sequences provided a useful educational support for teaching behavioral responses. The two features of the pictures specific of this study, namely photographs of the child and her personal environment, showed to enhance this teaching support. According to the participant, being an actor for recording the sequences was perceived as part of the game, hence a playful activity. Playfulness decreased the perception of being engaged in learning but did not decrease the effect of learning. The child managed to acquire a specific response within the performance context, and was able in one case to translate this knowledge in real life. The child herself being on the pictures prevented the participant from interpreting other individual's intentions through the pictorial sequences; adding a personal environment as a context for learning the desired behavior resulted in both behavior acquisition and recall from autobiographical memories when needed. If only the response itself would have been taught, the child would have had to spontaneously add the correct context during real life. This requires good context interpretation abilities, which are usually not mastered by children with ASD.

StepByStep was evaluated with one participant for a time period of three weeks. Involving more participants of various chronological age groups and different ASD conditions is planned to further validate the design. Further research should be done to define a balance between new information provided by new sequences and training periods according to the individual abilities of the child. The present study only touches upon the effects of playing with StepByStep for behavioral training in ordering sequences of daily events and generalization/translation of newly learned behavioral sequences to daily routine. Generalization over contexts by children with autism might be further explored, by evaluating if StepByStep can successfully train behavioral sequences that have been learned at school or other non-domestic environments.

Acknowledgments. The authors thank the family who participated passionately throughout the research and M. van Dijk, therapist at Expertise center Kentalis (Eindhoven, The Netherlands), for her support and cooperation in the design phase.

References

1. Alberto, P.A., Cihak, D.F., Gama, R.I.: Use of static picture prompts versus video modeling during simulation instruction. Research in Developmental Disabilities 26(4), 327–339 (2005)
2. Barakova, E., Gillessen, J., Feijs, L.: Social training of autistic children with interactive intelligent agents. Journal of Integrative Neuroscience 8(01), 23–34 (2009)
3. Baron-Cohen, S., Leslie, A.M., Frith, U.: Does the autistic child have a "theory of mind"? Cognition 21(1), 37–46 (1985)
4. Brok, J.C.J., Barakova, E.I.: Engaging autistic children in imitation and turn-taking games with multiagent system of interactive lighting blocks. In: Yang, H.S., Malaka, R., Hoshino, J., Han, J.H. (eds.) ICEC 2010. LNCS, vol. 6243, pp. 115–126. Springer, Heidelberg (2010)
5. Brown, A.K., Brown, J.L., Poulson, C.L.: Discriminating which fork to use: Teaching selective imitation to people with autism. Research in Autism Spectrum Disorders 2(2), 199–208 (2008)
6. Cihak, D.F.: Comparing pictorial and video modeling activity schedules during transitions for students with autism spectrum disorders. Research in Autism Spectrum Disorders 5(1), 433–441 (2011)
7. Corcoran, R., Frith, C.D.: Autobiographical memory and theory of mind: evidence of a relationship in schizophrenia. Psychological Medicine (33), 897–905 (2003)
8. Heflin, L.J., Alaimo, D.F.: Students With Autism Spectrum Disorders: Effective Instructional Practices. Prentice Hall (2006)
9. Heflin, L.J., Simpson, R.L.: Interventions for children and youth with autism prudent choices in a world of exaggerated claims and empty promises. Part I: Intervention and treatment option review. Focus on Autism and Other Developmental Disabilities 13(4), 194–211 (1998)
10. Hirano, S.H., Yeganyan, M.T., Marcu, G., Nguyen, D.H., Boyd, L.A., Hayes, G.R.: vSked: evaluation of a system to support classroom activities for children with autism. In: Proceedings of the SIGCHI Conference on Human Factors in Computing Systems, pp. 1633–1642. ACM (2010)
11. Qi, C.H., Lin, Y.L.: Quantitative analysis of the effects of video modeling on social and communication skills for children with autism spectrum disorders. Procedia – Social and Behavioral Sciences (46), 4518–4523 (2012)
12. Savner, J.L., Hyles, B.S.: Making visual supports work in the home and community: Strategies for individuals with autism and Asperger Syndrome. AAPC Publishing (2000)

Technologically Mediated Intimate Communication:
An Overview and Future Directions

Elham Saadatian[1], Hooman Samani[2], Arash Toudeshki[3], and Ryohei Nakatsu[4]

[1] Interactive and Digital Media Institute, National University of Singapore
[2] Department of Electrical Engineering, National Taipei University, Taiwan
[3] Department of Electrical and Electronic Engineering, University Putra Malaysia
[4] Department of Electrical and Computer Engineering,
National University of Singapore
Keio-NUS CUTE Center, NUS
elham@nus.edu.sg

Abstract. Emerging field of intimate computing relates to the technologies that aim to mediate affective communication across distance. Conventional telecommunication media are originally designed for collaborations and task oriented goals with the poor support of intimate experiences. Contemporary lifestyle changes leaded to design and adoption of technologies in support of long distance relationships. The present work is a study of existing prototypical systems and related conceptual studies in this realm of study. Their design perspective, mechanism and human factors are described. Challenges coupled to this domain are studied and future research directions are proposed.

Keywords: Telepresence, Mediated intimacy, Telematic emotional communication, User interface, Perspective.

1 Introduction

Intimacy is defined by social scientists as cognitive and emotional expressiveness, support, engagement, and physical contact [1]. Maintaining intimacy in the relationship is emphasized as a necessary factor of the romantic relationship [2]. However, increase of Long Distance Relationships (LDR), and poor functionality of current telecommunication system hampers the convergence of intimacy across distance.

Conventional technologies for mediated remote communication are originally designed for collaboration, teleoperation, and task oriented activities which are optimized for efficient exchange of information. This trend compromises the non-informative dimension of interaction. Therefore, intimate computing increasingly gained the attention of Human Computer Interaction (HCI) and Human Robot Interaction (HRI) researchers to support LDR and has opened a new area of study known as intimate computing. It resulted in a considerable amount of

J.C. Anacleto et al. (Eds.): ICEC 2013, LNCS 8215, pp. 93–104, 2013.
© IFIP International Federation for Information Processing 2013

studies and prototypes, by adopting the metaphor of remote or mediated intimacy. In these technologies the goal is promoting social bond rather than any information or data transition. The pioneering works in this area are three prototypical systems namely " Feather, Scent, and Shaker developed by Strong & Gaver [3] which affords remote intimate communication by providing ambient representation of the distant partner. It gave a new insight in telecommunication technologies. This paper takes and opportunity to survey the current state-of-the-art in intimate computing. It describes research and prototypes developed to date, and provide suggestions for future directions of research in this area.

2   Human Factor Elicitation for Design of Intimate Medium

Intimate communications are distinct form typical communications studied by HCI researchers, such as relationships amongst friends or colleagues [4]. Challenges on studying intimacy arises from their ephemeral nature, low informational content and emotional significant, self-disclosure and privacy, unsaid interactions and idiosyncratic nature. Also there is no predefined language for its description [5]. Since intimate behaviors are strikingly nuanced and often subtly vague to outsiders, involvement of users is unavoidable in design of its supporting technologies. One area of research in intimate computing relates to human factor elicitation and user experience of these technologies.

One of the approaches is using technology probes. For example: Lottridge et al. [6] explored the design space for remote intimate communication between couples. They realized the potential to draw on the daily routine "empty moments" of couples. Ambiguity, aesthetic, continuity, asymmetry, and movability were comforted by users as design space for sharing empty moments.

OBrien & Mueller [7] applied technology probe to investigate when partners in close relationships would want tactile exchange through holding hands while apart. However the experiment was not successful since the probe was too simple to encourage couples to use it. They realized a probe should be simple but aesthetically well designed to encourage participant to use it. Kaye & Goulding [8] developed personalized probes for long term study through the users proposed sketches. They studied how objects were used and how changed their communication pattern. This study was based on the advantages of personal over mass communication in the context of intimacy.

Another perspective focuses on scenario based design. For example, Battarbee et al. [9] tried to design in support of intimacy within an urban environment. It was done through observations within the city and developing scenarios. King [10] explored how people use interactive technologies in their relationships through legitimating the participates to explore the possible future, instead of being restricted to current technology.

Other studies on design space are: King & Forlizzi [11] used interview, web based diary study and photo journal. They found possibilities for emotional connectedness by designing reflective and slow interfaces which are linked to the sense of place. Pace et al. [12] studied virtual world as a source of intimacy and found permeability across virtual and real worlds, mundane as origin of intimacy, reciprocity and exchange, and temporality in shaping intimate experience. Gooch & Watts [13] proposed a framework to formalize the design space for intimate communication devices. They have highlighted the 6 factor of Personalization, Sensory Medium, Effort, Openness of the System, Metaphor of Use, and Fleeting vs Realized Output. These factors are based on the study of previous developed devices and more study is needed for validation and refining the framework.

There has been several attempts in exploring the effect of physiological and nonverbal signals on perception of intimate connections. For instance: Gooch & Watts [14] proved the impact of heat as an aspect of touch using thermal hug belt. Carpe Diem [15] proved the effect of eye contact in intimacy. Slovák et al. [16] Investigated people perception on heart rate feedback. They found heartrate feedback an affective connectedness signals as well as connector. In another study Janssen et al. [17] empirically proved the possibility of using heartbeat transition as an intimate signal through self-report and behavioral monitoring in an immersive virtual environment.

These are not the only attempts in studying intimate computing through user, however these are studies which dominantly focused on user perception. Other researches have also involved users in the system design and evaluation into some extents.

3   Prototypes for Mediated Intimacy

The design space for remote intimate couples has largely been populated with technologies that support and mediate intimacy via abstracted presence [18,19]. Gaver categorizes these technologies into two groups, those which mediate intimate behaviors and those which provoke intimate reactions [3]. The first group attempts to mediate intimate feelings or actions through reproduction, manifestation or imitation of them, using technology. Whilst the second group concentrates on evoking reactions instead of explicit expressions [20]. Gaver [5] has identified three common features in most of these technologies: use of evocative materials; use of poetic mappings rather than didactic metaphors; and reliance on physical materials.

Fig. 1 shows the relative distribution of some of these technologies that will be described in the following sections. They are classified based on degree of holism and realness versus abstract and poetic presence that they convey.

3.1   Technologies That Mediate Intimate Behaviors

In this group commonly pair of coupled interfaces transmit the intimate behavior requiring near body presence. Whereas the interface acts on behalf of the remote person to literally or symbolically reproduced the intimate expressions. In literal approach the intimate action is directly reproduced. Whilst in symbolic (poetic) simulation, intimate behavior is mapped to another form. Attempts on

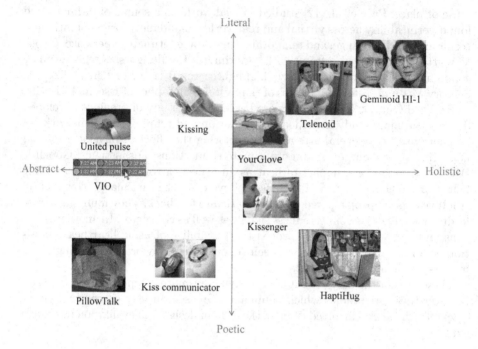

Fig. 1. Relative distribution of some of the telepresence technologies

this category includes different types of remote haptic communications such as hugging, kissing, grasping, shaking hand, hand holding. Other physical interactions such as, whispers, sound of heartbeat and body heat of significant others sleeping beside are in this category.

3.2   Technologies That Provoke Intimate Reactions

One perspective on intimate computing is implicit affective communication. In this approach abstract interfaces can convey the sense of presence in absence in an ambient way. They do not transmit any intimate behavior however they support emotional aspects of intimacy and provoke intimate reaction without explicit expression.

Ephemeral and Poetic Interactions. There has been several works that provoke intimacy through ephemeral interactions. The earliest of this type are "Feather, Scent, and Shaker" envisioned by Strong and Gaver [3]. They are paired devices that implicitly aware users when their remote partner thinks of them. In "Feather" interaction with a picture frame causes the feather drift in the air. Shaker facilitates the exchange of tactile gestures through a simple remote force feedback mechanism. And scents actuates ephemeral aroma at home when the traveling partner interacts with a photo frame. These prototypes convey romantic sensation through serendipitous and ephemeral attributes of interfaces.

Message	prototype	medium design	Stimulation
Kiss	Intimate mobiles [22] kiss communicator [23] Kissenger [24] CheekTouch [25], [26] Hkiss [27]	direct telepresence on mobile Symbolic mapping direct mapping on telepresence robot differnt vibration patterns haptic feedback from 3D avatar	hand loop, heat, wet sponge, airjet squeeze and blow vibration phone vibration and audio vibration on belt
Hug	The Hug [28] Hug over a distance [29] Huggy pajama [30] HaptiHug [31] Second Life HugMe [32]	via telepresence robot through wearable vest wearable hug jacket and hug trigger device autodetect hug keyword,visualization and haptics multimodal hug input	lights, vibration patterns, heat,sounds. air-inflation air pressure robotic hand pressure visuotactile on jacket and avatar
Co-Sleeping	Sensing Beds [33] Aura [34]	position tracking via mattress sensors sleep pattern sesning	slow heating music corresponding to pattern
Hand Touching	Tele-handshake [35] YourGlove [36] HotHands and HotMits [37] Feelybean [38] Stroking device while holding hands [39] The Withe Stone [40] VibroBod [41]	shared virtual interface and haptices paired robotic hands personalized hand shape augment touch to skype exchange stroke gesture paired stone interface detects gesture/voice	feedback through phantom hold and grip thermal insulation vibration servo motors under sponge beep sound and heat warmth and pose
Biological Signals	Mobile Feelings [42] united-pulse [43]	heart beat/breath sharing heartbeat share user heartbeat measured	LED blinking rhythmic pulses/ micro-ventilator ring vibration
Touch Gestures	Tug n' Talk [44] Poke [45] The ComSlipper [46] FootIO [47] InTouch [48] PillowTalk [49]	belt-buckle with chains surface augmented on mobile foot posture sensed emotion foot-stool paird rollers pillow detects hand gestures	chain moves inflation vibration/warmth/light different vibrations vibration ambient method
Holistic Presence	Geminoid HI-1 [50] Elfoid phone [51] Mebot [52] Callo and Cally [53]	Realistic humanoid robot miniature, generic humanoid robot robot and cellphone display robot and cellphone display	exact voice and some moves exact voice and some moves facial expression and gestures walk, dance, facila expressions

Fig. 2. Relative distribution of some of the telepresence technologies

"Hintouch" [21] is a Two-Way Ambient Communication prototype with support of context information around picture.

"LumiTouch" [22] is a pair of picture frames with the photo of remote users on each other's desks which are used as interface. When the sender squeezes the picture frame, her partner's picture frame displays area illuminates corresponding with input squeeze intensity. Different combination of of light intensities, colors, and pulses are decided by couples as a private language for their interaction.

Also "SmallConnection" [23] expresses faint information such as light, wind and touch using robotic technology. Light symbolizes presence by synchronically turning on and off between two distant homes. Winds detects the sound in remote place and spins in sync with it. And touch is transmitted by synchronized movement of paired buttons. "VIO" Virtual Intimate Objects (VIO) [24] transmits one bit message by clicking on a virtual circle on a task bar that brightens the remote persons' circle.In another study on VIO [25] users were evaluated using a logbook including open ended questions regarding the context of use. This Study also revealed that this simple interaction has a rich interpretation which suggest the importance of usage context in remote communication technologies.

Co-presence through Hybrid Sensory Interaction. There has been several prototypes that express intimacy through hybrid sensory mode. Such as: "Keep in touch" [26] that facilitates playful, visuotactile interaction by 'fabric screen'. Each persons' screen displays an out-of-focus video of his/her counterpart, that comes to focus after touching the fabric. "ComTouch" [27] augments touch to voice communication by sending vibrotactile feedback on the mobile phone during conversation. "Shake2Talk" [28] is a mobile messaging system that facilitates sending audio-tactile messages by SMS. Messages are composed by four gestures of stroke, tap, flick which are mapped to different audio-tactile message and played to the sender as they make the gesture. User evaluation showed it was most used by couples living apart.

Shared Experience. Bhandari& Bardzell [29] proposed four design concepts around these them: "Matchus board" and "Together aquarium" were based on the theme of experience sharing. In which the first one facilitates experience sharing by synchronized drawing on a board using multi-user touch input and output devices. And the later through coordination on taking care of online virtual aquarium. The second pair were based on the theme of awareness namely "Cancan" and "Audible gifts". Cancan was a button augmented on a watch which corresponds to "cannot be available now". Audible gift was inspired by significance of "letters" since they have tangibility, thoughtfulness, and require effort which is a pair of microphone and speaker for sending five minutes message.

"Lovers' Cup" [30] explores the idea of conveying the feelings of co-drinking as a communication channel for a couple in physically different places. Amount of liquid in each cup is shown in the partners' cup with LEDs and shaking the cups vibrate its remote pair.

Simple Awareness. "BuddyClock " [31] is a network-enabled alarm clock, which can share alarm status with alarm clocks within a social group. It is predicted such natural status sharing may enhance social awareness, facilitate self-reflection and intimacy. In case of distant romantic couples after a few days their sleeping pattern was synchronized.

"CoupleVIBE" [32] is an awareness unobtrusive privacy-friendly, communication channel on mobile. It shares location information of remote partners by sending specialized touch cues when users moves to each location. This medium allows them to keep updated without being distracted from their daily activity.

"Personal portraits" rises or dims a remote photo frame based on the existence or absence of key ring, which is ambience representation of presence at home. "Light sculptures" uses light bulbs to show presence at home. And in "SoftAir Communication" pressure and movements are detected through embedded sensors in the chair when they are touched and show the presence of remote person by embedded lights and sounds on the touched surface [33].

Effort and Mutual Exchange. Another abstract approach which affords self-disclosure, communicates moods and shows effort and individualization is "sharing emotion through self composed melodies" [34]. This system allows users to compose and share melodies via mobile phones. It synchronically shares emotional state of the sender. They founded self composed melodies have strong impact on receiver which is similar to the effect of crafted piece of art offered to a beloved person.

"Lovers' box" [35] is a digital artifact that aims to engage couples in reflection on their relationship. The role of refection which is through creation, exchange and sharing is examined using digital artifacts. Feeling communication interface was a box that could exchange self-created video messages between couples. The other factors that supported intimate interaction were being more customizable than text, private sharing, and giving & receiving. It also has ambiguity since it allows the users to interpret and analyze the message.

Fictitious Co-habiting through Sharing Everyday Artifacts and Objects. Another group of prototypes use the existing and adapting existing artifacts as a·communication medium instead of creating a completely new device. This theme is initiated by Dodge through a prototype named "The bed" [36]. By equipping the pillows with heating pads and vibrating motors presence and heartbeat of the remote person is symbolized.

"Peek-a-drawer" [37] facilitates virtually sharing drawers among remote family members. In this device when a user put something in the drawer its photo is taken and appears in the remote drawer. "Habitat" [38] is a series of joined furniture for background awareness between distant couples. The initial prototype consists of two, networked coffee table whereas each station consists of a computer, RFID tag reader and a video projector. Objects placed on the table are sensed by the RFID reader and its corresponding representation is projected on the remote table. When objects are removed their representation fades gradually.

"SyncDecor" [39] informs couples of each other's activity by synchronizing daily appliances. This system can remotely synchronize lamps lightness, trash door open, TV channel and smell between remote couples. "Magic Sock Drawer" [40] enables to create digital hand-drawn or typed messages and then automatically produce the physical printed version in the remote users' drawer. The system design supports four intimate computing design concepts including: exchange between dyads, personalization, tangibility and location sharing.

"Digital Selves" proposed by Grivas [41] proposes fictitious merge of the homes of remote couples. This system recognizes the positions of electronic objects inside the two disparate homes of a couple living apart. The advantage over simple ambient communication is adding spatiality and creating sense of place.

4   Discussions and Recommendations for Future Research

In this paper we have attempted to present a broad outline of the field of intimate computing, including relevant conceptual descriptions, human factor elicitation , technical mechanism, and current design trends, fueled by psychological attributes, as well as trends in affective computing, social technologies, and telepresence. The prototypical systems and design perspectives reviewed in the present paper have set the stage for future studies on intimate computing by inspiring researchers, designers, and developers by providing description of the state of the art.

However, it seems that in design investigation and point solutions, there is still ambiguity in approach that best support LDR. Deeper conceptual understanding on the nature of intimacy and practical experiments on the effects of mediated intimacy is needed. Due to the private and delicate nature of intimacy conventional user need exploration techniques such as ethnography are not efficient enough. There have been several attempts in use of cultural probes, but since the current attempts are still rudimentary, more encouraging and well designed cultural probes are still needed.

Although the field of intimate computing is largely populated by technologies that facilitate experience sharing, they have likeness and monotony and very naive approach to love and relationships [42]. Therefore technologies and design ideas that support different subjective love languages are needed.

To date very few objective evaluation techniques of the systems are available beyond the simple descriptions from users or quantitative analysis with few participants. Studying the long term effect of intimae interaction through developed mediums and benchmarking among different suggested designs is rarely experienced. We recommend more detail studies on the user acceptance of such novel trend of communication, and also studying potential cultural, gender and age differences in the degrees of acceptance and ethical issues. What the relatively new area of intimate computing would benefit most from at this early stage is more studies that put the assumed design decisions, described in the reviewed literature to the test and practice in the real world application.

Study on unmediated intimate communication, reveals unmet research questions. For instance an interesting question is whether people hold the same expectancies about the use of mediated intimacy as about the unmediated one. Whether or not the mediated has the same physiological and psychological effects. For instance in real-life scenario people have different reactions to opposite sex and to their own partner compared to same sex and stranger. Exploring the design solutions and engineering ideas that recreate the same sensation in mediated environments is also recommended.

Current technologies still do not support the same natural sensation of real intimate communication. Studies on real interaction offers a good solution to explore the necessary technical and design improvements. Experimental studies on physical properties of real intimate interactions could help to figure out the physical properties (e.g., required actuation amount, pattern) which may lead to more organic sensation.

Exploration on alternative solutions with the same physiological or perceived effect instead of literal simulation of intimate behaviors is suggested. For instance, approaches such as rubber hand illusion [43] could be adapted to provide the perception that the medium acting on behalf is the extension of self.

Also physical close interactions, causes the release of chemicals such as oxytocin and serotonin that help to feel happy and connected [44]. Studies on alternate technologies that stimulate brain for the same reaction could contribute to this field. Also since the nature of this study is multidisciplinary involvement of people from different fields can be promising.

Common theme of intimate computing technologies is pairing abstract devices that connected through internet and enable simple interactions. However, a holistic telepresence medium that provokes or expresses intimacy is not yet developed.

In intimate communication systems, there is a move towards investigating the use of touch. In current systems, it is usually done through simple vibration, pressures or other forms of actuation. Development of high fidelity mediums through advanced control of tactile stimulation algorithms, non-invasive sensing technologies or machine leaning is still needed.

Current telecommunication mediums such as video conferencing compromise the non-verbal signal of eye-gaze direction. Although there has been very few attempts in this area [45] they are still in their infantry. Technical improvements and integration in intimate computing interfaces could be promising. Another suggested research direction is development of intelligent agents to interfere and advice in the relationships instead of simply transmitting the nonverbal cues. Also improvement in usability (exp., non-disruptiveness, embedding in current communication medium instead of separate device, and portability.) is suggested.

5 Conclusion

To sum up, the studies reviewed in the present paper show variety of promising design perspectives of mediated intimacy, ranging from once in a while communicating a bit of data [24], to a complex telepresence robot [46]. However, to date, the developed interfaces are still prototype and needs cutting edge technical, design and usability improvements to be empirically applied in real-life scenarios. Doing so has consequence for the progress of the field, for science, commerce, and social health.

Acknowledgement. This research is supported by the Singapore National Research Foundation under its International Research Center Keio-NUS CUTE Center @ Singapore Funding Initiative and administered by the IDM Program Office.

References

1. Moss, B., Schwebel, A.: Defining intimacy in romantic relationships. Family Relations, 31–37 (1993)
2. Cheal, D.: Showing them you love them: gift giving and the dialectic of intimacy. The Sociological Review 35(1), 150–169 (2011)
3. Gaver, B.: Provocative awareness. In: Computer Supported Cooperative Work (CSCW), vol. 11(3), pp. 475–493 (2002)
4. Kjeldskov, J., Gibbs, M., Vetere, F., Howard, S., Pedell, S., Mecoles, K., Bunyan, M.: Using cultural probes to explore mediated intimacy. Australasian Journal of Information Systems 11(2), 102–115 (2007)
5. Vetere, F., Gibbs, M., Kjeldskov, J., Howard, S., Mueller, F., Pedell, S., Mecoles, K., Bunyan, M.: Mediating intimacy: designing technologies to support strong-tie relationships. In: Proceedings of the SIGCHI Conference on Human Factors in Computing Systems, pp. 471–480. ACM (2005)

6. Lottridge, D., Masson, N., Mackay, W.: Sharing empty moments: design for remote couples. In: Proceedings of the 27th International Conference on Human Factors in Computing Systems, pp. 2329–2338. ACM (2009)
7. O'Brien, S., Mueller, F.: Holding hands over a distance: technology probes in an intimate, mobile context. In: Proceedings of the 18th Australia Conference on Computer-Human Interaction: Design: Activities, Artefacts and Environments, pp. 293–296. ACM (2006)
8. Kaye, J., Goulding, L.: Intimate objects. In: Proceedings of the 5th Conference on Designing Interactive Systems: Processes, Practices, Methods, and Techniques, pp. 341–344. ACM (2004)
9. Battarbee, K., Baerten, N., Hinfelaar, M., Irvine, P., Loeber, S., Munro, A., Pederson, T.: Pools and satellites: intimacy in the city. In: Proceedings of the 4th Conference on Designing Interactive Systems: Processes, Practices, Methods, and Techniques, pp. 237–245. ACM (2002)
10. Howard, S., Vetere, F., Gibbs, M., Kjeldskov, J., Pedell, S., Mecoles, K., Bunyan, M., Murphy, J.: Mediating intimacy: digital kisses and cut and paste hugs. In: Proceedings of BCSHCI 2004, Leeds, UK (2004)
11. King, S., Forlizzi, J.: Slow messaging: intimate communication for couples living at a distance. In: Proceedings of the 2007 Conference on Designing Pleasurable Products and Interfaces, pp. 451–454. ACM (2007)
12. Pace, T., Bardzell, S., Bardzell, J.: The rogue in the lovely black dress: Intimacy in world of warcraft. In: Proceedings of the 28th International Conference on Human Factors in Computing Systems, pp. 233–242. ACM (2010)
13. Gooch, D., Watts, L.: A design framework for mediated personal relationship devices. In: Proceedings of the 25th BCS Conference on Human-Computer Interaction, pp. 237–242. British Computer Society (2011)
14. Gooch, D., Watts, L.: Communicating social presence through thermal hugs. In: SISSI 2010, p. 11 (2010)
15. Väänänen-Vainio-Mattila, K., Suhonen, K., Gonsalves, T., Schrader, M., Järvenpää, T.: Carpe diem: exploring user experience and intimacy in eye-based video conferencing. In: Proceedings of the 10th International Conference on Mobile and Ubiquitous Multimedia, pp. 113–122. ACM (2011)
16. Slovák, P., Janssen, J., Fitzpatrick, G.: Understanding heart rate sharing: towards unpacking physiosocial space. In: Proceedings of the 2012 ACM Annual Conference on Human Factors in Computing Systems, pp. 859–868. ACM (2012)
17. Janssen, J., Bailenson, J., IJsselsteijn, W., Westerink, J.: Intimate heartbeats: Opportunities for affective communication technology. IEEE Transactions on Affective Computing (99), 1 (2010)
18. Branham, S., Harrison, S., Hirsch, T.: Expanding the design space for intimacy: supporting mutual reflection for local partners. In: Proceedings of the Designing Interactive Systems Conference, pp. 220–223. ACM (2012)
19. Branham, S., Harrison, S.: Designing for collocated couples. Connecting Families, 15–36 (2012)
20. Davis, H., Skov, M., Stougaard, M., Vetere, F.: Virtual box: supporting mediated family intimacy through virtual and physical play. In: Proceedings of the 19th Australasian Conference on Computer-Human Interaction: Entertaining User Interfaces, pp. 151–159. ACM (2007)
21. Petersen, M.G., Hansen, A.B., Nielsen, K.R., Gude, R.: HOMEinTOUCH designing two-way ambient communication. In: Aarts, E., Crowley, J.L., de Ruyter, B., Gerhäuser, H., Pflaum, A., Schmidt, J., Wichert, R. (eds.) AmI 2008. LNCS, vol. 5355, pp. 44–57. Springer, Heidelberg (2008)

22. Chang, A., Resner, B., Koerner, B., Wang, X., Ishii, H.: Lumitouch: an emotional communication device. In: CHI (2001)
23. Ogawa, H., Ando, N., Onodera, S.: Smallconnection: designing of tangible communication media over networks. In: Proceedings of the 13th Annual ACM International Conference on Multimedia, pp. 1073–1074. ACM (2005)
24. Kaye, J., Levitt, M., Nevins, J., Golden, J., Schmidt, V.: Communicating intimacy one bit at a time. In: CHI 2005 Extended Abstracts on Human Factors in Computing Systems, pp. 1529–1532. ACM (2005)
25. Kaye, J.: I just clicked to say i love you: rich evaluations of minimal communication. In: CHI 2006 Extended Abstracts on Human Factors in Computing Systems, pp. 363–368. ACM (2006)
26. Motamedi, N.: Keep in touch: a tactile-vision intimate interface. In: Proceedings of the 1st International Conference on Tangible and Embedded Interaction, pp. 21–22. ACM (2007)
27. Chang, A., O'Modhrain, S., Jacob, R., Gunther, E., Ishii, H.: Comtouch: design of a vibrotactile communication device. In: Proceedings of the 4th Conference on Designing Interactive Systems: Processes, Practices, Methods, and Techniques, pp. 312–320. ACM (2002)
28. Brown, L., Sellen, A., Krishna, R., Harper, R.: Exploring the potential of audio-tactile messaging for remote interpersonal communication. In: Proceedings of the 27th International Conference on Human Factors in Computing Systems, pp. 1527–1530. ACM (2009)
29. Bhandari, S., Bardzell, S.: Bridging gaps: affective communication in long distance relationships. In: CHI 2008 Extended Abstracts on Human Factors in Computing Systems, pp. 2763–2768. ACM (2008)
30. Chung, H., Lee, C., Selker, T.: Lover's cups: drinking interfaces as new communication channels. In: CHI 2006 Extended Abstracts on Human Factors in Computing Systems, pp. 375–380. ACM (2006)
31. Kim, S., Kientz, J., Patel, S., Abowd, G.: Are you sleeping?: sharing portrayed sleeping status within a social network. In: Proceedings of the 2008 ACM Conference on Computer Supported Cooperative Work, pp. 619–628. ACM (2008)
32. Bales, E., Li, K., Griwsold, W.: Couplevibe: Mobile implicit communication to improve awareness for (long-distance) couples. In: Proceedings of the ACM 2011 Conference on Computer Supported Cooperative Work, pp. 65–74. ACM (2011)
33. Tollmar, K., Junestrand, S., Torgny, O.: Virtually living together. In: Proceedings of the 3rd Conference on Designing Interactive Systems: Processes, Practices, Methods, and Techniques, pp. 83–91. ACM (2000)
34. Shirazi, A., Alt, F., Schmidt, A., Sarjanoja, A., Hynninen, L., Häkkilä, J., Holleis, P.: Emotion sharing via self-composed melodies on mobile phones. In: Proceedings of the 11th International Conference on Human-Computer Interaction with Mobile Devices and Services, p. 30. ACM (2009)
35. Thieme, A., Wallace, J., Thomas, J., Le Chen, K., Kramer, N., Olivier, P.: Lovers' box: Designing for reflection within romantic relationships. International Journal of Human-Computer Studies (2010)
36. Dodge, C.: The bed: a medium for intimate communication. In: CHI, vol. 97, pp. 22–27 (1997)
37. Siio, I., Rowan, J., Mynatt, E.: Peek-a-drawer: communication by furniture. In: CHI 2002 Extended Abstracts on Human Factors in Computing Systems, pp. 582–583. ACM (2002)

38. Patel, D., Agamanolis, S.: Habitat: awareness of life rhythms over a distance using networked furniture. In: Adjunct Proceedings of UbiComp 2003 Fifth International Conference on Ubiquitous Computing. Citeseer, Seattle (2003)
39. Tsujita, H., Siio, I., Tsukada, K.: Syncdecor: appliances for sharing mutual awareness between lovers separated by distance. In: CHI 2007 Extended Abstracts on Human Factors in Computing Systems, pp. 2699–2704. ACM (2007)
40. Gooch, D., Watts, L.: The magic sock drawer project. In: Proceedings of the 2011 Annual Conference Extended Abstracts on Human Factors in Computing Systems, pp. 243–252. ACM (2011)
41. Grivas, K.: Digital selves: Devices for intimate communications between homes. Personal and Ubiquitous Computing 10(2-3), 66–76 (2006)
42. Kaye, J.: Love, ritual and videochat. In: The Connected Home: The Future of Domestic Life, pp. 185–202 (2011)
43. Tsakiris, M., Haggard, P.: The rubber hand illusion revisited: visuotactile integration and self-attribution. Journal of Experimental Psychology: Human Perception and Performance 31(1), 80 (2005)
44. Kuchinskas, S.: The Chemistry of Connection: How the Oxytocin Response Can Help You Find Trust, Intimacy, and Love. New Harbinger Publications Incorporated (2009)
45. Misawa, K., Ishiguro, Y., Rekimoto, J.: Livemask: A telepresence surrogate system with a face-shaped screen for supporting nonverbal communication. In: Proceedings of the International Working Conference on Advanced Visual Interfaces, pp. 394–397. ACM (2012)
46. Yim, J., Shaw, C.: Design considerations of expressive bidirectional telepresence robots. In: Proceedings of the 2011 Annual Conference Extended Abstracts on Human Factors in Computing Systems, pp. 781–790. ACM (2011)

Short Papers

2D vs 3D Visualization
and Social Networks Entertainment Games:
A Human Factor Response Case Study

Zlatogor Minchev

Institute of ICT, IT for Security Department, Bulgarian Academy of Sciences,
Sofia, Bulgaria
zlatogor@bas.bg

Abstract. In today's world modern 3D visualization screens are already entering the entertainment world of future smart homes together with the social networks popular games. The paper describes and experimental study of volunteers' focus group spontaneous EEG dynamic changes related to 2D/3D screen modes stimuli during short-time gaming activities. A quantitative difference between 2D and 3D gaming stimuli have been found by implementing relative power spectra approach.

Keywords: social networks entertainment games, human factor response, visualization, EEG.

1 Introduction

Nowadays modern personal 3D visualization screens are getting more and more popular for the regular computer gamers and the new smart homes that will encompass many new smart devices and technological solutions in the near future [7]. These are also producing and many negative effects like: fatigue, stress, addiction, physical discomfort, overweight, etc. [4], [9], [11].

Apart of this the recent appearance of lightweight cheap passive 3D personal glasses is strongly supporting the process of 3D visualization entering in the everyday life. Furthermore, the new emerging technologies in the field like simulated virtual and the upcoming augmented reality are opening a vast field for studying the multiple influence effects of all these technologies to the human factors (i.e. entertaining users) response in different smart environments and scenarios of usage.

An interesting direction for exploration in the field is related to the upcoming Web 3.0/Web 4.0 modern social networks games [6], [16] that are getting large popularity amongst social networks, to mention different Zynga games, hi5 - Pets and even the popular smart device Android applications like Rovio's Angry Birds. It is also important to note and the fact that according to [10], [13] the current trends in social network usage are more than fifty percent oriented towards entertainment activities opening a vast field for research concerning the effects of human-machine interaction related to cyber threats and the effects related to the human factors [2], [3], [5], [14].

J.C. Anacleto et al. (Eds.): ICEC 2013, LNCS 8215, pp. 107–113, 2013.

The present paper outlines shortly an empirical case study concerning the human factor 2D/3D brain activity response to the recently appeared in the most popular social network Facebook [15] and the famous entertainment game on-line modification – Angry Birds [1].

2 Methodology

A simple visual stimulation study of a volunteers' focus group of 25 people (23 men and 3 women, average age 36 years +- 3) EEG screening methodology was used.

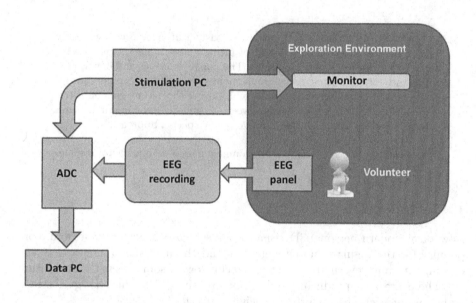

Fig. 1. General idea of the conceptual framework used in the study for EEG game response monitoring

As it is clear from Fig.1 the conceptual framework encompasses: (i) Monitor (a 2D/3D IPS LG D2343P was used during the experiments together with a set of passive glasses, implementing the build-in 2D/pseudo 3D regime switching), (ii) Simulation PC (a desktop Intel®CoreTM i5, 6 GB 1600 Mhz RAM station with NVIDIA 2 GB DDR3 video card connected to the LG monitor via HDMI interface) and (iii) EEG recording (utilizing Nation 7128W-C20 EEG panel wireless device together with a mobile HP8220 laptop station that encompasses the Data PC and 16 bit ADC block, fs = 512 Hz).

During the experiments a 6 lead recording mounted with T20 EEG conducting paste, plastic helmet and Ag/AgCl electrode leads were utilized following the international Jasper 10/20 system [12]: F3, F4, C3, C4, P3, P4; reference electrodes A1, A2 have been positioned on processi mastoidei of the studied volunteers with the ground electrode positioned on their foreheads.

The experimental series cover 3 minutes epochs (records) of the Angry Birds online game in the Facebook environment encompassing 3 game levels in 2D and 3D visual stimulation regime of the screen. All experiments were conducted in silent mode, normal working light office conditions and comfortable chair sitting position. The volunteers were using only a standard Creative®2 button optical mouse with a scrolling wheel as an input interface device and a known Facebook account for single player game access.

Fig. 2. A photo with a volunteer for the experimental implementation of the conceptual framework for EEG game response monitoring

The recorded spontaneous EEG series have been sorted and only artifacts free ones have been further used for further digital filtering. A Butterworth 12 dB/oct band pass zero-phase shift filtering within the following four frequency bands have been performed [12]: theta (4-8 Hz), alpha (8-13 Hz), beta (13-30 Hz), gamma (30-70 Hz). Additional notch filtering with Chebyshev 18 dB/oct digital filter in the frequency band 45-55 Hz have been implemented.

In order to achieve the 12dB/oct and 18 dB/oct filter characteristics a multiple 3 dB/oct filter base was used. Next, after the [17] algorithm a Fourier based Relative Power Spectrum calculation of the selected four frequency bands have been performed averaging the results for all monitored volunteers for both 2D/3D stimuli. It is important to note that the whole EEG signals processing have been performed in Matlab®2011b environment.

3   Results

The resulting averaged power spectra concerning F3, F4, C3, C4, P3, P4 leads are depicted on Fig.3 (for 2D) and on Fig.4 (for pseudo 3D):

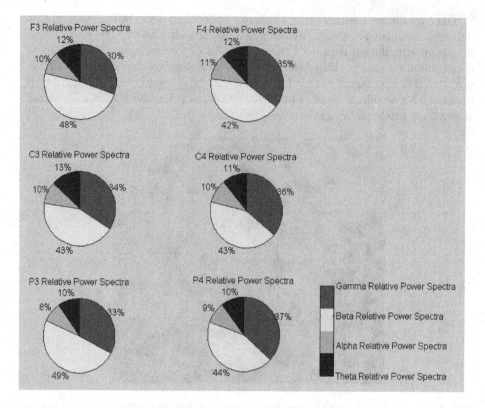

Fig. 3. Averaged Power Spectra for F3, F4, C3, C4, P3, P4 leads of theta, alpha, beta and gamma frequency bands during 2D visual stimulation with Angry Birds on-line social network game for 3 minutes epochs

The obtained results from both Fig.3 and Fig.4 are demonstrating an interesting quantitatively measured phenomenon concerning the gamma EEG frequency band with prominent difference of 8-10 % between the 2D and pseudo 3D visual stimulation. The other spectral parts differences are rather small - 1-2 %. These could be considered as an interesting finding that practically produces a higher fractal dimension of the measured signals [8].

Generally, the gamma frequencies are related to motor tasks and awareness rising from physiological view point [12] but the present finding being with an empirical character could be used for quantitatively differentiating between the generalized visual stimuli. A further emotions recognition work was initially planed but due to the fact that there exists an individual peculiarities that require single user calibration before every experiment an assumption for real-time on-line detection more accurate results is under development in the framework of [2].

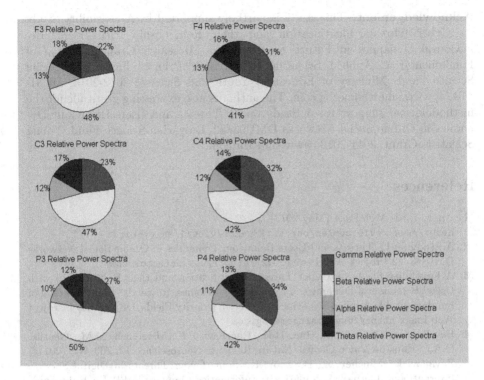

Fig. 4. Averaged Power Spectra for F3, F4, C3, C4, P3, P4 leads of theta, alpha, beta and gamma frequency bands during pseudo 3D visual stimulation with Angry Birds on-line social network game for 3 minutes epochs

4   Discussion

The briefly presented conceptual framework for studying the differences between 2D vs 3D visual stimulation in social network entertainment games concerning the human factors' EEG response is adding data to the vast discussion about the technological influence to the human factor in the new information 21st century. This very large problem is still unconsciously underestimated but sooner will become a significant player with the practical development of smart homes and cities ideas. Currently, the problem is not well studied and requires a more serious observation in the near future accentuating on the multiple human factor responses like: behavior, psychology and physiology correlates together with the fast progressing technological developments.

Acknowledgement. This study is partially supported by:A Feasibility Study on Cyber Threats Identification and their Relationship with Users' Behavioural Dynamics in Future Smart Homes, Research Grant 'Funding of Fundamental & Applied Scientific Research in Priority Fields', Bulgarian Science Fund, Ministry of Education Youth and Science, 2012-2014, DFNI-T01/4, www.smarthomesbg.com. The author is also expressing gratitude for the methodological support to: A Study on IT Threats and Users Behaviour Dynamics in Online Social Networks DMU03/22, Bulgarian Science Fund, Young Scientists Grant, 2011-2013, www.snfactor.com.

References

1. Angry Birds Web Page (May 2013),
   http://www.rovio.com/en/our-work/games/view/1/angry-birds
2. A Study on IT Threats and Users Behaviour Dynamics in Online Social Networks DMUO3/22 Project Web Page (2012), http://www.snfactor.com
3. A Feasibility Study on Cyber Threats Identification and their Relationship with Users' Behavioural Dynamics in Future Smart Homes, Research Grant 'Funding of Fundamental & Applied Scientific Research in Priority Fields, DFNI-T01/4 Project Web Page, http://www.smarthomesbg.com
4. Bavelier, D., Green, C.S., Han, D.H., Renshaw, P.F., Merzenich, M.M., Gentile, D.A.: Brains on Video Games. Nature Reviews, Neuroscience 12, 763–768 (2011)
5. Boyanov, L., Minchev, Z., Boyanov, K.: Some Cyber Threats in Digital Society. International Journal' Automatics & Informatics (January 2013) (in Bulgarian), http://www.syssec-project.eu/media/
   page-media/3/boyanov-autoinfo-2013.1.pdf
6. Codorniou, J.: Top Rated Social Games of 2012 (December 5, 2012),
   https://developers.facebook.com/blog/post/
   2012/12/05/top-rated-social-games-of-2012/
7. De Silva, L.C., Mirokawa, C., Petra M.I.: State of the art of smart homes. Eng. Appl. Artif. Intel. (2012), http://dx.doi.org/10.1016/j.engappai.2012.05.002
8. Georgiev, S., Minchev, Z., Philipova, D., Christova, C.: EEG Fractal Dimension Measurement before and after Human Auditory Stimulation. International Journal Bioautomation 12, 70–81 (2009),
   http://www.clbme.bas.bg/bioautomation/2009/vol12.1/files/122.3.pdf
9. Hazelle, R.: Effects of Technology on Younger Generations – Children (October 10, 2012), http://scienceray.com/earth-sciences/
   effects-of-technology-on-younger-generations-children/
10. Minchev, Z.: Cyber Threats in Social Networks and User's Response Dynamics, SMU 03/22 I Stage Report (December 2012) (in Bulgarian),
    http://www.it4sec.org/system/files/IT4SecReports1059.pdf
11. Minchev, Z.: Smart device q-based survey results (Context definition), DFNI-T01/4 III Project Meeting Report (April 29, 2013),
    http://www.smarthomesbg.com/files/dfnit014meetingtalksapril292013.zip
12. Niedermeyer, E., da Silva, F.L.: Electroencephalography, 5th edn. Lippincott Williams & Wilkins (2005)

13. State of the Media: The Social Media Report, Nielsen (2012),
    http://www.nielsen.com/us/en/reports/2012/
    state-of-the-media-the-social-media-report-2012.html
14. SySSec Project Web Page (2010), http://www.syssec-project.eu
15. Top 15 Most Popular Social Networking Sites (May 2013),
    http://www.ebizmba.com/articles/social-networking-websites
16. The Top 25 Facebook games (February 2013),
    http://www.insidesocialgames.com/2013/02/01/
    the-top-25-facebook-games-of-february-2013/
17. Mina, M.: Real Time Emotion Detection Useing EEG, The American University
    in Cairo (2009),
    http://www.cse.aucegypt.edu/~rafea/CSCE590/Spring09/Mina/Mina.pdf

A Game Design Analytic System Based on Data Provenance

Lidson B. Jacob[1], Troy C. Kohwalter[1], Alex Machado[2], and Esteban W.G. Clua[1]

[1] Instituto de Computação, Universidade Federal Fluminense - Niterói - RJ, Brazil
{ljacob,tkohwalter,esteban}@ic.uff.br
[2] Departamento de Computação - Instituto Federal do Sudeste de Minas Geral
Rio Pomba, MG – Brazil
alexcataguases@hotmail.com

Abstract. This paper presents a game system approach to assist game designers to make decisions and find critical points in their game through data provenance collected from a game. The proposed approach is based on generating graphs from collected data to quickly visualize the game flow. We test and validate our approach with an infinity run genre for mobile devices.

Keywords: Provenance, Game Analytics, Infinity Run.

1 Introduction

Developing a successful game that holds the user's attention for a long time in today's market is a challenging endeavor [3]. Due to this, it is essential to generate income for both games that contains advertisers and those that offer items for sale. [3] also says that thousands titles are published each year, generating a competition for players' time. Making game analysis one of the main resources for ensuring game quality, rate of success, understanding player behavior, and enhancing the player's experience. It also have led to a shift in development design strategies for digital games, bringing data-driven intelligence practices into the fray for help decision making.

A system capable of displaying played and captured game data would support game designers by finding expected patterns as confirmation of such functioning. On the other hand, it could also find unexpected patterns, which indicates critical points where the game designer should analyze for potential problems, like bad difficulty balancing or items values. It is very important that these data are displayed in a simple and clear way for a quicker understanding.

As a proof of concept, we use an infinity run prototype due to the large numbers achieved by this genre games. According to [10] these are in important demand from AppStore. Raising examples as Temple Run by Imangi Studios has more than 170 million downloads and Temple Run 2 has achieved the Top 10 most sold games on iOS. Another example is the Subway Sufers by Kiloo launched on June 2012 and it established itself as the top action title. This genre is characterized by making the player run an endless path. In it, the longer the player stays alive, or the distance achieved, greater are the chances of collecting more items and points.

J.C. Anacleto et al. (Eds.): ICEC 2013, LNCS 8215, pp. 114–119, 2013.

After collecting the relevant data provenance while running the game, it is possible to generate graph for an easier viewing and understanding of the game, from its beginning to its end. According to [2] we can observe that few systems address the issue of query game data, requiring the user to have knowledge of how to write queries in complex languages. However, the designer doesn't always have such knowledge. These queries are importance to game designer because they may be used to find critical issues. To solve this problem, this paper proposes to develop a system for assisting the game designer in making decisions and finding critical points in their games without necessarily knowing complex languages to query the data.

This paper is organized as follows: Section 2 presents the concept of data provenance, treating about the capture, storage and query of provenance data. Section 3 presents an approach for querying previously collected provenance data. Finally, section 4 presents the conclusions of this work and highlights the contributions and future work.

2   Data Provenance

According to [8][9], data provenance refers to the documentation of an art object, or the documentation process life cycle of digital objects allowing you to see all your history. Due to the historical documentation of an object, it gets some property, allowing the comprehension and the possibility to assess more accurately the importance and application context of the object. Computational methods must be transformed in order to build a qualified provenance, so that it can be retrieved and analyzed [8].

In [1], it is possible to see that the central foundation of provenance is to collect evidence about the time and place of object. Techniques of comparative analysis and expert opinions can also be used for this purpose, but what establishing the provenance is documentation of object. The provenance is the reference to the origin of data and contains identification, responsible, creation date and the processes applied to it.

According to [7], a provenance graph may be an object execution representation in past or present. Thus, provenance can only have information about up to where the player was able to reach. However, this information can be used to help understand why the player could not advance as far as was expected by game designer, showing possible fails at the game design process.

2.1   Provenance Components

According to [4], when referring to computational tasks, may be used a variety of mechanisms for modeling process. Tasks related to games are complex requiring the usage of other tools, data sources, specific libraries, or Web services. We use Web services for the collection and storage of data in order to simulate a real environment where users from different places can play the game.

There are two ways for approaching computational tasks in provenance: prospective and retrospective. Prospective provenance captures the steps (or processes) adopted for generation a product, allowing a record of specifications for the computational tasks. On the other hand, retrospect provenance is used for capturing the steps performed, in addition to information about the environment used for the derivation of a product specific data, such as detailed execution log of a given computational task. It is preferably captured information about the input and output of data, execution user and initial time and final time of execution. However, the retrospective provenance is not dependent on the presence of the prospective, because it allows capturing process execution without the need to know the sequence of activities involved [4].Assuming in a first case where the user take an item and not deviate from the obstacle. In a second case, the user doesn't deviate from an obstacle and get the item. These are different circumstances because, in the first case, the item may be influencing the user by not deviating he obstacle, while it was different in the second case. Thus the sequence of activities involved is relevant to our work.

According to [6][7], actions can be represented by a series of attributes in context which are related, allowing the creation of a provenance graph containing some information as reason, triggered, responsible, and time. A good reason of using provenance is to produce a graph containing details that can be determined why something occurred. Similar to this idea we propose to collect data and generate graphs leaving the analysis for the game designer.

3   Graphs Representation

A graph representation of the provenance is fundamental for fast and efficient view of the elements and events. From a game design point of view, it is necessary that this representation is associated with game design elements.

The graph representation of data is defined as a "distance by round" as illustrated in Fig. 1 representing in this case the distance that the user advanced during each round. By observing case 1, the users in the first rounds reached short distances. This may be a consequence of the first contact with the game, where obstacles were a novelty, thus quickly losing the game. Another factor that could have influenced is the unfamiliarity with the character controller. After getting used with the game, users reached greater distances. However, it stabilizes at 2000. This may be due to the increased difficulty as the distance increases.

These analyses can help the game designer in the following circumstances: First, the users spend many rounds to known the game. This can cause abandonment because it's might be very difficult for the player and frustrating. Developing a tutorial at beginning of the game would be a good solution to the problem. Second, the maximum distance that users were able to reach might not be the distance expected by game designer. For example, the coins distribution and special items are only available after 2000 distance, but users hardly reach this distance. The designer will have to rearrange the items or change the game difficulty.

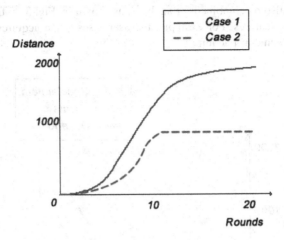

Fig. 1. Distance x Rounds

A large permanency in a distance as the Case 2 from Fig. 1 can demonstrate a difficult obstacle where users couldn't surpass. It may be necessary to remove or simplify the obstacle so users don't get frustrated and stop playing the game. This type of graph can be made to analyze the experience of a single or several users.

Another example is Case 1 from Fig. 2, which represents the number of acquired coins over the total advanced distance. This information can be used to reach conclusions about a uniform distribution for the coins. Perhaps the game designer wanted to benefit users who achieved greater distances, while also motivating to go farther. This is one of the main goals of the Infinity Run games. To represent a distribution in this context would be the case 2 of Fig. 2. A graph for special items would also be similar to the graph for coins.

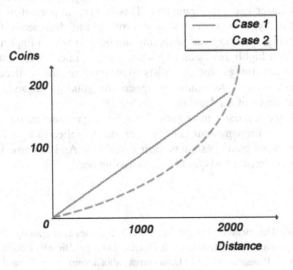

Fig. 2. Coins x Distance

Graphs can also be combined for analysis, as shown by Fig. 3, to find features that influenced other features. For example, the user loses when acquires a special item and pass only when don't acquire it.

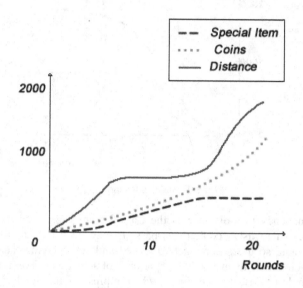

Fig. 3. Combined Analysis

4   Conclusion

This paper presents an approach for a system that helps the game designer by using visual representations of the data to facilitate understanding of the game flow and to make decisions faster and more punctual. This is very important as (Gaspar et al., 2012), where this type of system should provide the designer with facilities as features for viewing, querying and analyzing the data. It is also important for (Costa, et al., 2010), which highlights as an important issue to query these data to be one of the most important things for scientists that analyze the collected data from experiments. Experiments for game designer are your game and, therefore, it's necessary the existence of a system query such data.

Currently this work doesn't have gone through the implementation phase. The next phase consists of the implementation of this approach applied to a game and verify by experiments if it helps game designers during analysis. And to know if the proposed analyses approach is easier and quicker than existing ones.

References

1. Almeida, F.N.: Descrição da Proveniência de Dados para Extração de Conhecimento em Sistemas de Informação de Hemoterapia. Interunidades em Bioinformática (2012)
2. Costa, P.V.C., Braganholo, V.: Uma nova abordagem para consulta a dados de proveniência (2010)

3. Drachen, A.: GameAnalytics. [Online] GA, 02 de 11 de 2012. [Citado em: 22 de 04 de 2013.], http://blog.gameanalytics.com/blog/announcing-game-analytics-maximizing-the-value-of-player-dat.html
4. Freire, J., et al.: Provenance for Computational Tasks: A Survey. Computing in Science and Engineering, pp. 11–21 (2008)
5. Gaspar, W.A., Braga, R.M., Campos, F.A.: SWfPS: Um Sistema de Proveniência de Dados e Processos no Domínio de Workflows Científicos (2012)
6. Kohwalter, T.C., Clua, E.W.G., Murta, L.G.P.: Provenance in Games. SBGames (2012)
7. Moreau, L.: The Open Provenance Model core specification(v1.1). Future Generation Computer Systems, 743–756 (2011)
8. Moreau, L., et al.: The open provenance model(v1.00). Technical report, University of Southampton (2007a)
9. Moreau, L., et al.: The Provenance of electronic data. Communications of the ACM, 4:52-4:58 (2007a)
10. Todor, A.: Monetizing an Infinite Runner. GameAnalytics. [Online] GameAnalytics, 22 de 02 de 2013. [Citado em: 22 de 04 de 2013.], http://blog.gameanalytics.com/blog/monetizing-an-infinite-runner-guest-post.html

Evaluation of Interaction Methods
for a Real-Time Augmented Reality Game

Frederic Pollmann, Dirk Wenig, Mareike Picklum, and Rainer Malaka

University of Bremen
Bibliothekstr. 1
28359 Bremen, Germany

Abstract. Augmented reality is a way to enhance mobile games and can be easily implemented on today's powerful smartphones. Developers need to consider additional constraints when choosing the input method for such an AR game. We implemented three control methods for a mobile AR multiplayer fighting game using a virtual joystick, a touch interface and continuous crosshair tracking. We evaluated the effect of the control methods on the game experience with 43 participants and conducted a survey using a questionnaire for intuitive use (QUESI [1]) and individiual interviews. We found significant differences between two of the three implemented input methods, but in the interviews the test persons did not prefer the control method with the highest survey score.

1 Introduction

Mobile devices such as smartphones are no longer just used for communications but also as a calendar, for browsing, email and entertainment. Their incorporated sensing devices (eg. camera, GPS, microphone and acceleration sensor) and now powerful CPUs and large available memory enable them to run augmented reality (AR) applications such as games. Overlaying the real world with an image the game world can provide a higher level of immersion in the game and make for a more enjoyable game experience. While it is possible to just use sensors such as an accelerometer or a compass for the synchronization of the real and the game world this approach does not yet yield compelling results, so a common solution is to use special markers that need to be tracked while running the AR application. We implemented and evaluated three different interaction methods to control the movement of an avatar in a mobile AR game. In it two players fight each other with an avatar in a fighting ring that is displayed in an AR environment. Attacking is controlled by a virtual button drawn on the screen. Our focus was to find an input method that let the players quickly learn the game and to concentrate on winning, not moving the avatar.

2 Related Work

Vaijk et al. [2] used the sensor data of a mobile phone to turn it into a motion controller similar to Nintendo's Wiimote. It was tested in a multiplayer racing

J.C. Anacleto et al. (Eds.): ICEC 2013, LNCS 8215, pp. 120–125, 2013.

game where it proved to be intuitively applicable as well as fun to use. Chehimi et al. [3] used the sensors of mobile phones for input in 3D multiplayer games. The users controlled a space ship in a space battle by moving the mobile phone. The authors concluded that 3D accelerometers provide new interaction possibilities and that motion controlled games can be fun to play. Duh et al. [4] studied the effect of innovative control methods on mobile devices on game experience. Games that require high eye-hand-coordination may be hard to play due to small screens, small keypads or control difficulties. They concluded that it may be better to stick to well-tried interaction concepts. Oda et al. [5] extended a car racing game by adding an augmented reality component. The car can be driven around on a tracked surface and is controlled using a handlebar with an additional marker that is also tracked. Hürst and van Wezel [6] used the camera to track the user's finger and use it to interact with the virtual world and control an avatar. A challenge using this interaction method was the difficulty to keep the device steady when moving the finger. Lagerstam et al. [7] tested camera-based interaction techniques with an AR application for children aged 10-11. Their results suggested that the mental overhead of both keeping a marker in the viewfield of a camera and trying to control some avatar in the AR world may be to high for children this age. Gu et al. [8] developed an AR game in which two players can fight each other in a virtual arena. To enhance game interactivity the accelerometer can be used to control the character. Multi-touch gestures could be used to control the character or initiate attacks.

When using a marker-based AR environment, the marker has to be visible to the devices camera at all times or the syncronization of virtual and real world is lost. This poses additional constraints on the player and the way he may play the game. Picklum et al. [9] proposed six different interaction methods to such a scenario. After considering the feedback to a poster presentation at ICEC 2012, three of the six methods were chosen and are evaluated in this paper.

3   Interaction Methods

For the evaluation of the input methods an existing mobile real-time augmented reality game[1] is used. The first control implemented is a touch-based virtual joystick that behaves similar to its hardware pendant found in common arcade or PC games. A circle is drawn on the touchscreen that symbolizes the movement range of the virtual joystick. The position of a player's finger inside the circle relative to its center defines the movement direction and speed of the avatar.

For the second control method the player sets the target of the avatar by touching the screen. The avatar moves towards the corresponding position in the AR world until it reaches it. Tapping on another point before the movement is completed interrupts this movement and sets a new target position for the avatar. This method will be referenced as "touchplane" in the rest of this paper. An example using this control method can be seen in Fig. 1.

---

[1] The game is implemented using the graphics library libGDX and the AR framework Vuforia, both available for the mobile platform Android.

The third control method uses the field of view of the mobile device's camera. A crosshair is drawn in the center of the display. The avatar continuously follows the point where this crosshair is projected to in the AR environment. Controlling the movement of the the avatar is achieved by moving or tilting the mobile device (and with it the integrated camera) while tracking the AR marker to move the crosshair to a new point in the AR world.

Fig. 1. The view of the game   **Fig. 2.** The two player scenario

4   Evaluation

The evaluation was conducted by an observation of the test persons and a subsequent opinion survey about their personal attitude towards the control method that they used. A total number of 43 players took part in the experiment. 14 participants were female, 29 were male. The average age was 25 years (ranging from 17 to 49 years, $\sigma = 5.5$). More than half (28) of the test subjects were students, the remaining subjects answered *employed* or *miscellaneous* as occupation. Participants came both from technical (eg. computer science or engineering) and non-technical fields (linguistics, geography or sports). Most (28) of the test persons regularly used a smartphone, but only nine of those regularly played games on it. 16 subjects played console games regularly, five for less than two hours, ten for two to ten hours and two for more than ten hours a week.

We divided the test subjects into two groups for a singleplayer (23 members) and a multiplayer (20 members) condition. In the first group the players had to defeat a simple computer-controlled enemy while in the second group two player were fighting each other as shown in Fig. 2. To remove the effect of the tension of a multiplayer battle from the evaluation, we only let players rate the intuitive usability after the singleplayer scenario using the *Questionnaire for the Subjective Consequences of Intuitive use* (QUESI) [1]. To make sure that the order of the presentation of the prototypes did not affect the result of the evaluation, we balanced the experiment using a *latin squares* [10] order. The participants of the multiplayer scenario were interviewed about their experience and asked for difficulties and possible improvements of the used input method. Additionally each test person was asked to give a personal ranking of the control methods at the end of each test.

5   Results and Analysis

5.1   Statistical Evaluation of the Singleplayer Condition

In the singleplayer condition the joystick was rated as intuitively usable with a QUESI score of 3.81 ($\sigma = 0.79$), the touchplane with a score of 4.02 ($\sigma = 0.73$) and the crosshair with a score of 3.37 ($\sigma = 0.90$) (repeated-measures ANOVA, $F_{2,44} = 4.670$, $p = 0.014^*$. A detailed view of the scales that make up the QUESI score are shown in Fig. 3. When compared pairwise, the crosshair input method is significantly worse than the touchplane method ($p = 0.009^*$, Sidak-corrected). Comparing the different scale values of the QUESI results shows that the touchplane is significantly better than the joystick on every scale except for the perceived effort of learning and the perceived error rate ($p_K = 0.017^*, p_Z = 0.046^*, p_L = 0.206, p_V = 0.000^*, p_{Fe} = 0.110$). This suggests that the crosshair input method may be a new experience for the players that is easy to learn but not easy to master.

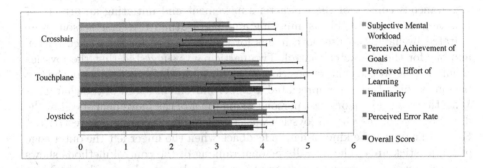

Fig. 3. Results of the QUESI survey of the input methods

5.2   Interviews of the Participants of the Multiplayer Condition

The interviews were conducted to get qualitative feedback on the different input methods.

Crosshair Interaction. Twelve participants thought of this control method as unusual and complicated to use. Six persons found interesting and innovative. Eleven had expected to control the AR world instead of the avatar and first steered into the wrong direction. Two criticized a lack of precision, while five criticized the sensitive reactions of the avatar to even slight camera movements. 15 test persons found it appropriate for the given application and preferred it over the touchplane or joystick input. This may be based on the fact that they could use their fingers for the fight interaction as they were not needed for the motion control. Four participants suggested a stabilization of camera movements, five wished for a larger fighting area.

Touchplane Interaction. Twelve of the participants called the touchplane easy, beginner-friendly or intuitive. Eight of the testers named a flaw of this input method: As the player taps on a point on the screen and then waits until the avatar has reached this position, the control method is not seen as suitable for games that require a high degree of response from the player. Seven mentioned the occlusion when tapping on the screen. Three said it was difficult to control the rotation of the avatar, which is important when attacking. The control method was rated as well-known from point and click games by three participants. Only six test persons gave the touchplane as their favorite input method. The analysis of the survey results and the interviews shows that an easy and intuitive control method may not necessarily be the most favoured by a player.

Joystick Interaction. Interviews show that the joystick is the most popular control of the three presented methods. 16 users described this method as easily understandable because it is simple and precise. Seven participants also mentioned the partial occlusion of the screen by the control elements as disadvantage. In addition, missing multitouch functionality of the test devices prevented simultaneous control of the character's movement and initiating an attack. 17 test persons regarded this as annoying and aggravating. Five test persons were irritated by having to use both hands for the game, one for the attack button and one for the character control. Two participants suggested that the joystick should appear at the contact position of the finger on the screen. Most of the test persons would also have appreciated a higher movement speed of the character. With the exception of one test person the mapping of the movement speed to the drag distance of the virtual joystick was considered as annoying and restrictive. Four wished for some kind of haptic feedback when the finger left the outer edge of the joystick area. The overall personal ranking of the control methods shows that the joystick is clearly preferred to the touchplane or the crosshair. 22 test subjects voted the joystick control as the most suitable input method for this kind of game.

Additional Feedback. Some of the criticism expressed by the participants was referring to the game itself and not the used control method. Missing haptic feedback was criticized as well as a lack of control over the avatar's rotation. Several users had little or no experience with AR applications and needed to get used to it first which made it difficult to differentiate between problems they had with the application and issues with the control method. Many participants asked for an input method based on physical control elements such as buttons. Unfortunately those are not available on all devices. Users preferred control methods which did not occlude the screen by the user's hands or virtual control elements. Extra features such as a dash function to speed up the characters movement or a jump function as well as additional levels were also mentioned to improve the overall game experience.

6   Conclusion

We evaluated three different interaction concepts for controlling a character in an augmented reality game using a questionnaire about the intuitive use of the control methods and with personal interviews about the individual preferences of the test persons. We found a significant difference between the intuitive usability of the touchplane and the crosshair input method, but in the interviews the test persons did not prefer the touchplane method over the joystick although it had the highest QUESI score. In the interviews some players indicated that they preferred the joystick because it was well known. Also the perceiverd error rate was higher for the touchplane which might have frustrated users and let the joystick seem better suited for this kind of game. Future research needs to be conducted to implement the suggested improvents and to measure their effect on the game experience.

References

1. Naumann, A., Hurtienne, J.: Benchmarks for intuitive interaction with mobile devices. In: Proceedings of MobileHCI 2010. ACM, New York (2010)
2. Vajk, T., Coulton, P., Bamford, W., Edwards, R.: Using a mobile phone as a "wii-like" controller for playing games on a large public display. International Journal of Computer Games Technology (2007)
3. Chehimi, F., Coulton, P.: Motion controlled mobile 3d multiplayer gaming. In: Proceedings of ACE 2008. ACM, New York (2008)
4. Duh, H.B.L., Chen, V.H.H., Tan, C.B.: Playing different games on different phones: an empirical study on mobile gaming. In: Proceedings of MobileHCI 2010. ACM, New York (2008)
5. Oda, O., Lister, L.J., White, S., Feiner, S.: Developing an augmented reality racing game. In: Proceedings of INTETAIN 2008. ICST, Brussels (2007)
6. Hürst, W., van Wezel, C.: Multimodal interaction concepts for mobile augmented reality applications. In: Lee, K.-T., Tsai, W.-H., Liao, H.-Y.M., Chen, T., Hsieh, J.-W., Tseng, C.-C. (eds.) MMM 2011 Part II. LNCS, vol. 6524, pp. 157–167. Springer, Heidelberg (2011)
7. Lagerstam, E., Olsson, T., Harviainen, T.: Children and intuitiveness of interaction: a study on gesture-based interaction with augmented reality. In: Proceedings of MindTrek 2012, MindTrek 2012. ACM, New York (2012)
8. Gu, J., Duh, H.B., Kitazawa, S.: A Platform for Mobile Collaborative Augmented Reality Game: A Case Study of "AR Fighter". In: Recent Trends of Mobile Collaborative Augmented Reality Systems. Springer, New York (2011)
9. Picklum, M., Modzelewski, G., Knoop, S., Lichtenberg, T., Dittmann, P., Böhme, T., Fehn, V., John, C., Kenkel, J., Krieter, P., Niethen, P., Pampuch, N., Schnelle, M., Schwarte, Y., Stark, S., Steenbergen, A., Stehr, M., Wielenberg, H., Yildirim, M., Yüzüncü, C., Pollmann, F., Wenig, D., Malaka, R.: Player control in a real-time mobile augmented reality game. In: Herrlich, M., Malaka, R., Masuch, M. (eds.) ICEC 2012. LNCS, vol. 7522, pp. 393–396. Springer, Heidelberg (2012)
10. Weathington, B., Cunningham, C., Pittenger, D.: 14 - Correlated-Groups Designs. In: Research methods for the behavioral and social sciences. Wiley (2010)

Exercise My Game:
Turning Off-The-Shelf Games into Exergames

Benjamin Walther-Franks, Dirk Wenig, Jan Smeddinck, and Rainer Malaka

Research Group Digital Media, TZI,
University of Bremen, Bibliothekstr. 1, 28359 Bremen, Germany

Abstract. Exercise video games (exergames) can motivate players to be more physically active. However, most exergames are controlled by confined and predefined movements and do not promote long-term motivation. Well-funded commercial games often excel at long-term motivation, but are not operated with motion input. *Exercise My Game* (XMG) is a design framework for turning off-the-shelf action games into full-body motion-based games. Challenges with this approach involve finding mappings from control input to game-action, as well as blending active input feedback with the game's interface. XMG facilitates transforming well-produced, non-exercise video games into captivating exergames by structuring the design space and outlining game requirements. We illustrate XMG with the example of turning the popular first-person action game *Portal 2* into the exergame *Sportal*.

Keywords: exergames, active games, design framework.

1 Introduction

Exercise video games (exergames) can motivate players to carry out physical exercises and can also provide guidance and feedback to the players. Yet current exergames are controlled by confined and predefined movements. This hinders immersion, since many patterns that players are used to from real-world embodied interactions cannot be employed when playing such games. Furthermore, the nature of current exergames is usually akin to mini-games (or casual-games), with limited story and repetitive game-play. In this manner, they do not make full use of the potential of videogames to create long-term motivation. Well-funded *AAA* games excel at providing deep story lines, high-quality assets and long-term motivation, but are almost exclusively created for standard sedentary input devices (gamepad, keyboard, mouse).

What if it were possible tap the benefits of well-produced, successful, non-exercise video games for exergames? What if one could turn an existing off-the-shelf game title with sedentary controls into an exergame? We present *Exercise My Game* (XMG), a design framework for turning regular video games into motion-based or even exercise-oriented games. It considers four stages:

1. *Choosing a game.* What are the factors in finding a suitable game to "exercise"? We discuss requirements and justify our choice of first-person action games.

J.C. Anacleto et al. (Eds.): ICEC 2013, LNCS 8215, pp. 126–131, 2013.

2. *Creating a control overlay.* How to map a broad range of natural motion patterns onto established game controls? Our examples encompass physical locomotion for continuous spatial input in combination with a range of exercises for discrete input.
3. *Designing a feedback overlay.* Full-body motion-based input requires different feedback than standard controller input. How to blend motion feedback with the existing game interface and maintain a consistent experience? We show an example overlay that adds necessary information without disrupting the game interface.
4. *Adapting workouts.* Adding motion input to games designed for standard controllers can result in gameplay that is physically too demanding or not challenging enough. Fortunately, many game studios offer authoring tools that allow players to design their own levels, which can greatly aid in creating appropriate workouts. We demonstrate how custom-built levels can provide effective exercise regiments.

We illustrate our framework by turning the popular first-person action and puzzle title *Portal 2*[1] into *Sportal*, a version of the game featuring a full-body motion-based interface. The XMG approach has the potential to bring non-gamers who are indifferent to sedentary gaming but eager to exercise to major gaming titles *and* to generate interest to exercise in avid gamers.

2 Game Choice

Games let the player step aside from everyday life and get immersed in a virtual world. In sports and physical exercising, the equivalent is a state of *flow*, a concept which has also found adoption in the game design literature [3]. In exergames, presence and flow ideally combine to form a unique mental and physical experience [5]. To this end, player motions should be mapped as directly as possible, and both game mechanics and game world must be adequately designed to allow for enaction of the input.

The most obvious type of game to support this are *character-based action games*. In these the player controls the movement of an avatar in order to reach destinations and often needs to physically overcome obstacles and enemies with various actions such as jumping, climbing and combat. Since the avatar is usually humanoid, this provides the perfect target for direct mapping of full-body input.

Games with a *first-person view* that show the world from the perspective of the avatar increase the sense of presence. Since there is no direct visual feedback of avatar motions, they can be used most gracefully in the XMG approach since they offer more leeway in mapping gestural input to standard game controls.

Unfortunately, direct controls restrict the design of mapping physical input to avatar motions. This makes the degree to which such active games can be used for exercising dependent on the design of the game world. In many action games the player needs to traverse long distances, which can be quite challenging if controlled by physical locomotion interfaces. The complexity and large variety of games available means that there are no simple rules for choosing game worlds for a certain workout. However, in many cases this can be addressed with customisable game worlds, as discussed below.

---

[1] http://valvesoftware.com/games/portal2.html, last viewed 2013-07-10

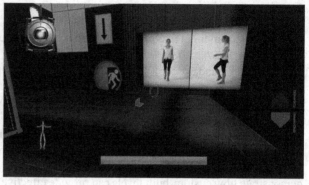

Fig. 1. *Sportal* control setup (left) and screenshot featuring feedback overlay (right, magenta interface elements). *Portal 2* game interface and game assets are copyrighted by *Valve Corporation*.

The two next steps in turning an existing first-person action game into an exergame are to design a *control overlay* that replaces standard game controllers by connecting motion detection to virtual device drivers, and the matching *feedback overlay* that augments original game feedback to support motion-based input. In the following, we illustrate these steps by reporting on how we turned the popular action and logical thinking game *Portal 2* (by *Valve*) into the exergame *Sportal. Sportal* features motion input through physical locomotion, a diverse range of exercises, and an augmented graphical display.

3   Control Overlay

The general design problem in exergames is to create full-body gestural controls that are also exercises. In the XMG approach, this is subject to a specific constraint: since the game controls are not changeable in terms of which actions the game avatar can be instructed to perform and which parameters can be used to detail these commands, the full-body motion-patterns need to map onto already defined traditional input-patterns.

While the specific controls of each game differ, standard input patterns have been established for certain game genres. Typical first-person game controls map continuous spatial input via mouse or joystick to continuous motions such as locomotion and aiming, discrete trigger input (hitting buttons or keys) to well-defined discrete motions such as jumping, activating, or firing, and discrete modal input (holding buttons or keys) to continuous input modes, such as crouched movement or aiming modes.

The foundation of the *Sportal* motion interface is physical locomotion. We chose a walking-in-place (WIP) technique, since it provides a good trade-off between natural interaction and technical requirements [1]. The motion tracking setup involves an infrared camera mounted on a gun prop and a Microsoft Kinect. For general locomotion, we used the state-of-the-art low-latency gait-understanding-driven (GUD) WIP algorithm [6] fed by accelerometer data gathered from sensors located on the player's shins. Avatar rotation (view direction) can be controlled by torso stance or aiming the gun.

Shoulder rotations of the player to the left or right commence a view rotation, the speed of which is given by angle between shoulder axis and sensor view plane. The alternative is to point the gun into the desired rotation direction. Heuristics on the relative vertical position of the pelvis enable discrete triggering for jumps and a discrete modal control for crouched walking.

We derived further input motions from interviews with physical training instructors and physicians and developed a gymnastics training regimen consisting of warm-up and workout. This also includes the following additional motion patterns: jumping jacks, a kickbox move, and two exercises of holding a stance. As with locomotion moves, exercise moves are detected using heuristically determined models based on the skeleton recognition provided by the Kinect SDK. Recognised commands are then sent to the game via the virtual gamepad controller vJoy[2].

4   Feedback Overlay

The multimodal feedback in most games is optimised for conventional game controls rather than motion-based input. With gamepads, or keyboard and mouse, players receive passive haptic and mechanic feedback from pressing buttons or thumbing joysticks in addition to the visual and audio feedback presented through the game world rendering. However, motion input requires additional feedback on gesture recognition.

Since the game interface usually cannot be changed without considerable effort, the challenge is how to *augment* the existing game interface in order to provide adequate exergame output. While every game interface is different, we can define some similarities. On the graphical level, every first-person game features a prominent view of the 3D game world, usually together with several overlaid 2D widgets. The challenge for a visual feedback overlay is to integrate additional visual information without diminishing the view or cluttering the display. Concerning audio, motion events such as jumping are often emphasised with a signature sound. This is usually clearly recognisable above ambient sound and music. The challenge for an auditive feedback overlay is not to interfere with in-game sound events. Across all available channels, the exergame feedback overlay designer has the choice of whether to integrate overlay as much as possible or to allow for a clear distinction between in-game and NUI controls. Our design choices in *Sportal* will serve to illustrate the discussion.

For *Sportal*, we integrated direct feedback on sensor image/skeleton recognition into the visual overlay. Since this should not be mistaken for a third person depiction of the avatar, we kept it small, stylised and off-centre. A progress bar was added for specific exercises where the player is required to hold a position for a time period. An arrow display at the side provides feedback on walking direction and speed. To support gun-based view orientation, a small marker in the form of an arrow pointing in rotation direction signifies where the gun is currently pointing. The arrow-shape makes it distinct from the in-game cross-hair, which is used for shooting portals in *Portal 2*. The feedback overlay was realised as a full-screen window with transparent background that is rendered on top of the game screen.

---

[2] http://vjoystick.sourceforge.net/, last viewed 2013-07-10

For the audio overlay, we integrated a voice overlay explaining the game controls for a tutorial mode, which was kept in the style of a talking artificial intelligence in order to maintain the game world atmosphere. While we did not experiment with explicit audio feedback, the discrete gestures would most likely benefit from a confirmation sound played when recognition is complete.

5   Adapting Workout with Custom Game Worlds

Control and feedback overlays facilitate turning a well-chosen off-the-shelf game into an active game. Depending on game design, this can result in an experience that is physically either too demanding or not challenging enough, since it was not designed with active input in mind. While we can influence this with gesture designs and gain factors in the control overlay to a certain extent, certain commercially available titles offer further means of adapting exercise workout—content editors.

Many games with a high development budget and large player communities sport tools for user-generated content. These empower regular users to create their own game content in the form of levels or maps. In the context of XMG, such tools offer authority over training regimens. For instance, the *Valve Hammer Editor*[3] is an authoring environment in which levels can be created for *Portal 2* via direct manipulation. We exploited this for *Sportal* by experimenting with map layouts and obstacle courses to influence order and frequency of exercises.

6   Related Work

With the introduction of motion detection systems such as the *Nintendo Wii*, *Sony Playstation Move* and *Microsoft Kinect*, a large number of exergames have entered the market. However, existing titles mostly comprise only simple games that require limited body movements. The market also offers controllers geared towards exercising, such as the PCGamerBike[4]. These can be used in place of regular controllers in order to work-out while gaming, but offer only a limited range of motion and often lack appropriate feedback.

Recent research has seen an increasing number of projects on motion-based games and their effects on player engagement and health, as well as investigations into their therapeutic use for specific patient groups. In most cases these involve custom games that are far away from commercial titles regarding quality of assets and game engagement. Only few works have considered adapting off-the-shelf non-active games for purposes of exercise. The GAIM software toolkit [2] facilitates developers of active games to work independently of the device level. This enables easy switching between concrete devices, and even input categories, which the authors demonstrate with two adaptations of existing games, adding pedalling input to a racing game and controlling a 2D spaceship game with player stances. This can aid in changing the input to more

---

[3] https://developer.valvesoftware.com/wiki/Valve_Hammer_Editor, last viewed 2013-07-10

[4] http://www.pcgamerbike.com, last viewed 2013-07-10

physically active modes, although not without editing game code. Augmenting existing game visuals has already been proposed in the context of biofeedback games [4]. This approach uses texture-based graphical overlays to obfuscate the underlying game based on the player's physiological state, but heart rate input and feedback do not figure into actual game control.

7 Conclusion and Future Work

Turning existing video games into motion-based games makes use of their virtues of high-quality assets and long-term motivation for exergames and motion-based games for health. In order to aid the transformation from off-the-shelf game to exergame, we proposed the *Exercise My Game* (XMG) design framework. This structures the process into four steps: choice of game, input overlay, output overlay, and game customisation. We applied XMG in turning *Portal 2* into the exergame *Sportal*, demonstrating that with an adequate choice of game, control and output overlay software, and the creative use of authoring tools one can truly *exercise* a commercial video game. This approach can potentially both acquaint exercise-eager non-gamers with major gaming titles, in addition to giving many traditional gamers an incentive to exercise.

We are currently evaluating our approach in an experiment investigating how gamification level affect the motivation in exercising. We also intend to transfer the XMG framework into a software toolkit in order to further facilitate *exercising* regular games.

Acknowledgements. We would like to thank all students involved in developing *Sportal*: Daniel Apken, Anna Barenbrock, Smitha Basavalingaiah, Nadezda Bogdanova, Dörte Brockmann, Darya Davydenkova, Nicole Hurek, Sergej Kozuhovskij, Yasser Maslout, Fariba Mostajeran Gourtani, Peter Szmidt, Xiaoyi Wang, Guangtao Zhang.

References

1. Bowman, D.A., Kruijff, E., LaViola, J.J., Poupyrev, I.: 3D User Interfaces: Theory and Practice. Addison-Wesley (2004)
2. Brehmer, M., Graham, T.C.N., Stach, T.: Activate your GAIM: A toolkit for input in active games. In: Proc. Futureplay 2010, pp. 151–158. ACM, New York (2010)
3. Chen, J.: Flow in games (and everything else). Commun. ACM 50(4), 31–34 (2007)
4. Mandryk, R.L., Kalyn, M., Dang, Y., Doucette, A., Taylor, B., Dielschneider, S.: Turning off-the-shelf games into biofeedback games. In: Proc. ASSETS 2012, pp. 199–200. ACM, New York (2012)
5. Sinclair, J., Hingston, P., Masek, M.: Exergame development using the dual flow model. In: Proc. IE 2009, pp. 1–11. ACM, New York (2009)
6. Wendt, J.D., Whitton, M.C., Brooks, F.P.: GUD WIP: Gait-understanding-driven walking-in-place. In: Proc. VR 2010. IEEE (2010)

How Do People Talk with a Virtual Philosopher: Log Analysis of a Real-World Application

Xuan Wang and Ryohei Nakatsu

Keio-NUS CUTE Center, Interactive and Digital Media Institute
NUS Graduate School for Integrative Sciences and Engineering
National University of Singapore
{wangxuan,elenr}@nus.edu.sg

Abstract. Conversation with computers is an important form of human computer interaction. Inappropriately designed conversational agents can easily lead to unsatisfying user experience and even frustration, and this is especially true when the application is deployed in the real world. Currently, research on casual non-task oriented systems and our understanding in how people interact with such agents are still limited. To gain more insights on this issue, we carried out both quantitative and qualitative content analysis of conversation logs collected from a real-world application, featuring a non-task oriented conversational agent as a virtual philosopher. We construct a taxonomy of user utterances to the agent and discuss a few strategies that an agent might employ to provide a better user experience.

Keywords: non-task oriented conversational agent, log analysis, virtual philosopher.

1 Introduction

A conversational agent (CA) is a computer system that is able to carry out natural language conversation with a human user. As an intuitive interface, CA has been used in a variety of ways, such as helping people to accomplish tasks, obtain information and learn about things[1–3]. When a CA is deployed in the real world, it can often face user utterances that are untrained before. The ability to handle the so-called "out-of-domain" questions is key to the lifelikeness of an agent [4], and coherence/appropriateness of the answer is important in maintaining engagement from the user [5], as user frustration can be caused otherwise. This is especially true for non-task oriented CAs, where there is no clear common user-agent goal [6], which means the user utterances are largely unbounded. As a result, common dialogue strategies in task-oriented CAs are no longer effective. In order to develop good strategies for non-task oriented CA to deal with open conversation, we need to have good understanding of how users talk to the agent first. This paper attempts to shed some light on this issue by presenting a qualitative and quantitative analysis of the conversation logs between users and a non-task oriented conversational agent in a real world

J.C. Anacleto et al. (Eds.): ICEC 2013, LNCS 8215, pp. 132–137, 2013.

setting. We situate our study in the case of a virtual philosopher, which is a conversational agent that mimics Confucius, a famous philosopher in ancient China.

2   Related Work

As compared to task-oriented agents where there is a well-defined task or well-circumscribed body of information sought by the users, non-task oriented conversational agents are designed to simulate human conversation for entertainment, learning, etc., usually within a certain domain. Some examples are virtual museum guides [2, 7–9], virtual historical persons[4, 10]. When evaluating such systems, besides user's subjective report through questionnaires, interviews, log analysis is a very informative way to understand the actual performance of an agent, and it can also help us to have a good understanding of how users behave when interacting with the system. In [11], Aggarwal et al. presents a large corpus of spoken conversation with two virtual museum guides, Ada and Grace, where common questions are identified and added to the characters' training data to improve their conversation ability. Kopp et al. carried out a more detailed content analysis on the conversation logs during the museum guide Max's employment in the Nixdorf Museum [2]. They categorized the utterances into "Greeting", "Farewell", "Flaming", "Feedback to agent", "Questions", "Answers", "Request to do something", and showed that people use human-like communication strategies when interacting with the system [2]. Robinson et al. also analyzed the content of dialogues carried out between visitors and the virtual character Sgt Blackwell in the Cooper Hewitt Museum [12]. They categorized user utterances into user initiated and reacted utterances, with finer categories within each category. By presenting a very detailed description of the utterance content, they provide a good picture of user's preference, which points out directions for the expansion of the agent's knowledge base. In this paper, we conduct a similar analysis in the context of a virtual philosopher, to see whether users have similar behavior and expectations, and also inform our design to handle the user utterances appropriately.

3   Content Analysis

3.1   Data Collection

The application used for data collection is called iSage Confucius. It is a conversational agent that mimics Confucius, the renowned philosopher and educator in ancient China. It models the problem of finding answers as an information retrieval task, and uses a combination of scripts and semantic analysis methods. More details of the system can be found in [13]. We published the application in Google Play Store for free download since September 2011. All conversations are logged anonymously, and users are notified the first time they open the application. Each user is identified by a UUID (Universally Unique Identifier). As of the end of 2012, the application has collected over 1500 conversation turns. A turn is defined here as one utterance from the user and one response from the virtual Confucius. We take the log files collected during the year of 2012 for the analysis, with a total of 1029 turns coming from of 115 different user IDs (which means on average 8.95 turns per user, assuming each user ID corresponds to one user).

3.2   Method

Following the method in [2], we also took a data-driven approach in the content analysis of log files. Different from [2], we distinguish the categories based on the nature and content of user utterances. The rationale for such classification is that the agent needs to be equipped with different techniques to respond to user utterances of different type and scope. Knowing the distribution of utterances can inform algorithm design and improve the agent's ability in carrying out open dialogues. To derive the classification scheme, two coders skimmed through all the log data and jointly came out with the initial categories. Then the coders coded the first 100 turns, discussed and modified the categories if necessary. After the categories were finalized, the coders independently coded the first 200 turns, and the inter-coder agreement was checked. A Cohen's Kappa value of 0.642 was computed, indicating satisfactory inter-coder agreement. The coders then proceeded to code the rest of the log files, each responsible for half of the data.

3.3   Classification Scheme

The resulting categories, selected examples and their frequencies are shown in Table 1. There are altogether 6 high-level categories. Some of the high-level categories are further classified into lower-level categories to reveal more details. The meaning of each of the high-level category is explained as follows:

1. *Confucius and Confucianism*: This category contains user utterances that are directly related to the agent. This is an important part of the intended usage of the application - to know more about Confucius and Confucianism through conversation. Many of the conversational agents reviewed in the related work section are designed mainly to handle this kind of questions.
2. *Factoid*: This category contains factoid questions that have a definite answer (which have been the subject of study in many question answering systems, e.g. [14]). Such questions are not related to the agent and are considered out-of-domain.
3. *Subjective*: As opposed to factoid questions, this category contains questions that do not have a definite answer. This is also an important part of the intended usage of the application - to get Confucius's subjective opinion on things. For utterances that contain only a single noun or noun phrases, we assume that users expect Confucius can give some comments on it. So we include such utterances in this category as well.

4. *Conversational*: This category contains user utterances which serve the purpose of starting a conversation and maintaining the flow. Such utterances are a main indicator of social interaction.
5. *Nonsense*: This category contains utterances that do not have any meaning or contribution to the conversation, as well as obscene language.
6. *Others*: Two of the utterances about the app itself turn out to fall out of the above 5 categories, so we put them in a separate category called others.

Table 1. A taxonomy of user utterances in the iSage corpus

No.	Categories	Examples	Count (%)
1	**Confucius and Confucianism**		**172 (16.7%)**
	1A. Biographical info	Were you ever married?	168 (16.3%)
	1B. Domain specific terms	What is the Way?	4 (0.4%)
2	**Factoid**	How many miles is it to Jupiter.	**47 (4.6%)**
3	**Subjective**		**546 (53.1%)**
	3A. Definition/explanation of abstract concepts	What is wisdom?	115 (11.2%)
	3B. Reasons	Why is life so complicated?	36 (3.5%)
	3C. Judgments, Predictions	Can machines love?	114 (11.1%)
	3D. Advice	How can I be successful?	105 (10.2%)
	3E. Statements	I am depressed.	61 (5.9%)
	3F. Single word, word phrase	love	115 (11.2%)
4	**Conversational**		**147 (14.3%)**
	4A. Feedback to agent	This is amazing.	91 (8.8%)
	4B. Greeting, goodbye	Hi.	56 (5.4%)
5	**Nonsense**		**115 (11.2%)**
	5A. Mistyped, meaningless	How many studenrs you have?	95 (9.2%)
	5B. Pornographic/abuse	Obscene words	20 (1.9%)
6	**Others**	What is the point of this app?	**2 (0.2%)**
		Can I go to main menu?	
Total			**1029 (100%)**

4 Discussions

From the frequency count of the categories, we can see, in general, users are willing to suspend their disbelief and act like talking to the real Confucius, asking questions regarding Confucius's life (16.3%), posing difficult philosophical questions, revealing their problems and seeking advice (53.1%). Conversational utterances can also be observed (14.3%). In accordance with findings in other studies [2, 12], we also observed flaming (obscene language, random keystrokes, meaningless utterances)(11.2%), or testing (by asking factoid questions) (4.6%).

From user's replies, we can have a partial idea of whether they enjoyed using the system. Some users appear to be satisfied with the answer given by the virtual Confucius, as we can observe them replying *"Oh I see."*, *"This is amazing."*. Enjoyment can also be observed: *"Hahaha"*, *"Funny"*. On the other hand, we also observe frustrations when the system was not able to give a good answer, or completely misunderstood user's question. Users expressed their unhappiness using utterances like *"You are not making any sense"*. It is observed that usually after getting a few irrelevant responses, users would stop using the system. Currently, when the agent is not able to find any good answer, its strategy is to honestly tell that he does not understand and ask the user to rephrase the question. The log analysis reveals that it is not effective. Very few people would rephrase the question as the agent requested.

Users of different CAs may have differing needs and expectations [12]. Different from the results found in the case of virtual museum guides [2] and virtual soldier [12], where users tend to ask questions regarding the agent itself, we found that for a virtual philosopher, users tend to share more about their own experiences or problems with the agent, expecting the agent to clear their doubts or provide guidance. It seems that the identity of the agent plays a large role in the types of questions users would ask. As the main purpose of using a virtual philosopher system is information-seeking or advice-seeking, traditional dialogue acts are less useful in this case. Therefore, when designing strategies for answering, it may be a good choice to refer to the taxonomy constructed from real user data. It is important for the agent to know the type of input utterance, so that it can either invoke appropriate answer finding technique, or provide an appropriate reply when no answer can be found in the knowledge base. A classifier can be trained to classify the utterances using the collected data, and corresponding strategies can be designed to respond to these utterances. For example, to improve the agent's ability to handle category 1 utterances, we can either ask domain experts to expand the knowledge base, or look for information online using QA engines. Category 2 questions can also be handled by consulting existing QA systems, or designing appropriate default responses to inform the user that it is not supposed to answer this kind of questions. Category 3 utterances are more difficult - users tend to share their own experience, or ask about subjects of their own interest, so we cannot predict the questions and prepare answers beforehand. Therefore, we need better semantic and pragmatic understanding to select the best answer from the repository of candidate answers. Category 4 utterances is also important, as it is essential in making the agent human-like. A simple and good solution is to use standard chatbot's techniques.

We believe that the taxonomy of utterances derived from real user data can help us to have a better understanding of how users talk to a virtual philosopher system in an unrestricted setting, and such understanding can inform the algorithm design for a more human-like agent. In future work, we plan to implement the discussed strategies and conduct experimentally controlled studies to find the optimal strategy for handling open conversation with a virtual philosopher.

Acknowledgments. This research is supported by the Singapore National Research Foundation under its International Research Centre @ Singapore Funding Initiative and administered by the IDM Programme Office.

References

1. Crockett, K., O'Shea, J., Bandar, Z.: Goal Orientated Conversational Agents: Applications to Benefit Society. In: O'Shea, J., Nguyen, N.T., Crockett, K., Howlett, R.J., Jain, L.C. (eds.) KES-AMSTA 2011. LNCS, vol. 6682, pp. 16–25. Springer, Heidelberg (2011)
2. Kopp, S., Gesellensetter, L., Krämer, N.C., Wachsmuth, I.: A conversational agent as museum guide – design and evaluation of a real-world application. In: Panayiotopoulos, T., Gratch, J., Aylett, R.S., Ballin, D., Olivier, P., Rist, T. (eds.) IVA 2005. LNCS (LNAI), vol. 3661, pp. 329–343. Springer, Heidelberg (2005)
3. D'Mello, S., Graesser, A., King, B.: Toward Spoken Human-Computer Tutorial Dialogues. Human-Computer Interaction 25(4), 289–323 (2010)
4. Marinelli, D., Stevens, S.: Synthetic interviews: the art of creating a 'dyad' between humans and machine-based characters. In: Proceedings 1998 IEEE 4th Workshop Interactive Voice Technology for Telecommunications Applications, IVTTA 1998 (Cat. No.98TH8376), pp. 43–48. IEEE (1998)
5. Artstein, R., Cannon, J., Gandhe, S., Gerten, J., Henderer, J., Leuski, A., Traum, D., Rey, M.: Coherence of Off-Topic Response for a Virtual Character. In: Proceedings of the 26th Army Science Conference (2008)
6. Bernsen, N.O., Dybkjar, L.: Evaluation of spoken multimodal conversation. In: Proceedings of the 6th International Conference on Multimodal Interfaces - ICMI 2004, p. 38. ACM Press, New York (2004)
7. Swartout, W., et al.: Ada and grace: Toward realistic and engaging virtual museum guides. In: Safonova, A. (ed.) IVA 2010. LNCS, vol. 6356, pp. 286–300. Springer, Heidelberg (2010)
8. Bell, L., Gustafson, J.: Child and adult speaker adaptation during error resolution in a publicly available spoken dialogue system. In: EUROSPEECH 2003, pp. 613–616 (2003)
9. Richards, D.: Agent-based museum and tour guides. In: Proceedings of The 8th Australasian Conference on Interactive Entertainment Playing the System - IE 2012. ACM Press, New York (2012)
10. Bernsen, N., Dybkjæ, R.L.: Domain-oriented conversation with H. C. Andersen. In: Proc. of the Workshop on Affective Dialogue Systems, pp. 142–153. Springer (2004)
11. Aggarwal, P., Artstein, R., Gerten, J., Katsamanis, A., Narayanan, S., Nazarian, A., Traum, D.: The Twins Corpus of Museum Visitor Questions. In: LREC 2012, vol. 3, pp. 2355–2361 (2012)
12. Robinson, S., Traum, D., Ittycheriah, M., Henderer, J.: What would you ask a Conversational Agent? Observations of Human-Agent Dialogues in a Museum Setting. In: LREC 2008 Proceedings, pp. 1125–1131 (2008)
13. Wang, X., Khoo, E.T., Siriwardana, S., Iroshan, H., Nakatsu, R.: Philosophy Meets Entertainment: Designing an Interactive Virtual Philosopher. In: Herrlich, M., Malaka, R., Masuch, M. (eds.) ICEC 2012. LNCS, vol. 7522, pp. 100–113. Springer, Heidelberg (2012)
14. Voorhees, E.M., Dang, T.H.: Overview of the TREC 2005 Question Answering Track. In: Proc. of TREC 2005 (2005)

Life-Like Animation System of Virtual Firefly Based on Animacy Perception

Daiki Satoi, Hisanao Nakadai, Matteo Bernacchia, and Jun'ichi Hoshino

University of Tsukuba, 1-1-1-#3M309 Tennodai Tsukuba, Ibaraki 305-8573 Japan
{satoi.daiki,nakadai.hisanao,bernacchia.matteo}@entcomp.esys.tsukuba.ac.jp,
jhoshino@esys.tsukuba.ac.jp,
http://www.entcomp.esys.tsukuba.ac.jp/

Abstract. In this paper, we propose a computational model to generate life-like motion for firefly-like creatures. By using a two-stage stochastic process and simple operational elements, we could generate various life-like motion patterns. Then, we incorporated these patterns in our animation system, where virtual fireflies move and emit light dynamically. We experimented and verified using surveys that the virtual fireflies look like living beings, and that different animations give rise to different impressions.

Keywords: Procedural Animation, Artificial Life, Firefly, Animacy Perception.

1 Introduction

The fireflies, with their typical glow and drifting movement, have been a popular summer tradition for a long time, and always had a relieving effect for the people watching them. With regard to the effects and principles of the fireflies' light emission, a number of studies have been conducted in areas such as engineering and physiology, e.g. there is a case that demonstrates their healing effect by using electroencephalogram data and surveys[1–3], also a virtual illumination system for welfare has been proposed[2].

In the art and entertainment areas, in order to produce contents such as games and movies, moving and glowing objects like fireflies (virtual fireflies) are widely used in the production of both real and virtual spaces[4–11]. To incorporate virtual fireflies it is necessary to generate fireflies' behavior automatically using computational models to allow for user interaction.

Reproduction technique by calculation model has been proposed for synchronization phenomena and emission pattern of firefly ever[2, 12–14]. On the other hand, in the field of cognitive science, the phenomenon of "animacy perception" is known as a research about the object to the behavior typical life[15–17]. The study of animacy perception, that appearance is an effect on the perception of life a sense of change in the speed or direction of motion change even a simple geometric shape is known. Therefore, it is conceivable in order to represent the quality of life of fireflies, making a model of how to move in consideration of the change in speed or direction change in motion is important. However, in past studies about firefly, it has not been taken up for the element of motion.

J.C. Anacleto et al. (Eds.): ICEC 2013, LNCS 8215, pp. 138–144, 2013.

In this paper, we propose a computational model for automatically generating and easy, the motion looks like like a creature light-emitting object, such as a firefly. Through the modeling of the movement of fireflies, it can be expected to become easily incorporate virtual creatures like fireflies to art and entertainment contents.

2   Generating Method of Life-Like Motion

In this chapter, we introduce a life-like motion generation method based on the concept of animacy perception.

Our method complies with rigid body dynamics. A firefly is treated as a single rigid body, and translations and rotations are performed according to the firefly velocity and angular velocity. In this paper, we assume a left-handed coordinate system, with the fireflies standard position facing the positive direction of the Z-axis.

2.1   Motion Modules and Two-Stage Stochastic Model

We define the motion of a firefly with two modules (we call "motion modules") that consist of "acceleration (including redirecting)" and "deceleration", that transition in a gradual manner. This method consists of a two-step probability selection processes, first it selects stochastically a model and then selects the stochastic parameters of the motion generated in the previous step. With this approach, even with a few parameters and models various realistic patterns can be obtained. This procedure is repeated at small time intervals, each time selecting a motion module, doing the relative computations and finally producing the data.

2.2   Selection Process of the Motion Module

In this stage, the next motion module is selected depends on current motion module. This can be expressed as a stochastic process (a simple Markov chain)(Fig.1) in a discrete time series, such as the following:

$$p(x_0, x_1, \ldots, x_r) = p(x_0)p(x_1|x_0)p(x_2|x_1) \ldots, p(x_r|x_{r-1}) \tag{1}$$
$$\text{State space: } \Omega = S_1, S_2$$

However, S_1 is the acceleration motion module and S_2 is the deceleration motion module. That is, the probability that a motion module is selected at the discrete time n depends only on which motion module has been selected at the discrete time $n - 1$. Transition probabilities should be given as constant parameters in advance.

2.3   Selection Process of the Parameters

The second stochastic control stage is performed in the acceleration motion module.

Acceleration Motion Module. In the acceleration motion module, at first we generate a force vector F has a random component on the local spherical coordinate system with the origin at the center of the firefly, as shown in Fig.2. r is the magnitude of F and is a given constant parameter. Arguments θ and ϕ are determined by the following equation:

$$\theta = 90 + R(a_\theta), \quad \phi = 90 + R(a_\phi) \tag{2}$$

$R(a)$ is a function that returns a pseudo random number in the range $-a$ to a. When $R(a_\theta), R(a_\phi) = 0$, the firefly goes straight without rotation at all. a_θ and a_ϕ are given constant parameters. Then, we convert F from the local spherical coordinate system to a local Cartesian coordinate system (left-handed) as follows:

$$x = r \sin \theta \cos \phi, \quad y = r \cos \theta, \quad z = r \sin \theta \sin \phi \tag{3}$$

Next, we determine the acceleration a and the angular acceleration α as follows:

$$a = \frac{1}{m}\begin{pmatrix} 0 \\ 0 \\ z \end{pmatrix}, \quad \alpha = \frac{1}{I}\begin{pmatrix} -y \\ x \\ 0 \end{pmatrix} = \frac{1}{mr^2}\begin{pmatrix} -y \\ x \\ 0 \end{pmatrix} \tag{4}$$

The mass m and the radius r are given constant parameters. I is the moment of inertia. Finally, we compute the velocity v and the angular velocity ω by integrating a and α.

Deceleration Motion Module. In the deceleration motion module, we subtract the velocity v and angular velocity ω as a drag that mimics the air resistance. The drag D exerted on the rigid body (firefly) in the fluid is proportional to the square of the speed, and is calculated by the equation $D = \frac{1}{2}C_D\rho u^2 S$. C_D is the drag coefficient, ρ is the density of the fluid, u is the speed of the firefly, and S is the representative area of the firefly. The values except u are given constant parameters.

3   Animation System of Virtual Firefly

In this chapter, we will build an animation system that incorporates the life-like motion generation method that was described in the previous chapter with virtual fireflies.

Fig.3 shows an example of the generated virtual fireflies. Virtual fireflies move in a virtual space and emit light at the same time. The configuration of the virtual fireflies

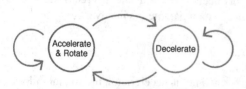

Fig. 1. Stochastic process to select motion module

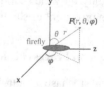

Fig. 2. Virtual firefly and force vector on spherical polar coordinates

contains two subsystems that stand side by side, the motion generation sub-system for generating motions and the emission control subsystem for controlling light emission (Fig.4). In order to focus on how virtual fireflies move, they do not possess a CG model representing their body. Their visible shape is generated as a circular particle, expressing pseudo glowing by changing size in conjunction with the light amount.

In the motion generation subsystem, we perform translations and rotations in the manner described in the previous chapter. However, in the acceleration motion module, because fireflies cannot assume a vertical orientation, the "attitude control biasing" works on the random component $R(a_\theta)$ that affects the pitch angle.

In the emission control subsystem, we control the glowing of the virtual firefly (i.e. changing size of the particle) in a simple way. This also uses a two-stage stochastic process as in the motion generation subsystem. The virtual firefly must select one state among "brightening", "keeping", and "darkening". The state continues to transition stochastically.

4 Evaluation Experiment

In this chapter, we experiment using surveys in order to verify if the virtual fireflies look like creatures and what impressions do they give. The subjects were 9 men, with an age ranging from 21 to 29. Seven of them had seen firefly with the naked eye. Two of them had never seen with the naked eye, but had seen moving fireflies in the video.

4.1 Equipment and Procedure

We present three animation sequences to subjects for 60 seconds each in random order, used the 21-inch LCD display. And then wait for them to fill out the questionnaire separately each time. At this time, we do not explain that we are mimicking the fireflies, nor the differences of each motion pattern. The difference of animations is as follows:

- The virtual fireflies does not move at all. (P1)
- The virtual fireflies perform linear motion with constant velocity. (P2)
- The virtual fireflies move according to our model. (P3)

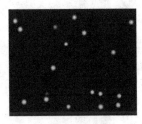

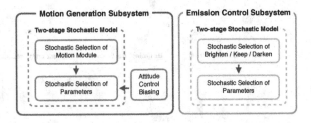

Fig. 3. Animating virtual fireflies (screenshot)

Fig. 4. Configuration of the animation system of the virtual fireflies

The portions that do not get involved in the motion generation, such as the emission control subsystem, are common to all patterns. A total of 15 virtual fireflies is generated in the virtual space with a random initial position. Parameters set in advance.

In the questionnaire, the subjects assign a score using a rating scale of 9 steps, from 1 to 5 points with 0.5 point intervals, regarding their impressions about the quality of the creatures currently displayed. There are 8 scoreing items: Not life-like/Life-like, Uninteresting/Interesting, Unfriendly/Friendly, Simple/Complex, Get bored easily/Get bored hardly, Not healed/Be healed, Unpleasant/Pleasant, Dislike/Like (1 point/5 points). In addition, if subjects have particular impressions or notice something while watching the scene, they are invited to write in the apposite blank space.

4.2 Results

Rating Impressions. The list of mean and standard deviation of the scores of the rating scale for each pattern is shown in Fig.5. The length of the bar indicate average score and the length of the error bars indicate standard deviations. Furthermore, as a result of the analysis of variance to analyze the effect on the impression of the differences in the pattern, a significant difference was observed in 4 of 8 items.

In "Life-like/Not life-like", there is significant main effect ($F(2, 26) = 25.436, p < .001$). The result of the multiple comparison using HSD method by Tukey has large significant difference between groups of P1–P3 and P2–P3 ($p < .01$). In "Interesting/Uninteresting", there is significant main effect ($F(2, 26) = 4.894, p < .05$). The result of the multiple comparison using HSD method by Tukey has significant difference between groups of P1–P3 and P2–P3 ($p < .05$). In "Complex/Simple", there is significant main effect ($F(2, 26) = 26.0183, p < .001$). The result of the multiple comparison using HSD method by Tukey has large significant difference between groups of P1–P3 and P2–P3 ($p < .01$). In "Pleasant/Unpleasant", there is significant main effect

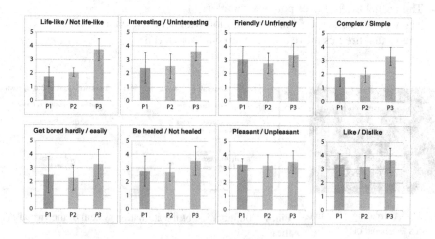

Fig. 5. Mean and standard deviation of the scores in each animation pattern

$(F(2, 26) = 5.131, p < .05)$. The result of the multiple comparison using HSD method by Tukey has significant difference between groups of P1–P3 and P2–P3 ($p < .05$).

Free Description. In the free description part of the questionnaire, there were many impressions on P1 about the light patterns being too simple, for example, "Felt like just sparkling lights" and "Looks like christmas lights". Mechanical impressions such as "Feels like looking at the flow of traffic" and "The movement is monotonous" were raised in P2. Impression about the creature-likeness, such as "Moves randomly like a creature" and "Creature-like" came to be seen in P3. In addition, for P3 many wrote comments about the glowing and the movement such as "I think acceleration and deceleration are too strong" and "Flickering slowly while moving fast does not feel natural".

5   Conclusion

In this paper, we proposed a computational model to generate life-like motion for firefly-like creatures. By using a two-stage stochastic process and simple operational elements, we generated various life-like motion patterns. By incorporating an object that mimics a virtual firefly, we built an animation system where virtual fireflies move and emit light dynamically. We experimented and verified using surveys that the virtual fireflies look like living beings, and made the subjects feel healing and fun.

References

1. Inagaki, T., Inuzuka, K., Agu, M., Akabane, H., Abe, N.: $1/f^n$ Fluctuating Phenomena in Luminous Pattern in Firefly and Its Healing Effect. Transaction of JSME Series C 67(659), 365–372 (2001) (in Japanese)
2. Abe, N., Inagaki, T., Ishikawa, H., Matsui, T., Agu, M.: Kansei Estimation on Luminescence of Firefly - Fluctuating Characteristics of the Light Emission Pattern -. Journal of Kansei Engineering 3(1), 35–44 (2003) (in Japanese)
3. Hoshiba, E., Inagaki, T., Kimura, N., Abe, N., Miyauchi, K.: $1/f^n$ Fluctuating Phenomena in the Hue of Light Emission Pattern of Firefly and Its Healing Effect. Transaction of JSME Series C 72(714), 109–117 (2006) (in Japanese)
4. Square Enix: Agni's Philosophy (2012), http://www.agnisphilosophy.com/
5. Eubanks, A.: Catching Fireflies: A Persuasive Augmented Reality Game for Android Phones. In: ACM-SE 2011 Proceedings of the 49th Annual Southeast Regional Conference, pp. 363–364 (2011)
6. Matsuo, T.: Floating Light (2003), http://www.monoscape.jp/
7. Matsuo, T.: Phantasm (2006), http://www.monoscape.jp/
8. Matsuo, T.: Aquatic Colors (2009), http://www.monoscape.jp/
9. Yoon, M.: White Noise White Light, Athens (2004), http://www.mystudio.us/
10. United Visual Artists: Array (2008), http://www.uva.co.uk/work/array/
11. Q Entertainment, Ubisoft: Child of Eden (2011)http://www.ubisoft.co.jp/coe/

12. Buck, J., Buck, E.: Synchronous Fireflies. Scientific American 234(5), 74–85 (1976)
13. Raghavachary, S.: Firefly flash synchronication. SIGGRAPH 2003 Sketches & Applications (2003)
14. Nishi, H., Sakurazawa, S., Mima, Y., Yamamoto, T.: Interactive Illumination System Simulating Entrainment Phenomenon of Fireflies. IPSJ Interaction 2012, 385–390 (2012) (in Japanese)
15. Michotte, A.: The perception of causality. Basic Books (1946/ English Transl. 1963)
16. Heider, F., Simmel, M.: An Experimental Study of Apparent Behavior. The American Journal of Psychology 57(2), 243–259 (1944)
17. Scholl, B.J., Gao, T.: Perceiving animacy and intentionality: Visual processing or higher-level judgment? In: Rutherford, M.D., Kuhlmeier, V.A. (eds.) Social perception: Detection and interpretation of animacy, agency, and intention. MIT press (in press)

Posters

A Model-Driven Engineering Approach for Immersive Mixed-Reality Environments

Marija Nakevska[1], Jasen Markovski[2,*], and Matthias Rauterberg[1]

[1] Department of Industrial Design,
[2] Department of Mechanical Engineering,
Eindhoven University of Technology,
P.O. Box 513, 5600 MB Eindhoven,
The Netherlands
{m.nakevska,j.markovski,g.w.m.rauterberg}@tue.nl

Abstract. We propose a model-based engineering approach for development of immersive mixed-reality environments based on supervisory control theory that provides for automated software synthesis. The proposed approach greatly improves the consistency of the design process by employing models as means of communication, whereas supervisory control synthesis caters for system flexibility and evolvability.

1 The ALICE Installation

Cultural computing is a new human-computer interaction paradigm that aims to provide an interactive experience, closely related to the core aspects of a culture [5]. The ALICE project [4] implements an immersive mixed-reality installation that aims to address important cultural determinants, such as perception, rationality, logic, and self. Immersive mixed reality merges real and virtual worlds to produce new environments that confronts the user in an intense and a seemingly real experience [6]. The ALICE project creates an experience based on the novel "Alice's Adventures in Wonderland" by L. Carroll. The installation comprises six stages over two floors of 12 by 12 meters, employing a large palette of hardware and techniques, such as sensors, actuators, virtual reality, and embodied and virtual agents.

Each stage simulates a certain environment, e.g., nature mimicking, simulation of falling, or changes of the perception of the relative size of the space, corresponding to different parts of the narrative. The participant is engaged in an interactive experience, which includes movements, distortions of the concept of space, and counter-intuitive interactions [9]. The narrative scenario is implemented into a centralized control software, which relies on a unifying communication interface with the sensor and actuator components that we developed.

The production of immersive mixed-reality environments demands efforts from contributing experts from various fields, like artists, interaction designers, and software and electrical engineers. The collaboration within such a diverse

* Supported by Dutch NWO project: ProThOS, no. 600.065.120.11N124.

J.C. Anacleto et al. (Eds.): ICEC 2013, LNCS 8215, pp. 147–150, 2013.

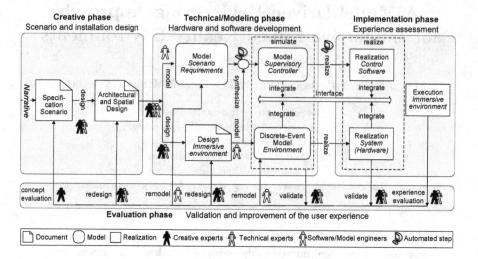

Fig. 1. The proposed model-driven engineering framework

environment requires additional clarity in the architectural, spatial, and control design. Moreover, the user experience is constantly evaluated and improved, demanding changes and additions to the existing features, e.g., additional audio or lighting effects. As a result, the installation is constantly changing and evolving.

Taking in consideration the number and diversity of the involved components and technologies, the maintenance and development of this installation becomes a daunting task. To mitigate system complexity and to ensure user and system safety, we search for engineering approaches that can guarantee safety and cater for flexibility and evolvability of the system. One such advocated approach is model-driven engineering, where models play a central role as means of communication between the involved parties [7].

2   A Synthesis-Based Model-Driven Approach

In this paper we propose a model-driven approach for design and development of immersive mixed-reality environments that relies on supervisory software synthesis [8,2]. The synthesis is based on the models of the underlying hardware and the coordination requirements, which implement the desired interactive scenario as interplay between the sensors and the actuators.

We distinguish four phases in the design and development of immersive mixed-reality environments: creative, technical and modeling, implementation, and evaluation phase, as abstractly depicted in Fig. 1. We also recognize three groups of contributing parties: (1) creative experts, e.g., media designers, (2) technical experts, e.g., system engineers, and (3) software and model engineers [1].

The modeling process begins with the narrative that inspires the immersive mixed-reality user experience. An informal specification of the scenario follows, made together by the creative and technical experts. The scenario is most importantly influenced by the various design and implementation decisions, like choice of the medium or implementation of the hardware control. These decisions result in an architectural and spatial design of the environment.

The technical phase begins with modeling of the components, such as sensors and actuators. The environment behavior is specified as the parallel composition of the models of its components [2,3] that may synchronize to deliver the desired experience. Once the environment is modeled, the software engineers model the scenario requirements by specifying safety properties of the system.

The models of the environment and the scenario, as given by the coordination requirements, are input for the synthesis tool which automatically generates a model of a controller. The latter can be coupled with the model of the environment to analyse the scenario by interactive simulation or formal verification [3], before the physical environment and control software are actually built.

In the implementation phase, the control software is generated based on the synthesized models. The scenario and control structure are integrated with an interface to the physical realization of the environment, depicted below in Fig. 1. Once the realization is completed, the interactions of the users are studied, evaluating the implemented concepts and user experience [9].

The scenario is adapted often to enrich the user experience, requiring changes in the requirements. We reuse the models to re-synthesize supervisory control software for the new scenario. The framework of Fig. 1 enables model reuse, whereas the automated synthesis significantly improves system evolvability.

3   Case Study: Eat Me, Drink Me

"Eat Me, Drink Me" is one of the stages in the ALICE project. Upon entering the stage, detected by a pressure floor sensor, the participant is 'trapped' by a sliding door that closes behind. The room has transparent walls with backside projections, which alter the perception of the relative size of the room by a virtual reality projection dependent on the interactions.

The virtual reality is implemented as a five-sided CAVE, see *www.crytek.com* for synchronization of the audio and video streaming. As interaction props in this stage, we use a cookie box labeled 'Eat Me', and a bottle labeled 'Drink Me'. The cookie box is equipped with an infrared motion sensor that detects whether a user takes a cookie, whereas the bootle is equipped with a tilt sensor that detects the action of drinking. Users in the CAVE are detected by pressure sensors on the floor and the actuation of the doors implemented with motors.

We depict the hardware and its interface to the control architecture in Fig. 2. We provide for a unified interface to the hardware resource control by employing a Blackboard interface implemented using the Robot Operating System (ROS), see *www.ros.org*. The supervisory controller is implemented as a state machine in SMACH, as a component of the system. The model of the controller is synthesized by employing Supremica, see *www.supremica.org*.

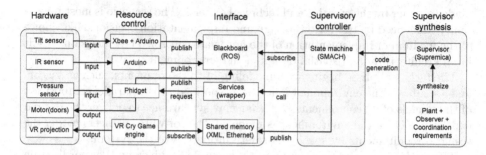

Fig. 2. Control architecture and hardware interfaces of stage 3 of the ALICE project

4   Concluding Remarks

We proposed a model-driven approach for design and development of immersive mixed reality environments that relies on supervisory control synthesis to automatically generate the control software that implements the interactive scenario. We find that the use of formal models is a key element for successful application of a synthesis-based engineering process. The proposed framework most importantly affects the control software development process, switching the focus from interpreting requirements, coding, and testing to analyzing requirements, modeling, and validating the behavior of the system. The proposed control architecture and software generation approach greatly improves model reusability and the flexibility and evolvability of the mixed reality environment.

References

1. Alcorn, S.: Theme Park Design: Behind the Scenes with an Engineer. Theme Perks Incorporated (2010)
2. Cassandras, C., Lafortune, S.: Introduction to discrete event systems. Kluwer Academic Publishers (2004)
3. Forschelen, S.T.J., Mortel-Fronczak, J.M., Su, R., Rooda, J.E.: Application of supervisory control theory to theme park vehicles. Discrete Event Dynamic Systems (4), 511–540 (2012)
4. Hu, J., Bartneck, C., Salem, B., Rauterberg, M.: ALICE's adventures in cultural computing. International Journal of Arts and Technology 1(1), 102–118 (2008)
5. Kooijmans, T., Rauterberg, M.: Cultural computing and the self concept: Towards unconscious metamorphosis. In: Ma, L., Rauterberg, M., Nakatsu, R. (eds.) ICEC 2007. LNCS, vol. 4740, pp. 171–181. Springer, Heidelberg (2007)
6. Milgram, P., Kishino, F.: A taxonomy of mixed reality visual displays. Transactions on Information and Systems 77(12), 1321–1329 (1994)
7. Ogren, I.: On the principles for model-based systems engineering. Systems Engineering 3, 38–49 (2000)
8. Ramadge, P.J., Wonham, W.M.: Supervisory control of a class of discrete-event processes. SIAM Journal on Control and Optimization 25(1), 206–230 (1987)
9. Rauterberg, M.: From personal to cultural computing: how to assess a cultural experience. uDayIV–Information nutzbar machen, 13–21 (2006)

A Technique to Improve Freehand Sketches of Multi-touch Interactions

Gil Barros, Leandro Velloso, and Luis Carli

FAU-USP: Faculty of Architecture and Urbanism, University of São Paulo
Rua do Lago, 876 - 05508.080 - São Paulo - SP - Brazil
{gil.barros,leandrovelloso}@usp.br, info@luiscarli.com

Abstract. Sketching is a core activity in design, but sketching practices in interaction design are sometimes insufficient, especially in the case of freehand sketching. In this article we indicate how a technique developed originally for the WIMP paradigm was extended to include multi-touch interfaces. We describe the technique, provide examples and show some future directions.

Keywords: Sketching, multi-touch, freehand, technique, ActionSketch.

1 Introduction

Sketching is a core activity in design [8] with great importance during early stages of the design process [11]. It is a well-established practice in many areas of design but is still in its infancy in the field of interaction design [5]. The field poses particular challenges for sketching and so current sketching practices are sometimes insufficient [5].

Several studies address this issue [7], but we focused on a particular approach: sketches as freehand drawings on paper. A review of the literature shows that it is still unexplored, despite being usually adopted and fostered as good practice [6, 10].

In previous works we proposed a technique to improve the process of sketching for interaction design [4]. The technique was designed for the WIMP paradigm (Windows, Icons, Menus, Pointer) and focused on rich interactions. We found that the technique improved the representation of the interaction on sketches and had positive effects in terms of the cognitive process of the designers and in the communication between professionals.

In this article we propose an extension to the technique to encompass its use for multi-touch interfaces, focusing particularly on tablets and smartphones.

2 Extending the Technique

Our first step was to understand the specific needs for the touchscreen environment. We analyzed the underlying technology by looking at available APIs for

J.C. Anacleto et al. (Eds.): ICEC 2013, LNCS 8215, pp. 151–155, 2013.

touchscreen [2, 3] as well as articles which proposed new forms of multi-touch interfaces [1, 12].

Based on the particularities found on this material, such as new events and parameters, we selected several multi-touch interactions, mostly from native applications of the iOS system, such as Safari, Mail, Weather and Springboard (Home Screen).

We then used our technique to represent these interactions, in order to compare our technique with the needs of multi-touch interfaces and to verify how it should be changed. From this comparison we found that the technique only needed minor extensions to be used with multi-touch interfaces. We now present the extended version of the technique, indicating the changes made in this version.

3   The Technique: Frames, Colors, Symbols and Rules

Frames are used to represent the interaction happening over time, arranged as a storyboard. This is a common practice in interaction design [5] and we found it to be the suitable for our technique.

Colors are applied to represent steps of the interaction. Each frame can have up to three steps: initial state, user actions and system actions. In order to indicate these steps in the same frame we use colors to separate them, following this association: initial state in black; user actions in green; system actions in orange.

Symbols are defined to represent basic user actions and responses from the system. The WIMP version of the technique has 12 symbols to represent operations that the user can do with a pointing device and a keyboard. Four for mouse clicks: click, dou-ble click, mouse down and mouse up. Four for mouse movements: mouse over, mouse out, mouse move and scroll. And four for actions on the keyboard: key click, key down and key up and typing.

The only part of the technique that needed to be extended was the symbols for user actions. This extension was done in three ways, shown on the three columns of Figure 1 and described on the following paragraph.

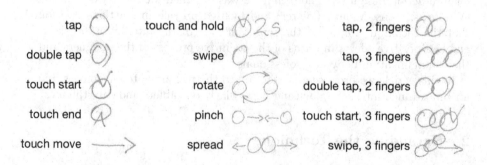

Fig. 1. Symbols for user actions on the extended version of the technique

On the first column we have five symbols using icons that already existed on the previous version. We only changed their names to match the terminology used in multi-touch. *Click* became tap; *double click* became *double tap*; *mouse down* became *touch start*; *mouse up* became *touch end*; and *mouse move* became *touch move.*

On the second column we have five symbols for new actions for multi-touch inter-faces: *touch and hold, swipe, rotate, pinch* and *spread.* On the *touch and hold* symbol, the "2s" to the right of the touch indicates the duration of the touch, two seconds in this case.

On the third column we have multi-touch versions of the basic symbols. We indi-cate each touch (a point of contact) with a circle, so *taps* with two and three touches use two and three circles respectively (first two examples). We also combine the number of circles with the other symbols; for example, a *double tap* with two touches combines the *double tap* symbol with two circles (third example). The last two exam-ples demonstrate how to represent *touch* start and *swipe* with three touches.

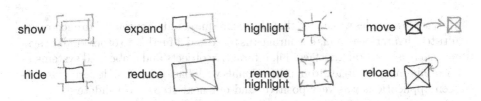

Fig. 2. Symbols for system actions, same for WIMP and multi-touch versions of the technique

Symbols for system actions didn't require any changes. Figure 2 presents the eight symbols that represent actions that the system can produce on elements presented on the screen: *show, hide, expand, reduce, highlight, remove highlight, move* and *reload.*

Three rules are the last part of our technique. 1) Draw *only what changes* between frames. 2) On each storyboard stay focused on *just one task.* 3) The goal is to express an idea, *employ the technique when useful and modify it as needed.*

We now provide two examples of the technique being used to describe multi-touch interactions. On the two frames to the left of Figure 3 we present an example of delet-ing a message from the Mail application of an iPhone. On the first frame the user swipes over a message and the system shows a delete button. On the second frame the user taps the button and the system removes the deleted message, moving up the following messages.

On two frames to the right of Figure 3 the user selects a word on an email message, again on the Mail application of an iPhone. On the first frame the user touches and holds the touch for two seconds and the system presents a contextual menu. On the second frame the user taps the "select" option and the system highlights the selected word.

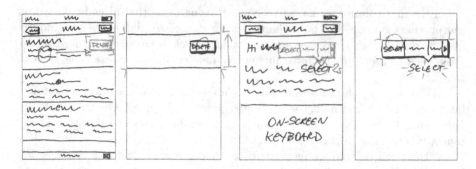

Fig. 3. Two frames on the left: representation of swipe gesture (first frame) followed by tap (second frame). Two frames on the right: representation of touch and hold (first frame) and tap actions (second frame).

4 Conclusions

From these examples we can see that the technique could be extended to encompass multi-touch interfaces. This encourages us to extend it further to other kinds of systems, such as gestural interfaces [9], interactive objects and embedded systems.

A preliminary feedback from professionals with background in designing touch-screen applications was very positive, and our next step is to validate it.

References

1. Agarawala, A., Balakrishnan, R.: Keepin' it real: pushing the desktop metaphor with physics, piles and the pen. In: Proceedings of the SIGCHI Conference on Human Factors in Computing Systems, pp. 1283–1292. ACM, New York (2006)
2. Apple Inc.: Cocoa Event Handling Guide. Apple Inc., Cupertino (2013)
3. Apple Inc.: Event Handling Guide for iOS. Apple Inc., Cupertino (2013)
4. Barros, G., Carneiro, G.: A technique to improve sketches of rich interactions. In: Proceedings of the 12th Brazilian Symposium on Human Factors in Computing Systems, IHC. Brazilian Computer Society, Manaus (In press) (forth-coming)
5. Buxton, B.: Sketching User Experiences: Getting the Design Right and the Right Design. Morgan Kaufmann, San Francisco (2007)
6. Cook, D.J., Bailey, B.P.: Designers' use of paper and the implications for informal tools. In: Proceedings of the 17th Australia conference on Computer-Human Interaction: Citizens Online: Considerations for Today and the Future, pp. 1–10. Computer-Human Interaction Special Interest Group (CHISIG) of Australia, Narrabundah (2005)
7. Johnson, G., et al.: Computational Support for Sketching in Design: A Review. Found Trends Hum-Comput Interact 2(1), 1–93 (2009)
8. Lawson, B.: How designers think: the design process demystified. Architectural Press, Oxford (2005)

9. Saffer, D.: Designing gestural interfaces. O'Reilly, Beijing (2009)

10. Stolterman, E., et al.: Designerly Tools. Undisciplined? Design Research Society Conference 2008 (2009)

11. Verstijnen, I., et al.: Sketching and creative discovery. Des. Stud. 19(4), 519–546 (1998)

12. Wobbrock, J.O., et al.: User-defined gestures for surface computing. In: Proceedings of the SIGCHI Conference on Human Factors in Computing Systems, pp. 1083–1092. ACM, New York (2009)

An Artificial Emotional Agent-Based Architecture for Games Simulation

Rainier Sales, Esteban Clua, Daniel de Oliveira, and Aline Paes

Universidade Federal Fluminense, Brazil
{rsales,esteban,danielcmo,alinepaes}@ic.uff.br

Abstract. Emotions are fundamental in in any person's life, and would be no different in games. While games are based at the gameplay for achieving the necessary fun factor, emotive elements are becoming common and in some cases even necessary. In some computing entertainment based systems, including and bringing emotional aspects from the real world may aspects of reality, turning the virtual characters more believable. This poster proposes a novel architecture for supporting Non-player character (NPC) behavior modeling, enhancing emotive agents. Personality, mood and emotive features are determined to the agents, based on well-established models developed in psychology. We validate our system in simulation games.

Keywords: Emotional Agents, Digital Games, Artificial Intelligence, NPC.

1 Introduction

Digital games are often considered closed systems, in the sense that there is no direct communication with the outside world events. Usually, they are only updated by the developers, either to improve playability or to fix bugs. However, the game may be-come more attractive to the player if real world events capable to interfere in the game are captured. The objective of this research is the creation of affective agents, also called emotional agents, and its inclusion at the gaming environment. The use of such agents in NPC follows the idea of the convenience for interpreting external events and bringing them inside the game. This research contributes with a novel architecture that aims to model NPC emotions and feelings more similar to the real humans. To achieve that, NPC in the game are mapped to artificial emotion-based agents, built from personality, emotion and mood models, previously developed in psychology science. In this sense, emotion is recognized as a central element of human behavior, and we intend to simulate within the game real situations regarding the game's domain.

2 Representation and Modeling of Psychological Aspects with Emotional Agents

The representation of real psychological aspects of characters in games is an essential part of this research. In this section we present the models of psychology

J.C. Anacleto et al. (Eds.): ICEC 2013, LNCS 8215, pp. 156–159, 2013.

that we will adopt in our architecture. The characters will be built based on four models that can communicate in an acceptable manner, namely: Personality model, emotion model, mood model and response model. Games traditionally implements agent events as game triggers that executes some kind of specific action. Our proposal intends to capture and compute events or inputs from the external world, in order to increase human aspects, such as personality, mood, emotion and response.

2.1   Models: Personality, Emotion, Mood and Response

The psychology model chosen for modeling the personality of the artificial agent in the proposed architecture is known as the Big Five model, taken from [1]. This is the model commonly used in recent research to describe personality of individuals ac-cording to a number of defined features.

Emotion is recognized as a central feature of human behavior. Because of that, it has been extensively studied in various areas of knowledge such as Psychology, Neu-roscience, Philosophy and Artificial Intelligence. In [2] emotions in the theory of evaluation are defined as the evaluation process, where events are classified and their emotional intensity is determined by the goals, beliefs, attitudes and risk of the person or agent. In the search for a suitable model for this process, we have chosen for this research the model of Cognitive Ortony, Clore and Collins (OCC), due to its simplicity of implementation in logic programming.

Mood and emotion are different in terms of intensity and duration [3]: mood dif-fers from emotion in the sense that are considered more durable and result from small events or stimuli generated from emotions. Because of that, besides mapping the basic personality and emotions of the artificial agent, it is also necessary to consider features based on its mood. Traditionally, the mood is represented in a one-dimensional scale, where the extremes are "good" and "bad" [4]. In order to describe and assess mood states, we used the PAD model (Pleasure, Arousal and Dominance) [5].

In our model, the agent will respond to some event that is linked to the three states of mood reactions described in the PAD model [6]. Such an answer defines the final behavior of the agent and is obtained directly from the eight possible combinations of mood, which in turn are related to the personality and emotional model of the agent. We resort to logical reasoning to conclude that the agent responds to an event in the game. When modeling human behavior to an artificial agent, personali-ty/emotional/mood features are not usually only totally true or false. They rather admit intermediate values between true and false. The fuzzy logic enables the capturing of vague information, commonly present in the natural language, in order to convert the results arising from the PAD model to a numeric value. For this research we define the Fuzzy Logic as a tool capable of capturing vague information, generally described in a natural language, as the results obtained in the model of mood PAD, mapping them to a numeric value, capable to be computationally manipulated.

3   Model Simulation

This topic aims to present a simple simulation to test the applicability of the use of agents in games and emotional changes possible. It is believed that the theory and practice based here can add much in the way the players understand and play current games.

With the goal of presenting results, we developed a simple simulation, initially, it is necessary to introduce values in the five basic guidelines personality parameters. Then, from the personality, the simulator computes in real time which is the base mood of the agent. With the baseline mood set, the simulator calculates the current emotion of the agent. An emotion will be assigned only when this is greater than the minimum intensity perception. A particular action will be relevant to the agent when it has an associated emotion. When an event is perceived by the agent, we have to change its current emotion parameters. In this way, the emotion value assigned to the agent is no longer derived from the personality and base mood, but it also takes into account the external events.

There are several games that can make use of the architecture proposed here, among these we can highlight PES 2013^{TM}, NBA2K13^{TM}, UFC UNDISPUTED 3^{TM}, NHL 13 ^{TM}, where the events represented internally to the game are the same hap-pened in the real world. In order to show the applicability of the architecture present-ed in this poster, we introduce a simulation of the game FIFA 13^{TM}, where we used the original data of the same. In the database of FIFA 13 game each player has a specific configuration based on the performance of the real world, which is going to be the way in which the performance intensity alters the actions of the player. This example has simple configurations for results, initially the system searches for the values in the database to display the information agent. By modifying the performance intensity of the agent from the entrance of an event, we are going to have a different value related to attribute penalties. To validate the results we used as basis the test presented below.

[**Test 1**]: "A Positive input event maximizes positive outputs response". In this case, a positive emotion maximizes the positive results. We considered the average results for each attribute in 100 tests for each of the 11 positive emotions, generating a total of 1100 tests to check this test. As results presented, all positive events produced positive results, changing to greater than half of the original value.

[**Test 2**]: "A Negative input event maximizes negative outputs response". In this case, a negative emotion maximizes the negative results, the average results for each attribute in 100 tests for each of the 11 negative emotions, generating a total of 1100 tests to check this test. As results presented, all negative results changed to less than half the original value.

[**Test 3**]: "Positive input events intensity generates different results of different intensity, respecting the test 1". To check this test will make use of the attribute performance minimum intensity equal to 0.5. As the logic applied is the same in all emotions we chose emotion Admiration for example. The results obtained from 100 tests were conducted for each of the three intensities using emotion generating a total of 300 tests. As the results show, higher intensities tend to positive results and to the maximum value of default agent value. For lower values of intensity, but above the minimum value, intensity measure will have more distant performance of the maxi-mum value of the agent.

[Test 4]: "Entries intensity of negative events generates different results of different intensity, respecting the test 2". To check this test will make the use of attribute performance minimum intensity equal to 0.5. As the logic applied is the same in all emotions we chose emotion Anger for example. The results were obtained from 100 tests, conducted for each of the three intensities adopted in the emotion, yielding a total of 300 tests. As the results show, higher intensities have larger negative results, tending in the opposite direction to the default value. For lower values of intensity, but above the minimum value intensity, values indicate performance measures farther from the opposite value of default agent value.

4   Conclusion

Currently the globalized world has made information available quickly and in many cases free, the information of an agent as a real football player, basketball or cricket are quickly available in different media, especially the Internet. The approach of this poster believes that this fatality of the contemporary world is favorable towards add-ing veracity to the games. The approach adopted here goes further, seeking not only to insert changes of the external environment, but work internally as the consequences of external world internally modifying the game. We believe that the proposal presented here may make games more fun for the player, since it event outside the game will have a direct impact on the performance of NPC, increasing the degree of reality between the game and the world of the player. Is important to note that the topics discussed here are part of an ongoing research and so the approach was only to evaluate and test the proposed structure, this new mechanism with the insertion of personality mood and emotion can generate emotional NPC.

References

1. Gazzaniga, Heatherton, Michael, S., Todd, F.: Psychological Science: Mind, Brain and Behavior. Artmed, Porto Alegre (2005)
2. Strongman, Kenneth, T.: The Psychology of Emotion. John Wiley and Sons, Chichester (2003)
3. Vinayagamoorthy, Vinoba, Gillies, M., Steed, A., Tanguy, E., Pan, X., Loscos, C., Slater, E.M., et al.: Building expressions into virtual caracteres. In: Eurographics Conference State of the Art Reports, Vienna (2006)
4. Picard, Rosalind: Affective Computing. MIT Press, Boston (1997)
5. Mehrabian, Albert: Pleasure-arousal-dominance: A general framework for describing and measuring individual differences in temperament. Current Psychology (1995)
6. Leite, F.N.H.F.: Impact of emotional experiences in customer satisfaction: A study in medical offices. Universidade Federal de Fortaleza, Fortaleza - CE (2006)

An Enriched Artifacts Activity
for Supporting Creative Learning:
Perspectives for Children with Impairments

Michail N. Giannakos and Letizia Jaccheri

Norwegian University of Science and Technology (NTNU), Trondheim, Norway
{michailg,letizia}@idi.ntnu.no

Abstract. In this paper we present the results of a creative development pro-gram for young students with the name, OurToys. In our empirical evaluation, a group of researchers and artists designed and implemented two workshop pro-grams of a total of 66 pupils, exploring their experiences with open source software and hardware. The workshops were based on Reggio Emilia philoso-phy of creative reuse and the open-source software Scratch. The results showed that: software and hardware intensive activities raise awareness of technology, intensify the experience, and invite students to explore boundaries and increase collaboration and the exchange of views and ideas.

Keywords: Creative activities, empirical evaluation, software and hardware development, physicaldigital creativity.

1 Introduction

Digital artifacts that enable people to exchange, create, and distribute information have, in the past couple of decades, profoundly reshaped the way we work and live [1] [4]. Artifacts allow children to learn by iteratively testing and rebuilding their designs [2]. The interactions between the children and the artifacts in a creative activi-ty are vital [5]. A better understanding of several aspects from childrens perspective could be valuable in designing effective creative activities. The purpose of the re-search presented in this paper is to build an understanding of the main interactions between children and the tools in creative activities and to consider improvements on the current processes. The clarification of this goal is expected to contribute to the understanding of how children face these activities and might increase their willing-ness to enroll in them.

This paper focuses on our efforts to develop an authentic environment for creative learninga workshop program (called OurToys[1]) that helps school children, to build their own digital game/story based on physical objects. We believe Our-Toys repre-sents a good example of novel directions in the creative learning. In particular, in this paper we present experiences from designing and conducting

---

[1] http://ourtoysntnu.wordpress.com/

J.C. Anacleto et al. (Eds.): ICEC 2013, LNCS 8215, pp. 160–163, 2013.

the workshop program where children collaboratively engaged in creating interactive artworks that react to events in the physical world [6]. Children used the open source software Scratch, Arduino sensors, and recycled materials.

2   OurToys: An Approach to Enhance Creative Learning

In our approach, we designed and developed a workshop program with the name: OurToys. OurToys was based on open source software and hardware and consisted of tutorials on open source tools, artifacts enriched creative sessions and students demonstrations/presentations. Up to date, OurToys has organized five workshops (Figure 1, top left). The number of children who participated on each workshop was among 10 to 15 (Figure 1, top left). Most of the children who participated in the pro-ject were 12 years old (except the last one), and on each workshop we had groups (comprised of 2-4 children).

Fig. 1. The list of our field studies (top left); examples of children's responses

OurToys took place at creative centers of University and ReMida center, ReMida is a center that collects and offers a variety of materials for use in creative and educa-tional projects. The center is a cooperation between the municipality, the education project Reggio Children, the municipal waste company (recycling) and the local busi-ness community. Students worked according to Reggio Emilia education principles [3], where the main idea is that the initiative for creative actions should spring from the child himself/herself and the child takes different kinds of leadership roles at dif-ferent times. ReMida centers are creative places with a lot of appealing objects where children start to work without being activated by adults (Figure 2, left). The adults act as assistants.

Children attending the workshops were instructed and assisted by programming artist, the leader of the ReMida center, and 5 HCI researchers. During the whole workshop at least three members from them were present. Children use Scratch (S4A[2]) software and Arduino boards to animate the physical characters

---

[2] http://seaside.citilab.eu/scratch/arduino

Fig. 2. Left, The physical part of the activity on ReMida Center. Middle, Children connecting the physical with the digital. Right, An example of interactive artworks (installations).

middle). The children completed and published in total six interactive works and eleven installations (see example, Figure 2 right) based on the software/hardware and the recycling materials of the center. Record of the childrens activities was kept through photographs, surveys, interviews and observation reports and used as data in this research.

3   Preliminary Findings

As aforementioned, a wide range of data was collected to address our research. In the data collection, a semi-structured interview guide was used in the personal in-depth interviews with the children. Interview questions were designed to probe different aspects of motivation and creativity. After the childrens interviews were collected (see examples of children's responses in Figure 1), we proceeded with a content anal-ysis. The content analysis procedures led us to several conclusions about the creative activities. Specifically, we can say that the creative development activities:

a) Raise **awareness** for technology,
b) Make the **experience** more intense,
c) Invite children to **explore** boundaries,
d) Increase **collaboration** and the exchange of views and ideas.

In addition to the qualitative study, a survey based on important aspects (con-structs) identified on the literature was implemented. Participants took the survey two days after the workshop, evaluating the following measures: Intention to Participate, Enjoyment, Satisfaction, Usefulness and Easiness. The level of enjoyment (6.29/7) and satisfaction (5.80/7) are high. The level of usefulness (5.42/7) and easiness (5. 53/7) are slightly lower. The participants intentions to participate in similar activities (4.26/7) are not in at such a high level. In general we can conclude that childrens attitudes were very positive, but there is space for improving several aspects, like increasing their intention to participate.

4   Discussion and Conclusion

In this paper we presented the results from the design, deployment and evaluation of OurToys program. Children engaged in programming languages (i.e., Scratch) and programmable hardware platforms (i.e., Arduino), which enabled them to engage in the world of creativity with digital enriched artifacts, like robots and interactive instal-lations.

The early results of our study showed that creative activities have certain and di-verse benefits to offer and improve childrens learning. In addition, children face these activities with positive attitude and great interest. However, several areas for improvement in the design and implementation of these activities exist.

The multiplicity of viewpoints the data yielded were useful as those provided in-sight and depth in the children's experiences, perspectives and opinions, and strength-ened this mixed method research. As creative activities are now widely used, an in-depth understanding of these activities in diverse and multiple settings has become a necessity.

We are in the process of extending our program to explore how programming in-tensive creative activities can offer benefits to children with impairments. Our hy-pothesis that will guide these future studies is that computing and creativity which are "extra languages" are even more important for people with communication impair-ments, like visual and hearing impairments. In view of the above we will take the advantage of (e.g., sign language) and introduce children with impairments into the world of the creative development via computing. In particular, our future work aims to produce a set of guidelines for how to customize digital creative technology for children with impairments.

Acknowledgements. The authors would like to thank the participants, P. Byesen, A. Eriksen I. Leftheriotis & R. Proto. The project has been recommended by the Data Protection Official for Research, Norwegian Social Science Data Services.

References

1. Buechley, L., Eisenberg, M., Catchen, J., Crockett, A.: The LilyPad Arduino: Using Computational Textiles to Investigate Engagement, Aesthetics, and Diversity in Computer Science Education. In: Proc. CHI 2008, pp. 423–432. ACM Press (2008)
2. Cassell, J.: Towards a Model of Technology and Literacy Development: Story Listening Systems. Journal of Applied Developmental Psychology 25(1), 75–105 (2004)
3. Edwards, C., Gandini, L., Foreman, G.: The hundred languages of children: the Reggio Emilia approach to early childhood education, 2nd edn. Ablex Publishing, NJ (1998)
4. Jaccheri, L., Giannakos, M.N.: Open source software for entertainment. In: Herrlich, M., Malaka, R., Masuch, M. (eds.) ICEC 2012. LNCS, vol. 7522, pp. 604–607. Springer, Heidelberg (2012)
5. Papert, S.: Mindstorms: Children, Computers, and Powerful Ideas. Basic Books, New York (1980)
6. Price, S., Rogers, Y.: Lets get physical: the learning benefits of interacting in digitally-augmented physical spaces. Computers & Education 15(2), 169–185 (2004)

Automatic Emotional Reactions Identification:
A Software Tool for Offline User Experience Research

Pedro A. Nogueira[1], Vasco Torres[2], and Rui Rodrigues[2]

[1] LIACC – Artificial Intelligence and Computer Science Lab., University of Porto, Portugal
[2] INESC TEC and Faculty of Engineering, University of Porto, Portugal
{pedro.alves.nogueira,rui.rodrigues}@fe.up.pt,
vascoptorres@gmail.com

Abstract. Current affective response studies lack dedicated data analysis procedures and tools for automatically annotating and triangulating emotional reactions to game-related events. The development of such a tool would potentially allow for both a deeper and more objective analysis of the emotional impact of digital media stimuli on players, as well as towards the rapid implementation of this type of studies. In this paper we describe the development of such a tool that enables researchers to conduct objective *a posteriori* analyses, without disturbing the gameplay experience, while also automating the annotation and emotional response identification process. The tool was designed in a data-independent fashion and allows the identified responses to be exported for further analysis in third-party statistical software applications.

Keywords: Player modelling, digital media, emotional reaction identification.

1 Introduction

User experience research studies generate large amounts of data that are *a)* difficult to manually analyse and *b)* require expert personnel to interpret. Furthermore, although there is some work on using biometric data for game research, there is no standard for automatic analysis or interpretation of this data [1, 2]. Therefore, there is a current need of tools capable of automatic psychophysiological data classification and emotional reaction identification. To address this issue we have developed a tool for the automated analysis of psychophysiological-measured emotional reactions to in-game stimuli. The developed tool allows game researchers to import and synchronise gameplay session videos with their corresponding psychophysiological readings [3]. Using the recorded gameplay videos allows players and game researchers to revisit past game events, thus eliminating the need for in-game interruptions. Also, using the emotional classification signal, the system is then able to automatically isolate the emotional responses to each annotated event via a two-dimensional peak detection algorithm. Throughout this paper we succinctly describe the developed tool, as well as report on its accuracy in detecting emotional responses.

J.C. Anacleto et al. (Eds.): ICEC 2013, LNCS 8215, pp. 164–167, 2013.
© IFIP International Federation for Information Processing 2013

2   Developed Tool

2.1   Requirement Analysis

Prior to starting the tool's development we held a small focus group with psychology researchers, which led to the following system requirements:

1) Provide an easily interpretable measure of the volunteer's emotional state
2) Provide a real-time and synchronised view of the volunteer's gaming session from both an audio-visual and psychophysiological perspective
3) Allow free manipulation of the experiment's rate of time passage
4) Allow for a simple and straightforward annotation of relevant events, with as few clicks and parameter selection as possible
5) Present time markers for each of the annotated events, as well as the ability to quickly cycle through and edit them
6) Allow for subjective data to be included for each event, if necessary
7) Automatically compute which events triggered emotional reactions
8) Incorporate a save/load feature for resuming the annotation process in relatively large data collections and posterior analysis/verification.

2.2   Tool Development

Given the modular nature of our framework, we choose to divide it into various independent components, so that any future additions or changes could be performed in an expeditious manner. These components are described in the following paragraphs.

Emotion Recognition Module (ERM)
The first step in the annotation process is determining a simplified, although relevant to our needs, image of the user's current emotional state (*ES*). Following requisite 1, we adopted one of the most popular dimensional (i.e. quantifiable) interpretations of emotions – Russell's Arousal and Valence dimensional theory [4].

ERM uses a two-layered system based on four distinct physiological sensor inputs (skin conductance, heart rate and facial electromyography at the cheek and brow muscles). The first classification layer uses several regression models to normalize each of the sensor inputs both across participants and experimental conditions, while also correlating each one to either Arousal or Valence. The second classification layer then employs a residual sum of squares (RSS) weighting scheme to merge the computed regression outputs into one optimal Arousal/Valence prediction (see Fig. 1) [3].

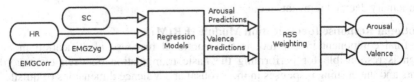

Fig. 1. High-level overview of the employed emotional classification system [3]

Details on how the method was designed, developed and validated can be found elsewhere [3]. The current paper only presents a high-level overview of the system as a part of the whole emotional reaction annotation process. Using this methodology, the authors have achieved convincing accuracy ratings – 85% for Arousal and 78% for Valence –, while at the same time successfully predicting these states in a continuous manner and without requiring lengthy calibration or parameter tuning procedures. Given these properties we deemed the method appropriate for our needs and incorporated it in the designed tool.

Event Annotation Module (EAM)

Since a considerable percentage of our requisites (55%) were related with how to visualise and annotate the recorded material, we devoted a great deal of attention to the development of this module. To fulfil requirements 1 and 2, we decided to combine a custom video player with a time series graph drawing library (ZedGraph). Timestamps were logged for both the gameplay videos and the physiological data, which were then used to synchronise the emotional classification and gameplay video streams. The video player component was designed to allow the user to quickly skip through the video using a simple slider or to accelerate the video through a fast-forward and backwards button (requisite 3).

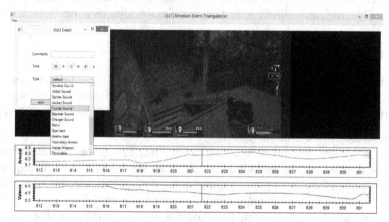

Fig. 2. The add event window, super-imposed on the developed tool

Regarding the event annotation process itself (requisites 4-5), we decided to limit the user input to the barest essentials in both terms of actions and input required. To insert a new event, the user needs only to perform a right-click on the video player window or right-click on the emotional classification time plot and choose "Add new event" (see Fig. 2). This will add a new event at the current time and bring forth a pop-up form where the user can choose which event took place and any subjective commentary deemed relevant (requisite 6).

Emotional Response Identification Module (ERIM)

The final component in our tool is the emotional response identification module, which is responsible for performing the basic triangulation between the recorded events and the ensuing responses in the Arousal and Valence dimensions (requisite 7). The triangulation process was automated by developing a simple local peak detection algorithm. Let $c=[c_1,c_2,...,c_n]$ be the continuous, uniformly sampled emotional state classification signal for a dimension of the AV space. Furthermore, consider the signal to be smoothed using the unimodal kernel with compact connected support and unit action $w\Upsilon(t) \geq 0$, and $\Upsilon > 0$ bandwidth parameter through the following process:

$$c_\gamma(t) = w_\gamma(t) * c(t) = \int_{-\infty}^{\infty} w_\gamma(t-s)y(s)\, ds$$

The peak detection process occurs in parallel for both dimensions and is contained in a standalone iteration for each event e_i, within a time region $\Omega = [max(T(e_{i-1}),T(e_i)-\alpha, min(T(e_i)+\beta, T(e_{i+1}))]$, where T is the mapping function between an event and its corresponding timestamp. Moreover, both α and β are parameterisable event horizon variables (in this paper $\alpha=2$ and $\beta=10$, as determined by an empirical analysis of the available data). For each iteration of the peak detection process, the smoothed signal $c\Upsilon(t)$ is taken and the maximal peak $|p|$ is extracted from a set of candidate peaks $\tilde{P}$:

$$\tilde{P} = \left\{ t \in \Omega : \dot{c}_\gamma(t) = \frac{dc_\gamma(t)}{dt} = 0, |c_\gamma(t) - c_\gamma(T(e_i))| \geq \varphi \right\}$$

Where φ is a minimum absolute local variability threshold, $\varphi = (\mu_{e_i} + 2\sigma_{e_i})$, such that μ_{e_i} and σ_{e_i} denote the mean and standard deviation values of the considered AV dimension in the processed event's time region. A light validation of the proposed algorithm using a total of 210 gameplay-related events randomly sampled from all the participants revealed that the algorithm was able to identify local maxima and minima with an approximate success rate of ~93%. Although further validation is required, this seems to hint that our approach is adequate for our described needs. In future work we will present a larger validation of the algorithm and more in-depth description of the system's interface.

3   Conclusions

Current UX research methods are unable to perform in-game evaluations without disrupting – and thus potentially contaminating – the gameplay experience. Moreover, emotional state classification methods are difficult to integrate in these studies due to their complex development nature and technical skillset. The methodology presented in this paper has the potential to contribute to a wider accessibility of emotional response studies by, not only easing the aforementioned issues, but also by removing the necessity of developing standalone emotional state detection systems – which in itself contributes to a standardisation and comparability of the annotation process.

References

1. Matias Kivikangas, J., Nacke, L., Ravaja, N.: Developing a triangulation system for digital game events, observational video, and psychophysiological data to study emotional responses to a virtual character. Entertainment Computing 2, 11–16 (2011)
2. Mirza-babaei, P., Nacke, L.E., Fitzpatrick, G., White, G., Mcallister, G., Collins, N.: Biometric Storyboards: Visualising Game User Research Data. In: CHI 2012 Extended Abstracts on Human Factors in Computing Systems, pp. 2315–2320 (2012)
3. Nogueira, P.A., Rodrigues, R., Oliveira, E.: Real-Time Psychophysiological Emotional State Estimation in Digital Gameplay Scenarios. In: 14th Conference on Engineering Applications of Neural Networks (EANN) (to appear)
4. Russel, J.A.: A Circumplex Model of Affect. Journal of Personality and Social Psychology 39, 1161–1178 (1980)

Evaluating Paper Prototype for Tabletop Collaborative Game Applications

Marylia Gutierrez, Maurício Cirelli, Ricardo Nakamura, and Lucia Filgueiras

Escola Politécnica da Universidade de São Paulo, São Paulo, Brazil

Abstract. Identifying the natural gestures for a tabletop application is one of the most challenging tasks developers must accomplish in order to achieve a good system user interface. This problem is even more difficult in a collaborative environment. Cooperative Gestures allow richer interaction and must be evaluated when designing a new multi-user tabletop interface. In this paper we present the use of paper prototyping to analyze user interaction on a tabletop collaborative game application. Our results show that it is possible to extract natural gestures for an application using this technique, regardless of some limitations.

Keywords: Paper prototyping, game design, tabletop interfaces, test.

1 Introduction

The success of a digital game depends on several factors including technology, development process, risk management and marketing. Central among them is the design of the experience the game brings to players, which includes the game's interaction design.

For this reason, game development projects often include a pre-production phase that involves the creation of prototypes. Paper prototyping is a technique used to design and evaluate user interfaces. Its appeal comes from the flexibility, ease of changing the prototype and testing different scenarios. The simplicity makes users feel comfortable criticizing the system and besides being a low-fidelity prototype it leads to almost the same quantity and quality of critical user statements.

Multitouch interfaces allow cooperative gestures, which are single and combined commands executed from interactions made by more than one user [9]. One important concept when dealing with multitouch interfaces is the idea of groupware, which combines hardware and software to assist group interaction [10].

It is necessary to define an adequate set of gestures for the interface. Experiments such as the one by Hinrichs and Carpendale [1] show that gestures are not free of context, depending on the antecedent and subsequent gestures, as well as on the social context (e.g., user's age, sex). In the case of developing engaging games, there are several guidelines [2], but they do not explicitly take into account the special needs of every type of users. Tabletop multitouch interfaces allow the exploration of different types of applications [3,4]. Games are

J.C. Anacleto et al. (Eds.): ICEC 2013, LNCS 8215, pp. 168–171, 2013.

suitable for experimenting with interface design methods because of the freedom in designing the tasks involved in their operation.

In this paper we present a experimental method and the results achieved testing on a common role-playing game (RPG) designed to be used with tabletop multitouch devices. We also discuss the feasibility of paper prototyping for the task of determining a set of most adequate gestures for multitouch-based digital games.

1.1   Related Work

In [6] we see two prototypes for a farm game tested with children which, after successive iterations, evolved into a product. Since the users were playing the game just for the fun, unexpected gestures were discovered.

Some insights regarding user behavior towards gesture definition can be found in [7]. The study indicates that users rarely care about the number of fingers they employ, that one hand is preferred to two, among other results.

Other studies have shown that there are not significant differences between low fidelity and high fidelity prototypes. The choice of prototyping technique should be based on the group's composition and the desired focus [8].

2   Paper Prototype

Our prototype was tested using a RPG game. To create this game all the gestures for the activities needed to be chosen, which is not trivial, since it is not possible to know which gestures are the most natural and intuitive for the players. The paper prototype was developed to help in this task.

Another advantage of this early prototype is that some usability issues could be found and fixed before the development started. At last, after defining which gestures should be used, the gesture recognition system could be developed.

There are different types of prototypes, but in this case we needed a simple one that could represent the game satisfactorily. A paper prototype is simple to make and can be employed to analyze how the application is used.

In this prototype, an ordinary table was used with delimitations representing the screen; characters and life points were made out of paper as well. Cards representing the action areas were also created in paper so that the players could know the exact space which the skills could be performed. The prototype was then tested with four users and the results are presented in the next section. Before the test, the game was explained to the players, but none of the gestures were defined, leaving the players free to choose them.

3   Results

Different actions caused different reactions from the players. Gestures for movement were made naturally, which means the players did them intuitively, by dragging the characters to the place they wanted them to go. This gesture was made exactly the same way by all players. The simple attack/healing action was performed with small differences.

The special skills gestures required more thinking and discussion. When the gesture was individual, the player would stop for a while to think how to represent it and sometimes consult the other players. For collaborative gestures, there was always a time of discussion, where the players suggested gestures and voted to select one; sometimes the decision was no unanimous, which resulted in different gestures for the same action [1] .

For the special skills, their names had a huge influence on the resulting gesture since the players were always trying to find gestures that would symbolize it. Therefore, if the exact same test was repeated with the same users but using different names for the special skills the resulting gestures could be totally different. Figure 1 shows the move gestures.

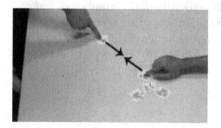 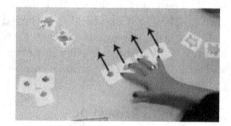

Fig. 1. Movement gestures

Despite being a successful approach in selecting gestures for actions, we have identified some limitations for tabletop applications design. The prototype was very similar to the final tabletop application, helping the players to imagine the game was real, but since it was not a real-time game, the speed and dynamics were compromised, creating a match that lasted far longer than on the real application.

In a real tabletop application, when the user touches the table, the targeted object is not necessarily going to move, but when we are working with paper, any touch would make the objects move and this inhibited the players. During the game players needed to make gestures that would not imply moving a character, and because they did not want to take the risk of moving them, the gestures were made above the "screen". This was a problem because sometimes the players made gestures in three dimensions, but our tabletop only works with 2D gestures. When this 3D gestures were made, the testers reminded the players that they were not acceptable gestures, making the players think even more on which gesture to do for the special skills, reducing the naturalness of some gestures.

4   Conclusion

Finding out which gestures are the most natural for an application is a challenging issue, and the paper prototype presented itself as one of the possible solutions to solve it. It has the ability to show some natural and intuitive gestures made by the players during the interaction.

The prototype helped not only at finding out these gestures, but also elements of the game that were missing or that were not clear to the players and other elements that were unnecessary. With the results of this test, changes could be made and the development of the could start, avoiding a series of changes during or in the end of the development, when the game goes through tests with the users.

Further user studies still need to be performed in order to evaluate the relationship between skill names, social context, user's age and gender and the gestures performed.

References

1. Hinrichs, U., Carpendale, E.S.: Gestures in the wild: studying multi-touch gesture sequences on interactive tabletop exhibits, New York, NY, USA, pp. 3023–3032 (2011)
2. Malone, T.W., Lepper, M.R.: Making learning fun: A taxonomy of intrinsic motivations for learning. In: Snow, R.E., Farr, M.J. (eds.) Aptitude Learning and Instruction: III Conative and Affective Process Analyses, vol. 3, pp. 223–253. Lawrence Erlbaum Associates, Hilsdale (1987)
3. Kim, Y.-M.: Interactive Communion Tabletop- Graduate School of Advanced Imaging Science, Multimedia, and Film, Chung-Ang University, 221 Huksuk-Dong, Dongjak-Ku, 156-756, Seoul, Korea
4. Mori, T., Hamana, K., Feng, C., Hoshino, J.: Narrative Entertainment System with Tabletop Interface- 1-1-#3M309, Tennodai 1-chome, Tsukuba-shi, Ibaraki, Japan
5. Bachl, S., Tomitsch, M., Wimmer, C., Grechenig, T.: Challenges for Designing the User Experience of Multi-touch Interfaces- 1 Research Group for Industrial Software (INSO), Vienna University of Technology, Austria; 2 Faculty of Architecture, Design and Planning, The University of Sydney, Australia
6. Marco, J., Baldassarri, S., Cerezo, E.: Bridging the Gap between Children and Tabletop Designers- Advanced Computer Graphics Group (GIGA) - Computer Science Department, Engineering Research Institute of Aragon (I3A) - University of Zaragoza, Spain
7. Wobbrock, J.O., Morris, M.R., Wilson, A.D.: User-Defined Gestures for Surface Computing - CHI 2009 Tabletop Gestures, Boston, MA, USA, April 7 (2009)
8. Johansson, M., Arvola, M.: A Case Study of How User Interface Sketches, Scenarios and Computer Prototypes Structure Stakeholder Meetings. In: Proceedings of HCI 2007 (2007)
9. Morris, M.R., Huang, A., Paepcke, A., Winograd, T.: Cooperative Gestures: Multi-User Gestural Interactions for Co-located Groupware. In: CHI 2006, Montréal, Québec, Canada, April 22-28 (2006)
10. Ellis, C., Wainer, J.: Groupware and Computer Supported Cooperative Work

Initial Perceptions of a Touch-Based Tablet Handwriting Serious Game

Chek Tien Tan, Junbin Huang, and Yusuf Pisan

Games Studio, University of Technology, Sydney
{chek,yusuf.pisan}@gamesstudio.org

Abstract. This paper aims to evaluate a handwriting serious game that makes use of popular modern touch-based tablets to preserve traditional handwriting practice. A first playable prototype was built and a pilot study performed on an initial group of twenty participants. Significantly positive results were observed in the perceptions of usefulness and also across all gameplay dimensions except for flow.

Keywords: Serious Games, Player Experience, Handwriting.

1 Introduction and Related Work

In today's developed countries, people mostly communicate via electronic means and the practice of physically writing on pen and paper is getting rare. In young children, the problem of not getting enough handwriting practice is even more severe [13]. However, even in this era of electronic communication dominance, handwriting still serves as an important cornerstone of basic language literacy. Individuals with clear and legible handwriting skills have been shown to have significantly better literacy skills [15].

Game-based learning is a mature domain that has demonstrated to be successful [14] but research in the area of handwriting games is however scarce. Maxim and Martineau [8] created a handwriting game for children on a tablet-PC and reported highly positive scores. However, the basis of their metrics was unclear and the description of their game mechanics did not portray a clear a level progression. They also mentioned that players are required to play mini-games in-between each handwriting task, which were possibly confounding variables that affected their results. The use of a hybrid tablet-PC meant for traditional keyboard and mouse inputs might not appeal to children as well.

In the related domain of handwriting rehabilitation, there is also some activity, though also minimal. Curtis et. al. [2] have created several mini-games for this purpose. However, it is targeted at patients with motor disorders with the goals of improving physical and mental health which are not the primary goals in this paper. Nevertheless, their qualitative evaluation have shown that all patients seemed to be motivated by the game premise and that direct feedback of their performance was an important feature of the system.

J.C. Anacleto et al. (Eds.): ICEC 2013, LNCS 8215, pp. 172–175, 2013.
© IFIP International Federation for Information Processing 2013

2   Penmanship Design and Evaluation

Motivated by the above reasons, we create and evaluate a touch-based tablet handwriting serious game called Penmanship. As a first playable prototype, the goal was to keep the game as minimal as possible to demonstrate handwriting as the core gameplay mechanic. Having only one core mechanic to allows for a clear and concise test of the initial research questions we have set out to answer so that we can clearly correlate the responses to just the handwriting mechanic. A screenshot of the game can be seen in Figure 1.

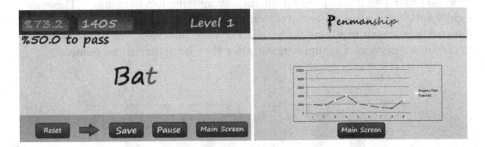

Fig. 1. Screenshots of the Penmanship game. The left picture shows the game state after a player tried to trace the word bat in a game level. Black lines indicate the player's trace and the red line represents the correct word template. Near the top left is a similarity percentage (updated in real-time so that player gets instant feedback) indicating the performance of the player in the current level, in terms of how well the trace matches the template. To the right of the percentage is a cumulative score for the player. The right picture shows the progress chart screen of the player's performance over time.

The game objective is simply to mimic word templates to reach a pre-set passing percentage in each level, in order to obtain as high a cumulative score as possible over time. Each successive level gets harder in terms of the word complexity, the similarity percentage required to conquer it, as well as the number of words required to clear a level. The gameplay premise was inspired by traditional handwriting tracing worksheets that we often see in the early years of education. The word templates were implemented based on the Segoe Print font, which closely resembles that of the New South Wales Foundation style handwriting[1] taught in all schools in New South Wales, Australia, where this research has taken place. Hence we hope to keep that traditional premise but with game elements added in the hopes of making it more engaging and fun.

As a pilot study, our goals were basically to find out initial perceptions on whether the game is useful for handwriting improvement and whether it provides a good gameplay experience even if it is a serious game. 20 participants (6 females) took part in the study with a mean age of 24 years ($SD = 2.14$). Penmanship was implemented in GameMaker Studio with the game compiled

---

[1] http://www.schoolfonts.com.au/Fonts_NSW.html

on a Motorola Xoom MZ604 Android tablet and participants played using a capacitive stylus.

Participants completed a user survey performed after they have played for 20 to 25 minutes. The survey is based on the iGEQ [6] with an additional "usefulness" dimension for us to evaluate the perceptions on whether the game is useful to improve handwriting. A two-tailed one-sample t-test was performed against the midpoint average of 2.5 for the likert scores. This was because we wanted to find out whether each mean score was significantly different from merely an "on the fence" opinion. All the mean scores were significantly different ($p < 0.05$) except for the items "I felt content", "I felt good", "I found it impressive" and "Did you find Penmanship useful for improving your handwriting?". These insignificant responses were removed and the summarised mean scores for each dimension is shown in Figure 2. An unstructured interview was also conducted to obtain suggestions for improvement after they have played the game.

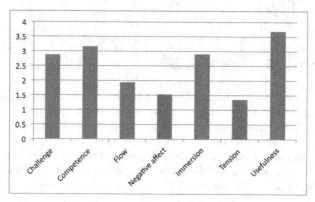

Fig. 2. Mean scores for each dimension in the survey. The y-axis represents the mean scores and the x-axis represents each dimension. Positive affect is absent as the mean scores for both its constituent questions were statistically insignificant. Blue bars indicate positively phrased questions (higher is better) whilst red bars indicate negatively phrased questions (lower is better).

3   Results and Conclusion

The results show much promise for just a first playable prototype of Penmanship with a single handwriting mechanic as the core gameplay. From the summarised mean scores (Figure 2), it can be seen that the dimensions challenge, competence, immersion and usefulness means were significantly higher than average. This shows that players did experience these important gameplay experiences even with the minimalistic prototype we have made with just a single handwriting mechanic. The negatively phrased dimensions negative affect and tension also had means significantly lower than average which shows that players were not dismissive of the game. It should also be highlighted that the usefulness dimension had the highest mean score which gives us confidence on the "serious" aspect of the game.

It can also be seen from Figure 2 that the flow dimension had a mean score that was significantly lower than average. Penmanship is built to be a casual game where players can stop and continue at anytime and hence is fundamentally different from highly immersive 3D games which focus more on providing a flow experience[1]. Moreover, this was a first prototype which did not have the full level progression dynamics that contains more varied game mechanics.

Abundant feedback was also provided during the interviews. Many participants suggested that more varied challenges should be incorporated at higher levels. Other comments were mainly to improve the visual and aural aspects of the game in order to improve player feedback.

The feedback provided highlights our main limitation, which is the maturity of the gameplay elements. Although most dimensions were positive, scores were mostly modestly above average. Hence more work needs to be done on improving the implementation the game resources, the challenge progression, as well as adding premise, story and characters. These are hence left as future work.

References

1. Csikszentmihalyi, M.: Flow: The Psychology of Optimal Experience. P. S. Series, vol. 54. Harper & Row (1990)
2. Curtis, J., Ruijs, L., de Vries, M.: Rehabilitation of handwriting skills in stroke patients using interactive games: A pilot study. In: CHI 2009 Extended Abstracts on Human Factors in Computing Systems, pp. 3931–3936 (2009)
3. Fullerton, T.: Game Design Workshop: A Playcentric Approach to Creating Innovative Games. Elsevier Morgan Kaufmann (2008)
4. Gee, J.P.: What video games have to teach us about learning and literacy. Computers in Entertainment 1(1), 20 (2003)
5. Graham, S.: Want to Improve Children's Writing? American Educator, 20–28 (2010)
6. IJsselsteijn, W.A., De Kort, Y.A.W., Poels, K.: The Game Experience Questionnaire: Development of a self-report measure to assess the psychological impact of digital games. Technical report, TU Eindhoven (2007)
7. Jeffries, S.: The death of handwriting. The Guardian (2006)
8. Maxim, B.R., Martineau, N.D.: Running head- Learning via Gaming- An Immersive Environment for Teaching Handwriting. Meaningful Play, pp. 1–12 (2008)
9. McGregor, R., Meiers, M.: Writing K-12: A guide to assessment & reporting. English Club (1987)
10. Michael, D., Chen, S.: Serious games: Games that educate, train, and inform. vol. 1. Thomson Course Technology (2006)
11. Nacke, L.E.: Affective Ludology, vol. 2. Blekinge Institute of Technology (2009)
12. Prensky, M.: Digital Game-Based Learning. Paragon House (2007)
13. Sheffield, B.: Handwriting: A neglected cornerstone of literacy. Annals of Dyslexia 46(1), 21–35 (1996)
14. Susi, T., Johannesson, M., Backlund, P.: Serious games: An overview. Institutionen för kommunikation och information (2007)
15. Wray, D., Medwell, J.: The links between handwriting and composing in primary aged children. Cambridge Journal of Education 39(3), 329–344 (2009)

Motivation-Based Game Design: A Framework for Evaluating Engagement Potential

Charles Butler

The Norwegian School of Information Technology, Oslo, Norway
charlesabutler@gmail.com

Abstract. Video games excel at capturing and maintaining the interest of players all around the world. However, actually moving a game from an initial concept to an attention-grabbing best-seller is quite a difficult and unlikely event. Even though the best games seem to have an almost magical ability to generate engagement among players, the vast majority of games fall far short of this mark. Likewise, many serious games and gamified products have considerable difficulty achieving their desired levels of engagement. Success with in these areas can be even more elusive as they are burdened with some disadvantages of traditional games without being able to leverage all of the advantages. This paper presents a motivation-based framework intended to evaluate the engagement potential of a game design, whether it be a traditional game, serious game, or gamified product.

Keywords: game design, game mechanics, gamification, motivation, serious games.

1   Introduction

Video games are often labeled (both positively and negatively, depending on the audience) with terms describing the duration and/or intensity of the engagement that they create, terms such as immersive, stimulating, or addictive. These traits are typi-cally very desirable from the perspective of the game's creators, and they can, at least in part, determine the extent to which a game is successful. Judging by the low percentage of commercial video games which actually turn out to be profitable, we can confidently say that achieving a sufficient level of engagement is a tremendously difficult endeavor, even for professional game studios with ever-increasing budgets which are at time approaching or even exceeding $100 million.

If massive commercial studios funded or owned by the largest video game publishing companies in the world have trouble with engagement, then consider how the makers of educational games, serious games, or gamified products could hope to compete when they are likely to have access to far fewer resources. To compound the difficulty, these alternative games tend to suffer similar difficulties to traditional vid-eo games (complexity, difficulty estimating proper schedules and budgets, etc.) as well as the additional difficulties that arise when making a

J.C. Anacleto et al. (Eds.): ICEC 2013, LNCS 8215, pp. 176–179, 2013.

non-entertainment-based product (less appealing subject material, low production quality when compared to the expectations that are set by traditional video games, creators are often subject matter experts as opposed to game design experts, etc.).

Despite these difficulties, this paper presents a framework for evaluating a game's engagement potential by mapping player motivations to the various game mechanics being utilized by the game. In addition, this framework can be used to pinpoint areas where a game could add or modify mechanics in order to increase its engagement potential. Of course, this doesn't directly address all of the issues (ever-increasing production values and their corresponding budgets, for example), but it can help a team with limited resources focus their efforts in order to achieve the best results from the work that its members are able to do.

2 Motivation

2.1 Motivation Frameworks

There have been prior attempts at creating a model of player motivations. Bartle's work, for example, attempts to identify the motivations that guide a player's action within a game context. Starting with a 4 point model and later evolving into an 8 point model, Bartle asserts that different types of players want different things from their games and that by intentionally planning a game's features around a set of assumed player types, the developer could control, to some extent, the mix of player types actively using the game.

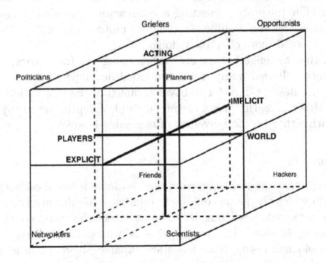

Fig. 1. Player Types (Bartle 2003)

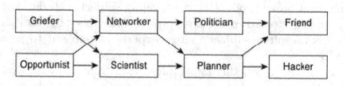

Fig. 2. Player Type Progression (Bartle 2003)

However, these models deal primarily behind in-game motivations and their resulting behaviors. This keeps the model at least one step removed from the basic human emotions that drive all of our day-to-day behaviors, whether we're playing a game at home, performing a task at work, or basically any behavior in any setting. To remedy this, I instead want to look at game features and/or mechanics through a lens which addresses the fundamentals of human behavior. The perspective chosed for this model is Maslow's Heirarchy of Needs, which addresses and prioritizes our innate human needs.

2.2   Driving Engagement

A recurring issue that I've noticed with less successful commercial games as well as with most educational/serious games (and to an even greater extent with gamifica-tion attempts) is that they tend to be more focused on the creator's objectives than on the players'. If a game isn't created with the users motivations in mind, it shouldn't be surprising when it fails to sufficiently engage them. The simple theory is that the more types of needs and motivations that a game can incorporate, the higher the chance of the game being especially engaging to a given player. The purpose of creating a framework is to allow developers to if their game is addressing a sufficient range of motivations and to help identify areas where it could more effectively do so.

However, the challenge is that even when using the framework, the path of least resistance will lead many well-intentioned developers into excessively superficial feature designs in order to cover as much of the motivational roadmap as possible. Unless a feature has a certain amount of depth, the engagement that it creates with either be short-lived or of negligible intensity.

2.3   Evaluation

When looking at any game design, we should evaluate it based on both the number of ways in which the game could help fulfill a particular need or motivation. In addi-tion, we should also consider to what extent that need could be filled.

In considering Maslow's Hierarchy of Needs, we can likely disregard the base level of physiological needs, but games are capable of providing at least some elements in the remaining four tiers. *Safety* can include any potential assets created as a result of the game. Even though they may not be tangible, have the potential to consume non-trivial amounts of actual time and effort to accumulate, thus providing a real sense of loss aversion if they are put at risk.

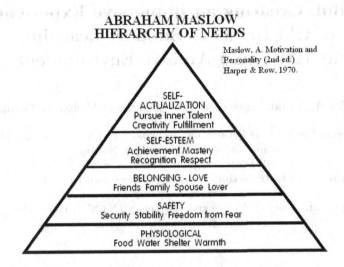

Fig. 3. Maslow's Hierarchy of Needs (Maslow 1970)

The elements of *Belonging*, friends, family, and intimacy, can be brought about though any game where cooperation is possible. Games are particularly good at *Self-Esteem*, naturally encouraging achievement and mastery while also providing a medium through which status can be displayed and recognized. The final tier, *Self-Actualization*, can be accessed via mechanics that offer self-expression or the opportunity for emergent gameplay.

3   Future Work

Judging by any substantial collection of players, it is clear that there are many per-sonality types represented, and by nearly any model of personality model, we can see that different types of people respond more or less strongly to various types of needs and motivations. A very interesting area for future development would be identifying which needs and motivations were most strongly represented by each personality type. Furthermore, identifying these types dynamically in-game and altering the gameplay experience accordingly could provide a leap in advancement for many games.

References

1. Bartle, R.A.: Designing Virtual Worlds. New Rider Publishing, Indianapolis (2003)
2. Maslow, A.: Motivation and Personality. Harper & Row (1970)

Mubil: Creating an Immersive Experience of Old Books to Support Learning in a Museum-Archive Environment

Alexandra Angeletaki[1], Marcello Carrozzino[2], and Michail N. Giannakos[3]

[1] Norwegian University of Science and Technology (NTNU) University Library,
Gunnerus branch, Trondheim, Norway
alexandra.angeletaki@ub.ntnu.no
[2] PERCRO, TECIP Institute, Scuola Superiore Sant'Anna, Pisa, Italy
m.carrozzino@sssup.it
[3] Norwegian University of Science and Technology (NTNU), Trondheim, Norway
michail.giannakos@idi.ntnu.no

Abstract. In this paper we present our design approach of transposing old books and manuscripts using 3D technology in a game frame. MUBIL is an interdisciplinary collaboration initiated by the NTNU University library of Trondheim and PERCRO at Scuola Santa Anna in Pisa. The books are enriched with 3D objects, additional explanatory content, in pictures, drawings, videos audios and texts in both Norwegian and English. This experimental setting is also supplemented by a game, the Alchemist's lab with content related directly to the book of medicine by Adam Lonicer written in 1590. The experiment to be carried out in the digital lab is a reconstruction of a distillation process described in this particular book that can be played as an interactive game using a stereo Powerwall and Nvidia 3D glasses in our MUBIL digital Laboratory in Trondheim. The applications are under development and we present here the system description and the workshop design adapted to visits of school children in our 3D lab.

Keywords: Augmented Books, Cultural Heritage, Immersive Systems, 3D, Archives and Libraries, XVR Systems.

1 Introduction

Browsing pages of books, fragile to be handled, manipulating manuscripts or gaining a tactile experience of books as digital objects has long been surveyed [10]. Research on augmented books with 3D-representations has seen progress the last 10 years [4]. New types of interfaces, interaction techniques and tracking devices are developing at a rapid pace and become integrated into multi-modal interactive VR and AR interfaces [7]. MUBIL aims to explore the evaluation methodology around user interfaces in such immersive environments. Our focus is mainly on the user learning experience in such combined or hybrid environments where 3D technological representations of books and gaming applications blend

J.C. Anacleto et al. (Eds.): ICEC 2013, LNCS 8215, pp. 180–184, 2013.

together [2]. We believe as it is already pointed out by several studies that gaming activities provide structure for collaboration and promote knowledge seeking skills in many learning contexts [8]. Students are often motivated to interact and to be engaged throughout the learning process in a way that is meaningful for them[3].In our case study social conduct seems to both create engagement and meaning. Learning by playing in groups seems to stimulate collaboration and enriches the user experience of the book content transposed in virtual applications [6] as the ones presented here.

2   System Description

The technological tool we use to promote archive content in this study is 3D technology. Manuscripts are presented in the form of an interactive 3D book (augmented book). Users can freely explore the original pages of the book or access their translations into several languages.

Fig. 1. Augmented book (left) and Virtual Lab (right)

An enhanced interaction modality enables the exploration of additional content purposely developed for the project such as 3D texts, images, movies, audios, real-time animated 3D models. In Figure 1 left, a page from the 3D transposition of Lonicer's treatise on medical distillation is presented. A second interaction level is represented by a virtual laboratory (Figure 1, right), where the user exploits knowledge from the previous level into an interactive lab application. The reader becomes an apprentice alchemist that must perform a real experiment based on the distillation notions acquired from the Lonicer treatise. A point-and-click interaction metaphor enables players to discover information, combine objects and perform all the operations involved in the distillation of a medicine. Thanks to the flexibility of the architecture (Fig. 2) and of the XVR underlying technology, both applications have been realized as *blank* container applications which can load a set of resources (XML schemas describing the application flow, textures, 3D models, videos, audios, music) in order to implement different books (in the case of augmented books) or to different experiments (in the case of the

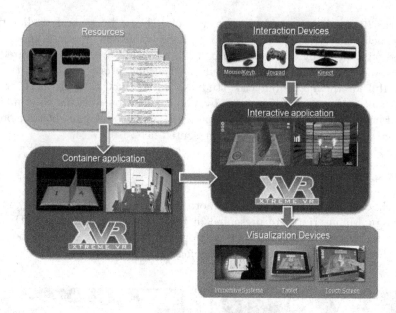

Fig. 2. Mubil high-level architecture

virtual lab). Several interaction metaphors have been implemented based on different devices (mouse, joystick, Microsoft Kinect etc.); all of these devices can be used to move a virtual pointer on the scene and execute actions of different types.

The same applies to visualization metaphors; this means that the 3D environment can be visualized on a simple flat screen, on a stereo screen or on a system of screens, therefore adapting to tablets, notebooks, and even immersive visualization systems such as CAVE. The software used for this prototype has already been used in several other applications [1].

3   Workshop Design

The first MUBIL prototype was evaluated by 40 High School students, invited to a day-workshop at our library-lab, last November 2012. They interacted with the applications in an environment of a simple Powerwall where the students used 3D Nvidia glasses and a simple mouse to browse through the book. The visit was organized as a field trip embedded in their curriculum and as a study activity on the history of chemistry. Two groups browsed first through the augmented book and the game prototype with no specific instruction or background information.

Two other groups were introduced, first to the content of the book and to the actual experiment described in the book of Adam Lonicer. A focus-group of 6 students, the "experts" was interviewed after the interaction and will

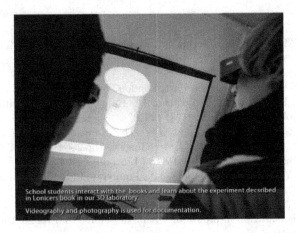

Fig. 3. School students interact with the books

evaluate the development of the applications in successive visits. They interacted through social conduct with both applications in the lab. All of the above was documented by 12 hours video recordings. All answered also pre- and post-tests and knowledge tests prepared by their chemistry teacher.

4 Conclusions

At present, we are still working with the development of the final applications and the design of the workshop visits. A usage interface evaluation is also under development based on guidelines proposed by other scholars [5]. A visit in such an environment or exhibition is defined here as a "cultural learning experience that occurs through observation, instruction, trial and error" [2]. The 3D book is tailored for our library as a digital version substitute protecting the original book from being handled. In the next step of this ongoing research after the completion and the launching of the applications at the end of 2013, we will invite more schools to participate in the Mubil work-shops, collect data on their performance and collaboration pattern, while in the XVR environment and try to analyze our results with a combined qualitative and quantitative methodology. We hope then to be able to define and compare different factors that affect their learning process.

Acknowledgements. We would like to thank the National library of Norway for the financial support of our project and Professor Letizia Jaccheri from NTNU, IDI for her support and supervision. We would like also to thank all our collaborators for their dedication to our work.

References

1. Carrozzino, M., Brogi, A., Tecchia, F., Bergamasco, M.: The 3D interactive visit to Piazza dei Miracoli, Italy. In: Advances in Computer Entertainment technology, pp. 192–195 (2005)
2. Champion, E.: Playing with the Past, London, vol. 178 (2011)
3. Costabile, M.F., Ardito, C., Lanzilotti, R.: Enjoying cultural heritage thanks to mobile technology. Interactions 17(3) (2010)
4. Shiaw, H.-Y., Jacob, R.J.K., Crane, G.R.: The 3D vase museum: A new approach to context in a digital library. In: Proceedings of the 2004 Joint ACM/IEEE Conference on Paper Presented at the Digital Libraries (2004)
5. Bowman, D.A., Kruiiff, E., La Viola, J.J., Poupyrev, I.: 3D User Interfaces Theory and practice. Addison Wesley (2004)
6. Liarokapis, F., Sylaiou, S., Basu, A., Mourkoussis, N., White, M., Lister, P.F.: An interactive visualisation interface for virtual museums. In: Proc. of the VAST 2004, pp. 47–56 (2004)
7. Mikalef, K., Giannakos, M.N., Chorianopoulos, K., Jaccheri, L.: "Do not touch the paintings!" the benefits of interactivity on learning and future visits in a museum. In: Herrlich, M., Malaka, R., Masuch, M. (eds.) ICEC 2012. LNCS, vol. 7522, pp. 553–561. Springer, Heidelberg (2012)
8. Riva, G.: Towards cyberpsychology: mind, cognition and society in the internet age. IOS Press (2005)
9. Rogers, Y.: Introduction to distributed cognition. In: Brown, K. (ed.) The Encyclopedia of Language and Linguistics, pp. 181–202 (2006)
10. Almeida, R., Cubaud, P., Dupire, J., Natkin, S., Topol, A.: Experiments towards 3D immersive interaction for digital libraries. In: Pan, Z., Aylett, R.S., Diener, H., Jin, X., Göbel, S., Li, L. (eds.) Edutainment 2006. LNCS, vol. 3942, pp. 1348–1357. Springer, Heidelberg (2006)

Suspended Walking:
A Physical Locomotion Interface for Virtual Reality

Benjamin Walther-Franks, Dirk Wenig, Jan Smeddinck, and Rainer Malaka

Research Group Digital Media, TZI,
University of Bremen, Bibliothekstr. 1, 28359 Bremen, Germany

Abstract. We present a novel physical locomotion interface for virtual environments. It suspends the user in a torso harness so that the feet just touch ground. Low friction materials allow walking motions with ground contact similar to real walking, while maintaing the user in the same position. We detail the hardware and motion tracking setup and outline results of a first user study.

Keywords: physical locomotion interfaces, virtual environments, games.

1 Introduction

We propose a novel physical locomotion interface for virtual reality that enables more natural walking by suspending the user so that the feet just touch the ground. The user rests in a harness that is mounted to the ceiling or a frame, and stands upon a low friction surface wearing special slippers. This allows for a high degree of freedom of movement, most importantly a full walking motion, while still maintaining the sensation of touching the ground and remaining in the same location.

Torso harnesses are used in healthcare and rehabilitation for walking-impaired patients. They are designed for maximum comfort while giving optimal support. In addition to a torso harness, our technique requires two leg-mounted 3-axis accelerometers for the detection of walking-patterns.

Suspended walking has advantages over existing physical locomotion techniques. It does not require large area tracking space and technology like actual walking techniques do. Unlike many devices simulating walking, the harness allows full freedom of movement for the legs, and does not suffer from device lag (unlike, for instance, a treadmill, which requires time to stop). It also enables turning motions and can be extended to support jumping.

The application areas for suspended walking are diverse. Apart from general physical locomotion in virtual realities for increased presence, it can be used for specific applications requiring "natural" full-body motions from the user or it can be employed in the context of games for health. From a therapeutic perspective, suspended walking opens up intriguing perspectives for rehabilitation and physical therapy. It can make the capacity of motion-based virtual environments for motivation, feedback and guidance available to people who suffer from impaired mobility.

J.C. Anacleto et al. (Eds.): ICEC 2013, LNCS 8215, pp. 185–188, 2013.

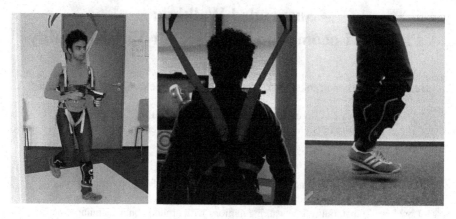

Fig. 1. Suspended walking (left, middle); walking-in-place (right)

2   Related Work

Physical locomotion techniques employ the user's body motion to facilitate moving through virtual environments. The physical exertion of the user has been shown to increase the self-perceived sense of presence in comparison to sedentary techniques [1]. Virtual reality research distinguishes three categories: walking, walking-in-place (WIP) and devices simulating walking. Virtual travel interfaces using actual walking transfer the user's physical locomotion directly into the the virtual space. These can only be used for small areas, due to the restricted tracking range of sensing devices. WIP techniques require the user to imitate a walking motion on the spot. Although this does not require the full leg motions of real walking, it is a good compromise between completely virtual travel and real walking, supporting presence better than the former but less than the latter. Keeping recognition latency to a minimum poses a challenge for WIP interfaces. State of the art algorithms approach this matter with prediction heuristics based on biomechanics [6]. Simulation devices address the tradeoff between area constraints and natural motions by mechanically supporting the user in making full walking motions without actually moving. These devices range from treadmills to spheres [2] or low friction surfaces [3,4]. However, such devices often suffer from balance problems, lag or limiting the freedom of movement of the user.

Our technique enables a high freedom of movement and the sensation of natural walking. Since it does not spacially translate the user, the tracking requirements remain confined to tracking the user's actions in a specific location.

3   Technique and Setup

The harness was originally developed for aiding walking-impaired patients in therapy. It consist of straps for the lower torso and loops for the thighs, which are attached to a yoke above the head. It requires a suspension that should safely carry at least twice the maximum weight expected for users. We experimented with low friction materials for the floor and feet, wool slippers or socks and a PVC sheet provided good characteristics.

The suspension setup works with both vision-based as well as accelerometer sensing, and we experimented with both. Our goal was to match our suspension setup with state of the art, low-latency walking recognition. Although skeleton recognition with the Microsoft Kinect worked well with the harness setup, we did not find it accurate enough for our purposes. We thus employed the signals of two 3-axis accelerometers (in the form of Nintendo WiiMotes), each attached to one lower leg of the user via shin guards.

Our walking detection is based on a state-of-the-art low-latency walk phase detection algorithm [6], which we have already successfully used for a WIP technique [5]. The recognition algorithm identifies the current step section of the leg movement using a series of optional conditions that need to be matched. These conditions include a min/max acceleration in each cardinal direction, a maximum amount of time the previous step section is valid, a masking time in which no next step section may be detected and a min/max difference between the two most important accelerations: Y (vertical) and Z (depth). A step is only completed, when each of the step sections occur consecutively. Step frequency is then transformed to walking speed using the heuristics of the gait-understanding-driven (GUD) WIP technique [6]. With small adjustments, we utilised the resulting predictions to implement a very low latency starting, stopping and walking speed detection. Although initially developed for WIP, this algorithm works with our suspended walking as well. Due to the "floating" movement in our suspended setup however, the pattern recognition algorithm does not deliver the same accuracy as for WIP, since distinct accelerometer spikes that normally occur when the feet touch the ground or are lifted from it are missing.

Suspended walking can be used with any kind of display setup. Since the user remains stationary, a heads-up solution is not required. In our working prototype, we achieved reasonable immersion with one large planar display. However, this only allows relative orientation gestures. In order to allow absolute orientation, a more immersive cave setup or heads-up display would be necessary.

4 Evaluation

To get first insights on our approach, we evaluated suspended walking in a user test against walking-in-place and the default keyboard and mouse setup. 18 test persons aged between 22 and 30 (average 26.3) took part in the experiment. 7 of the participants were male, 11 of them were female. Each participant used each technique to play an exergame adaptation of the action game *Portal 2* [5]. The treatment consisted of an obstacle course specifically designed for the experiment with a level editor. While none of the participants found the suspension setup most comfortable, which was attributed to a not well fitting harness, 6 of them would use it again and 3 rated it to be the most natural and intuitive user interface. However, none of the users found that suspended walking is easier to use than walking-in-place and the combination of keyboard and mouse. Some of the test persons criticised that contrary to walking-in-place, the suspension setup did not allow walking backwards. Others suggested to use a treadmill instead of a harness.

5   Conclusion

We presented a novel physical navigation technique for virtual environments. Like walking-in-place and walking simulation devices, it does not require large-scale tracking spaces. It enables the user to perform a whole step cycle and approximates real haptical feedback from touching the ground, while providing more freedom of movement than simulation devices. We adapted a state-of-the-art low-latency WIP algorithm for the full walking requirements. Results of a qualitative study indicate its potential as a natural walking device, but also point out the importance of a correct harness adjustment. While the harness setup was not perceived as the most comfortable solution when compared to walking-in-place and sedentary keyboard and mouse controls, we argue that the potential to make motion-based games with walking elements accessible to previously excluded player groups, as well as the potential that lies in the implementation of additional motion patterns, such as high jumping, warrant further explorations. As future work, we intend to add support for jumping and crouching by integrating springs into the suspension setup. We will also assess the quality of omnidirectional walking with a swivel and heads-up-display.

Acknowledgements. We would like to thank all students involved in developing *Sportal*: Daniel Apken, Anna Barenbrock, Smitha Basavalingaiah, Nadezda Bogdanova, Dörte Brockmann, Darya Davydenkova, Nicole Hurek, Sergej Kozuhovskij, Yasser Maslout, Fariba Mostajeran Gourtani, Peter Szmidt, Xiaoyi Wang, Guangtao Zhang as well as the participants of the evaluation.

References

1. Bowman, D.A., Kruijff, E., LaViola, J.J., Poupyrev, I.: 3D User Interfaces: Theory and Practice. Addison-Wesley (2004)
2. Medina, E., Fruland, R., Weghorst, S.: Virtusphere: Walking in a human size VR "hamster ball". Proc. HFES Annual Meeting 52(27), 2102–2106 (2008)
3. Swapp, D., Williams, J., Steed, A.: The implementation of a novel walking interface within an immersive display. In: Proc. 3DUI 2010, pp. 71–74. IEEE (March 2010)
4. Virtuix, http://www.virtuix.com (last checked July 11, 2013)
5. Walther-Franks, B., Wenig, D., Smeddinck, J., Malaka, R.: Sportal: A first-person videogame turned exergame. In: Proc. Mensch und Computer 2013. Oldenbourg Verlag (2013)
6. Wendt, J.D., Whitton, M.C., Brooks, F.P.: GUD WIP: Gait-understanding-driven walking-in-place. In: Virtual Reality Conference 2010. IEEE (2010)

Usability Evaluation of an Application Designed for the Older Adults

André Luiz Satoshi Kawamoto[1,2], Valéria Farinazzo Martins[3], and Flávio Soares Corrêa da Silva[2]

[1] Federal University of Technology - Paraná
Via Rosalina Maria dos Santos, 1233, Campo Mourão - PR, Brazil
kawamoto@utfpr.edu.br
http://www.cm.utfpr.edu.br
[2] University of São Paulo, IME
R. do Matão, 1010 - Cidade Universitária, São Paulo, Brazil
fcs@ime.usp.br
http://ime.usp.br
[3] Universidade Presbiteriana Mackenzie
Rua da Consolação, 930, São Paulo, Brazil
valfarinazzo@gmail.com
http://www.mackenzie.br

Abstract. Nowadays, population aging has attracted the interest of research areas such as Health, Social Sciences, and Economics. Aging can trigger unwanted phenomena associated to muscle weakness, loss of memory and loss of autonomy. This paper presents a computer application based on the Corsi Test designed for the elderly audience, which can be used for testing and for training of the visuospatial memory. The application development is presented, as well as the results of an Usability Evaluation. This work aims to contribute to the usability evaluation of gesture interfaces, especially in applications aimed to the elderly audience.

Keywords: Gesture-based interface, Usability Evaluation, Kinect.

1 Introduction

According to the IBGE (Brazilian Institute of Geography and Statistics) [7], by the year of 2050, one fifth of the Brazil population will be formed by people over 60 years-old. This increase in the elderly population is due to factors related to medical and technological advances, like basic sanitation improvements, reduction of the mortality rate and the augment of the life expectancy.

Despite the clear advantages associated to seniority, aging can also have negative physical, cognitive, and social consequences. The average visual and auditory acuity decline considerably with age, as well as the average strength and speed of response. Some people may experience loss of at least some kinds of memory functions, declines in perceptual flexibility, slowing of "stimulus encoding" and increased difficulty in the acquisition of complex mental skills [10].

J.C. Anacleto et al. (Eds.): ICEC 2013, LNCS 8215, pp. 189–192, 2013.

It is possible to compensate, at least partially, cognitive deficits [1, 4]. In fact, stimulating the memory in the elderly improves considerably the cognitive aspects [1, 3, 4]. In this sense, playing games can have positive effects on the emotional and physical well-being of elderly people, and can motivate them to maintain a basic level of physical and memory activity [2, 8].

Non-conventional devices, such as the Microsoft Kinect, may offer a good opportunity to create games able to motivate the physical and memory features of older adults. However, such games can provide real danger to these people [6]. Thus, it is necessary to consider usability criteria, such as exertion management, age-inclusive design and simple setup routines [5]. This work presents the development of a digital memory application based on Microsoft Kinect that reproduces the Corsi Test, and the results of an Usability Evaluation performed to determine usability issues.

2   Application Development and Evaluation

Prior to the development of the application, a professional specialized in memory issues was consulted. He suggested creating a computer version of a test, named Corsi Test, which is used to analyze the amount of information stored as part of the treatment for visuospatial memory. The test consists of a table presented to the patient. On top of it, 9 blocks are randomly placed. The conductor of the experiment touches the blocks, one after the other, in a sequence that must be repeated by the patient. The first sequence is composed by only one block, the second one takes 2 blocks, and so on, until the maximum number of 9 blocks. Each sequence is different from the previous one. The average number of blocks remembrance is in the order of 4 or 5 blocks. The interface of the application is shown in Fig. 1.

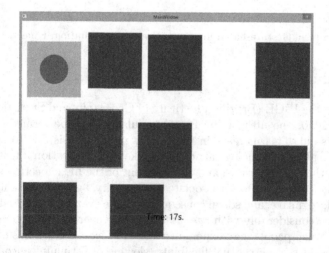

Fig. 1. Application Interface

The Usability Evaluation of the application was carried out with 11 people from both genders, with ages varying from 18 to 63 years old. The mixed age group is due the fact that, albeit being originally designed for the elderly audience, this first test aims to report enhancements and adjustments to the development team. In a second moment, the usability evaluation will be carried out with the target audience.

Three questionnaires were conceived for the evaluation: Profile, Expectations and Post-test. The Profile Questionnaire investigated the age, gender, computer games expertise, physical activities history and whether the user was familiar with the Microsoft Kinect or not. The Expectations Questionnaire was aimed to investigated the level of interest of the user on the application, ease of use, level of motivation, and whether the user like to try new technologies or not. The results of these two first questionnaires are not discussed in this paper. Finally, the Post-test questionnaire addressed usability issues pointed out by [9], like feedback, time of learning, and user satisfaction. This questionnaire attracts more attention, and its results are discussed in the next section.

3 Results

The answers of the Post-test Questionnaire pointed that the users considered undesirable not providing a feedback when they committed a mistake. This was not considered an error, because this version was designed to be used accomplished by a psychologist, with access to the error rate through a log file. Despite interacting with hands is not always as fast or as precise as with the mouse, the users were still interested in repeating the activity. The interface was considered intuitive, easy to learn, to play - even in the first time - and to remember. Playing for long periods of time was considered uncomfortable. Concerning the precision of the movements, the users did not consider annoying to have to repeat the action until reach the correct movement.

Two users, older than 60 years, attended an interview after the experiment in order to obtain more usability-related information. They revealed that had never used the Kinect before, and rarely use computer games. Both users had good expectations about the application, but in the beginning they were not sure whether it would be easy to use or not. They considered the game very motivational, and would certainly use it again. The users claimed to be able to master the game in very few time, with appropriate practice.

4 Final Considerations and Future Work

There are several studies for attenuating the memory loss in the elderly by means of stimuli, as well as there are studies in the Human-Computer Interface area to establish guidelines for building interfaces able to adapt themselves to the human memory characteristics. In Games Development area, it is possible to couple these interests and build games and interfaces adaptable to the memory characteristics, which can inhibit the memory loss in the elderly audience.

Computer games stimulate social interaction, enhance dexterity, and improve reaction time. Development for older adults requires a multidisciplinary team, including skilled health professionals able to provide guidance during the development, correctly focus the application, as well as to provide real test conditions and appropriate environments for the target audience.

This paper presented the development of a Kinect application for older adults. Its main contribution relies on the usability evaluation of applications for this particular target audience. Future work include applying usability tests with the target audience; verifying if the application can really improve the memory storage capacity of older adults; and make available to download the game.

References

1. Baltes, P.B., Baltes, M.M.: Psychological perspectives on successful aging: The model of selective optimization with compensation. Cambridge University Press (1990), http://dx.doi.org/10.1017/CB09780511665684.003
2. Bateni, H.: Changes in balance in older adults based on use of physical therapy vs the wii fit gaming system: a preliminary study. Physiotherapy 98(3), 211–216 (2012),
   http://www.sciencedirect.com/science/article/pii/S0031940611000472
3. Bäckman, L.: Varieties of memory compensation by older adults in episodic remembering. In: Poon, L.W., Rubin, D.C., Wilson, B.A. (eds.) Everyday Cognition in Adulthood and Late Life, pp. 509–544. Cambridge University Press, New York (1989)
4. Dunlosky, J., Hertzog, C.: Training programs to improve learning in later adulthood: Helping older adults educate themselves. In: Hacker, D.J., Dunlosky, J., Graesser, A.C. (eds.) The Educational Psychology Series, pp. 249–275. Lawrence Erlbaum Associates Publishers, Mahwah (1998)
5. Gerling, K., Livingston, I., Nacke, L.: Full-body motion-based game interaction for older adults. Game Design for Older Adults: Effects of Age-Related Changes on Structural Elements of Digital Games. In: CHI 2012: Proceedings of the 30th International Conference on Human Factors in Computing Systems, Austin, Texas, USA, pp. 1873–1882 (2012)
6. Gerling, K.M., Schild, J., Masuch, M.: Exergame design for elderly users: the case study of silverbalance. In: Proceedings of the 7th International Conference on Advances in Computer Entertainment Technology, ACE 2010, pp. 66–69. ACM, New York (2010), http://doi.acm.org/10.1145/1971630.1971650
7. IBGE: Perfil dos idosos responsáveis pelos domicílios no Brasil, 2000. ibge (2002)
8. Jung, Y., Li, K.J., Janissa, N.S., Gladys, W.L.C., Lee, K.M.: Games for a better life: effects of playing wii games on the well-being of seniors in a long-term care facility. In: Proceedings of the Sixth Australasian Conference on Interactive Entertainment, IE 2009, pp. 5:1–5:6. ACM, New York (2009), http://doi.acm.org/10.1145/1746050.1746055
9. Nielsen, J.: Ten usability heuristics (2005), http://www.useit.com/papers/heuristic/heuristiclist.html
10. Shneiderman, B., Plaisant, C.: Designing the User Interface: Strategies for Effective Human-Computer Interaction, 4th edn. Pearson Addison Wesley (2004)

Demonstrations

Demonstrating Hundreds of AIs in One Scene

Kjetil Raaen, Andreas Petlund, and Håkon Kvale Stensland

Abstract. This demo shows how a server can process heavy, game-enhancing workloads without sacrificing response time by implementing a highly parallelisable game server architecture. The architecture "LEARS" allows for the utilisation of more processing resources for tasks that will enhance the game experience. Using the A* path-finding algorithm, we demonstrate how the server distributes the resources under different levels of load, and how this impacts the response time for the game-clients. The demo allow the viewers to adjust game parameters such as the number of pathfinding entities, the number of player characters and the number of available threads and observe the impact on response time and CPU utilisation.

Introduction

Online massively multiplayer games have experienced a massive growth. Providers must deliver a stable service with short deadlines to please ever more demanding players. Technical limitations are however restricting the creativity of the designers. Increasing numbers of both clients and computer controlled oppo- nents (often referred to as Non-Player characters, NPCs) reduce the available computing power. To alleviate this problem, the traditional approach is parti- tioning the game world and limiting the number of player and NPCs present (collectively referred to as entities) in each partition. This approach restricts the social part of the game, which is an important aspect in many modern games.

Another important part of experienced Quality of Service (QoS) by the players is response latency from the server. Chen et al.(2006) [2] present some numbers as to what is acceptable latency, by investigating average session length as a function of response time measurements. They examine an online RPG, Shen-Zhou Online. Between 45 and 75 ms RTT, they find a linear correlation between increased latency and decreased game session length. For the standard deviation of latency which would represent "jitter", the correlation is even stronger. To allow for some network latency, we suggest that servers should keep processing time below 20 ms.

A proposed solution, termed LEARS, that allow both a high number of interacting entities and heavy computation for each is demonstrated by Raaen et al. [4] and analysed in [5]. However, that work focuses primarily on extreme num- bers of computationally cheap entities. The main costs in this work are collision between entities as well distributing information to clients. Potential uses of expanded access to computational resources on the server are numerous. The most computationally expensive tasks in games are usually 3D rendering of the world, and physics simulation. These, however are at the moment handled

J.C. Anacleto et al. (Eds.): ICEC 2013, LNCS 8215, pp. 195–199, 2013.

more or less exclusively on the client, with the server only run- ning an extremely simplified physics model. Moving physics, and basic awareness of how the world looks, to the server can allow players much more detailed inter- action with the environment at the cost of extreme computational demands. By running physics simulations on the server, we also enable much more detailed checking of the rules, eliminating cheating. Conversely, have chosen to focus on Artificial Intelligence (AI) as one of the most demanding subsystems typically run server-side. Describing the most commonly used AI techniques, Narayek [3] lists the two categories decision engines such as Finite State Machines, as well as movement including pathfinding and steering. For the purposes of this demo, the latter approach has the great advantage of being easy to visualize. Other advantages include the ability to easily scale the cost of the problem, either by varying the number of entities running the pathfinding, the frequency of updates or the complexity of the maze. Among the movement algorithms discussed, we chose to use the pathfinding algorithm known as A*, which is the most common as well as most efficient approach for navigating in games.

This work demonstrates how the LEARS approach can provide near-perfect resource utilisation on a multicore server, allowing for game-improving heavy-duty computations like A* in a complicated maze to be deployed to enhance the game without sacrificing server response time.

Design and Implementation

Traditionally, game servers are based around a main loop, which updates every active element in the game sequentially. These elements include for example player characters, non-player characters and projectiles. Since all updates are sequential operations all actions can be performed directly. The character reads input from the network, performs updates on itself according to the input, and updates other elements with the results of its actions. All this makes parallel execution tricky and modifications to this approach such as [1] show only limited success, implying a need for a system designed from the ground up with parallelism in mind. The LEARS architecture is described in detail in papers [4] and [5].

The system demonstrated here uses a thread-pool executor as the core of the execution engine. When an active element is created, it is scheduled for execution. When it excutes, the active element updates its state exactly as in the single threaded case, with the simple limitation that elements are not allowed to write to the state of other elements. When the task is finished for one time slot it can reschedule itself for the next slot, allowing active elements to have any lifetime from one-shot executions to the duration of the program. It also allows different elements to be updated at different rates, depending on the requirements from game designers.

To make elements in the game able to affect each other without the ability to write directly, inter-element communication must be implemented. Our solution is "blocking queues". These are queue implementations that are synchronised

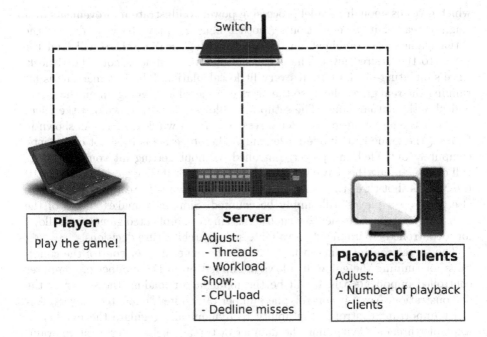

Fig. 1. Setup of the demonstration

separately at each end. Operations on a blocking queue are extremely quick, so the probability of blocking is low. Each active object that can be influenced by others has a blocking queue of messages. During its update, it will read and process the pending messages from its queue. Other active elements put messages in the queue to be processed when they need to change the state of other elements in the game.

Additions to [5] are in the form of a large, scalable maze, and computer controlled entities that will path-find through that maze. Implementation of the map and pathfinder is based on Keith Woodward's "StraightEdge" [6]. Each entity has a separate copy of the maze, to avoid resource contention. Scripted players characters are still included. These do not perform pathfinding, as they simply follow a scripted route through the maze, shooting at predefined times. Their purpose is to be targets for the pathfinding NPC to track and follow. Each of these also need to keep track of the position of all other entities, continuously reporting this information to their controlling clients, keeping the focus on thread-to-thread communications. Each pathfinding entity needs to keep track of all target entities to choose which to follow.

Demonstration

The demo setup consists of three machines and is illustrated in figure 1. One machine is the game server. For this purpose, we are using a quad-core CPU, which gives us enough parallel processing power to illustrate improvements over single threaded implementations. Another machine plays back a trace of the actual gameplay. Combined with the pathfinding entities, these will load the server to the desired level. The client simulation machine is not a bottleneck, since simulating clients requires very little calculation. The last machine is for running the real game client, so the users can see what is going on on the server and play the actual game. The setup also allows others to download the client and play the game during the demo session using a wireless LAN. As shown in figure 2 the game is a simple maze-game. The objective is to shoot opponents, computer controlled and player controlled, without getting hit yourself. NPCs will choose among the players, follow them and shoot if they get within range. If the NPC is shot three times, it will disappear for a while to reappear somewhere else. Hits on a player will simply be counted. Simplicity makes effects of the technology presented easier to visualise than more complicated games, and allows for a controlled environment to validate server architecture decisions.

The server control panel in figure 3 lets the experimenter control the conditions for running the game. It allows manipulation of the number of computer controlled opponents which will be the main factor loading the server in the demonstration. Next, it controls the number of scripted, emulated players. Another important control is the ability to dynamically regulate the number of available threads. Controlling the number of threads help experimenters evaluate how performance scales with the available parallel processing power. During the running of the game, the conditions on the server are displayed. Importantly the response time to clients is graphed, to show potential performance problems.

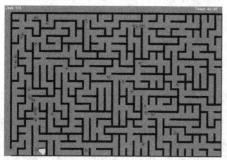

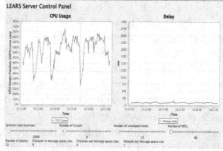

Fig. 2. Screenshot of the game   **Fig. 3.** Server control panel screenshot

Conclusions and Future Work

The setup demonstrated here show how our Lockless, Relaxed Atomicity State Parallel Game Server (LEARS) handles different conditions by adding and removing both computer controlled opponents, emulated players and real players. The demo allows us to thoroughly investigate how the system reacts when the described parameters are changed. Utilising this setup, we will be able to study how different classes of hardware, such as cloud and clusters will handle games requiring complex computation. Highly parallel server environments such as LEARS allow for hundreds of game clients to operate within the same virtual instance. Such environments pose challenges to inter-player network communications since a large number of players need updates on all events in their immediate vicinity. How to effectively handle the network challenges will be a focus for our upcoming investigations in game-server technology.

References

1. Abdelkhalek, A., Bilas, A.: Parallelization and performance of interactive multi-player game servers. In: Proceedings of IPDP Symposium, pp. 72–81 (2004)
2. Chen, K.-T., Huang, P., Wang, G.-S., Huang, C.-Y., Lei, C.-L.: On the Sensitivity of Online Game Playing Time to Network QoS. In: Proceedings of IEEE INFOCOM 2006 (2006)
3. Nareyek, A.: AI in Computer Games. Queue 1(10), 58–65 (2004)
4. Raaen, K., Espeland, H., Stensland, H.K., Petlund, A., Halvorsen, P., Griwodz, C.: A demonstration of a lockless, relaxed atomicity state parallel game server (LEARS). In: Proceeding of NETGAMES 2011 (2011)
5. Raaen, K., Espeland, H., Stensland, H.K., Petlund, A., Halvorsen, P., Griwodz, C.: LEARS: A Lockless, Relaxed-Atomicity State Model for Parallel Execution of a Game Server Partition. In: Proceedings of ICPP 2012 Workshops (2012)
6. Woodward, K.: StraightEdge, http://www.keithwoodward.com/straightedge/

Educational: 3D Design
for Mobile Augmented Reality

Ivar Kjellmo

NITH (The Norwegian School of Information Technology)

Abstract. Using Unity and the Vuforia platform in the course "3D design for Mobile Augmented reality" at The Norwegian School of IT. In the course students learned to make efficient, optimized and visually coherent content for Augmented Reality apps for mobile devices.

Keywords: Educational, Augmented Reality, Unity, Vuforia, 3D, IoS, Android, Mobile.

Overview

Making 3D content for mobile augmented reality consists of many challenges including both hardware limitations and design aspects when it comes to consistent content. The 3D graphics students of NITH (The Norwegian School of Information Technology) have designed augmented reality apps that addressed these challenges in their course "3D Design for Mobile Augmented Reality." This demonstration will show hands-on student work based in augmented reality on iPad and Android tablets as well as the technical workflow used when deploying the app on a tablet.

Background

With the increased use of smart phones and tablets, development of Augmented Reality apps in entertainment and in marketing for iPhone and Android has increased. As an example the Norwegian company Placebo Effects and Australian Labrat has created numerous AR apps for marketing. The latest product was a color game for children, created for the milk producer Tine in Norway[1].

In the beginning, creating augmented reality applications required a massive setup of hardware and custom work. A pioneer project among others was the research of AHO (The Oslo School of Architecture and Design) regarding the visualization of the Margaretha Church in Maridalen, Oslo in 2005[2]. The project was a recreation of an old church in 3D. The ruins of the church were covered by

---

[1] http://www.pfx.no/web_ar_tinekuer.html

[2] A lecture of Professor Søren Sørensens at AHO covering different early AR projects: http://www.ife.no/en/ife/departments/software-engineering/files/ar/ar-in-architectural-and-urban-planning.pdf

J.C. Anacleto et al. (Eds.): ICEC 2013, LNCS 8215, pp. 200–203, 2013.
© IFIP International Federation for Information Processing 2013

Fig. 1. AR markers placed on the ruin of the Margareta Church in Maridalen, Oslo, Norway

markers in order to project the 3D model in the right place. The project would be viewed from a custom made portable screen that the audience could carry around the area.

Unity

Today with the use of the game engine Unity and the Vuforia platform, creating augmented reality content has become much easier. However, there are still challenges to consider. The hardware limitations on mobile devices allows content creators to carefully design 3D content with a limited use of geometry, textures and visual effects. One of the many advantages of Unity is that it is a game engine that has the possibility to deploy to many different platforms as iOS and Android. This, combined with the Vuforia AR platform, makes it possible to assign a virtual camera in the 3D scene that is linked to an image tracker. This combination can then be deployed to a smart phone or tablet. Finally, it is possible to utilize the camera on the device in order to mix the 3D scene with the camera image.

Fig. 2. Screenshot from Unity with a scene for the song "Set Fire to the Rain" by Adele, made by Helene Roberts NITH 2012

The Course

The course "3D Design for Mobile Augmented Reality" focuses on the technical and aesthetic process of developing an augmented reality app for Android and iOS.

In the course the students worked on an assignment which was an AR app for a band or an artist. The students started by making a tracking marker as a CD cover and later designing a 3D scene with an animated figure as a cartoony version of the artist/band placed on the cover. Both the marker and the 3D scene with the figure reflected the band/artists visual style.

Creating AR markers or an image tracker that both is stable and visually coherent with the 3D content is a task in which the students must also take the visual design into account. They must create enough tracking points in the marker to create stable experience for the user while interactive with the app. The 3D design of the scene and the animated figure should both be optimized for mobile and reflect the visual style and concept of the artist/band. A 3D scene optimized for AR follows normal rules for creating games which means low-poly modeling of geometry and limited use of textures. Animating a figure would also mean a limited use of polygons and animation bones.

The Demonstration

The demonstration will be showing examples from several student works from the augmented reality course with different markers. The complete workflow will also be demonstrated, starting with a 3D scene in Unity and deploying to multiple mobile devices (an Asus tablet for Android and an iPad for iOS).

Fig. 3. Augmented Reality scene on iPad for the song "Set Fire to the Rain" by Adele, made by Helene Roberts NITH 2012

Interactive Arts

Moment of Memory

Karin Guminski and Franziska Tachtler

Art and Multimedia, Institute for Art Education
Faculty of History and the Arts
Leopoldstr. 13, 80802 Munich, Germany
karin.guminski@lmu.de,
franziska.tachtler@campus.lmu.de
http://www.kunstpaedagogik.uni-muenchen.de/

Abstract. Memories often consist of single pieces and sometimes cannot be put together temporally or contextually. Every now and then, you would like to erase your mind or you might wish to experience memories again or in another way. This will be possible with the interactive video installation "Moment of Memory". It was developed as a university art project by Franziska Tachtler with Karin Guminski as supervising lecturer. Super-8-movies combined with videos of today with an imitated super-8-video look are beamed on a vintage picture frame standing on the floor. The viewer can interact with the video by using a small pocket lamp as tangible user interface. He is able to play with the aesthetics of processing functions and super-8-films and to combine them in an individual way.

Keywords: Interactive art, video manipulation, memories, analog data media, Processing 2.0, OpenCV, blob detection, tangible.

1 Introduction

Old material like records and Polaroids are becoming more and more popular. A reason for this could be that especially the currently young generation is longing for the good old days which they can't really remember themselves. Furthermore, in today's digital age, analog data media creates a feeling of security and emotionality. Inspired by old personal super-8-movies (1970 - 1990) and the inspiring possibilities of processing, an interactive video installation was designed. By use of a pocket lamp pointed at the projection screen the user can filter, erase, paint, and recover the videos. The interaction involves the user; he has the possibility to create individual aesthetic video images. Such as the unsorted fragmentary pieces of our memory, the movie clips in this installation are not shown in chronological but rather in associated order and are mixed with current movie clips which have been reworked like a super-8-movie.

2 Related Work

This art project was inspired by music videos which experiment with super-8-style and show the current popularity of analog media material and interactive

J.C. Anacleto et al. (Eds.): ICEC 2013, LNCS 8215, pp. 207–208, 2013.

art installations like "Interactive wall" by Siddharth Mankad, Suni Vallu, Aashka Shah [1].These interactive installations have a very dream-like light appearance especially through control of the actions on the screen by touch or movement. For "Moment of Memory" an ordinary pocket lamp has been chosen as interaction tool because "light" fits the idea of "uncover memories" very well. The Khronos Project by Alvaro Cassinelli is an interactive art installation which consists of a tangible deformable screen where the user also creates new, individual images. "By touching the projection screen, the user is able to send parts of the image forward or backwards in time" [2].

3   Design and Implementation

The program behind the interactive art installation is coded by processing [3] and the library OpenCV [4]. For this video installation only the blobs()-function, which looks for contours in the webcam, video image has been used. Out of the information from the blob objects that have been tracked, the program receives the current coordinates of the spotlight in the webcam image. At these coordinates different processing functions are applied to the video pixels. If the video image has been filtered before or if another image is overlaying the video, the spot of light uncovers the original video. If the original video image is shown first, the recent video image gets filtered or erased by painting it black at the position of the light. It was a challenge to work with videos and not with fixed-images, but a very useful basis code for manipulating the pixels of a video image could be found in the Processing forum [5]. In order to guarantee a total aesthetic image and to show the personal view of the artist, the user cannot chose the type of manipulation and the order of the videos, but this could be an extension to this installation. As background sound, the sound of a super-8- projector has been added to increase the nostalgic impression of the old material.

4   Feedback

The video installation has been presented at LMU Munich and at the Aaber Award, an exhibition for young artists. The feedback of the visitors was that the art installation visualizes how they are thinking of memories.

References

1. Concept video, http://www.youtube.com/watch?v=OGoZktCzMS4 (accessed April 09, 2013)
2. http://www.k2.t.u-tokyo.ac.jp/members/alvaro/Khronos/ (accessed April 09, 2013)
3. Processing, http://www.processing.org/ (accessed April 09, 2013)
4. OpenCV for Processing, http://ubaa.net/shared/processing/opencv/ (accessed April 09, 2013)
5. Processing forum, http://processing.org/discourse/beta/num_1264466955.html (accessed April 09, 2013)

The Listening Walker

Interactive Sound Walk in a Virtual City

Cécile Le Prado[*]

Laboratoire CEDRIC, CNAM, 292 Rue Saint-Martin, 75003 Paris, France
cecile.leprado@free.fr

Abstract. The "Listening Walker" is an interactive sound installation designed as a video game with different levels of exploration. The player's reward is the discovery, via sound, of a virtual district of Paris. Success depends on his listening behavior: Non Player Characters (NPC) are moving around him, interpreting his moves, the direction he takes and the time spent listening particular sounds. Depending upon the listener's attitude, each NPC has his own reaction such as running away, getting closer to the listener, ignoring him or helping him to discover secret path in the city.

1 Description

The "Listening Walker" is produced as part of the "Terra Dynamica" project (www.terradynamica.com), funded by the French Government. The installation has been created for the exhibition "Urban stimulations" in Paris during the "Futur en Seine" Festival, in June 2013 and is proposed as an art installation for ICEC 2013. It is both an art piece by it self and a part of a research project. The research goal is to analyze writing styles used in interactive sound installations and to propose some new authoring tools for composers.

The Listening walker was designed and realized like a video game. It relies on the CryEngine and Fmod technologies. The writing style experimented in this piece first version of the "Listening walker" uses a "scripting design" style that considers the player as the narrator. The entire interactive story is written from a subjective point of view. The player controls his progression in the virtual city trough a Game pad. He gets almost all the informations needed for his progression through spatialized sounds: voices of NPC, ambient sounds located in given areas, cue sounds to trigger his attention.

The original installation in Paris used a WFS (Wave Field Synthesis) sound system. The image was projected on a large screen in front of the player. In this case, both the player and the audience were able to follow the spatial relation between the sound and the play. The same installation can use a binaural spatialization for the player and, eventually a 7.1 sound system for the audience with a smaller screen.

---

[*] Assisted by Romain Barthelemy (rbarthelemy@esba-lemans.fr) and Lubna Odeh (lubnaodeh@gmail.com).

When the walk begins, neither the plot, nor the buildings or the inhabitants are fully perceived. The city emerges from the ground, along with NPC that comes to meet the walker. NPC have the possibilities to reveal the history and the memory of what has happened. Compared to a "real game", there is no challenge, no objective and no time limit. Listening curiosity and the stability of the relationship with the NPC create the personality of the visit.

 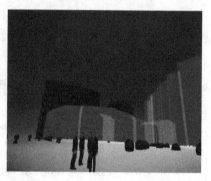

Fig. 1. Listening walker in the installation and communication with NPC

2   Conclusion and Future Works

The prototype can be optimized and lead to new versions. Our goal is to give the walker better feedbacks to his actions and a deeper relation with NPC. Currently the navigation in the city triggers audible or visual objects, but does not interfere with the soundscape itself. This also involves a method of writing more towards an emerging composition that we are working on.

3   Credits

Design: Cécile Le Prado

Assistants: Romain Barthélémy, Lubna Odeh with the help of Guillaume Tiger; Graphic design: Xavier Bouffault; Graphic Intégration: Lubna Odeh, Romain Barthelemy with the help of Pedro Alesio and Delphine Soriano; Programming development: Alexandre Topol, Guillaume Levieux; Project production monitoring: Stéphane Natkin; Administration CNAM : Viviane Gal; Co-production Clameurs.

VOLTE

Lisa van Noorden

Art and Multimedia, Institute for Art Education
Faculty of History and the Arts
Leopoldstr. 13, 80802 Munich, Germany
Lisa@lisavannoorden.nl

Abstract. Volte is an interactive kaleidoscopic art installation. Volte recreates our reality into an abstract video-animation where nobody and nothing is recognizable but is merged into a constant revolving detachment of that reality. Volte strips all imagery from its meaning and returns that imagery into an everchanging, colorful and continually recreated form, which is then again subject to a highly personal interpretation.

Volte has the power to recreate beauty out of the ordinary or grotesque.

Keywords: Interactive art, video manipulation, memories, analog data media, Processing 2.0, OpenCV, blob detection, tangible.

1   How Does It Work

Volte uses a software program which is installed on a computer. The software picks images created by Lisa van Noorden out of a folder. Volte then shows these images in a video-animation. A beamer or LED/TV screen is used to show the projection on an inside or outside surface.

2   Interactive Art

Volte can also be used as an interactive artwork. When a camera is connected it shows real time movement, for exampe people dancing. The camera can be connected to the computer directly, or through WIFI.

Volte also lets people upload their own pictures via a mobile website. Volte will pick those images from the images folder and show them in the videoanimation. To enable people to upload pictures with their Iphone or Android they get a login code. Once they uploaded their pictures, Volte will expose the images within the next minutes.

3   Day and Night

Volte comes with a day and night program. 24 images change every hour, creating a 24 hour program. The animations rotate at a lower speed during the night and at a higher speed during the day. These parameters are adjustable and will be set by the artist to fit the circumstances.

J.C. Anacleto et al. (Eds.): ICEC 2013, LNCS 8215, pp. 211–212, 2013.

4   Team

The Volte team consist of Lisa van Noorden as owner and designer of the concept; Duncan Champney for WareTo, who developed the software and Stephan Grevelink, who created the website with database for uploading images. The creation of Volte took around 4 months.

5   Requirements

Volte uses the following:

- 24 drawings or images created by Lisa van Noorden
- Volte software with software license exclusively for the event
- Mac Mini server or laptop
- Camera
- 2500 Lumen beamer

Costs involved: $ 300,- for the software licence.

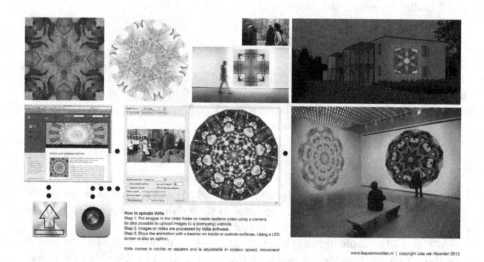

Fig. 1. Volte presentation

References

1. Project website, http://www.lisavannoorden.nl/projecten/volte.html
2. Volte animation 1, http://www.youtube.com/watch?v=8DotjcPgObo
3. Volte animation 2, http://www.youtube.com/watch?v=pRWpoWjYTbc

Author Index